MW01504609

Miscellaneous Essays

DE QUINCEY'S WRITINGS.

THOMAS DE QUINCEY'S WRITINGS.

UNIVERSITY OF ST. MICHAEL'S COLLEGE TORONTO LIBRARY

MISCELLANEOUS ESSAYS.

BY

THOMAS DE QUINCEY,

AUTHOR OF

'CONFESSIONS OF AN ENGLISH OPIUM-EATER, ETC., ETC.'

BOSTON:

TICKNOR AND FIELDS.

M DCCC LXI.

Entered according to Act of Congress, in the year 1853, by

TICKNOR AND FIELDS,

In the Clerk's Office of the District Court of the District of Massachusetts.

CAMBRIDGE:
THURSTON AND TORRY, PRINTERS.

CONTENTS.

MISCELLANEOUS ESSAYS.

THE KNOCKING AT THE GATE

IN MACBETH.

FROM my boyish days I had always felt a great perplexity on one point in Macbeth. It was this: the knocking at the gate, which succeeds to the murder of Duncan, produced to my feelings an effect for which I never could account. The effect was, that it reflected back upon the murder a peculiar awfulness and a depth of solemnity; yet, however obstinately I endeavored with my understanding to comprehend this, for many years I never could see *why* it should produce such an effect.

Here I pause for one moment to exhort the reader never to pay any attention to his understanding, when it stands in opposition to any other faculty of his mind. The mere understanding, however useful and indispensable, is the meanest faculty in the human mind, and the most to be distrusted; and yet the great majority

[9]

of people trust to nothing else ; which may do for
ordinary life, but not for philosophical purposes. Of
this out of ten thousand instances that I might produce,
I will cite one. Ask of any person whatsoever, who is
not previously prepared for the demand by a knowledge
of perspective, to draw in the rudest way the com-
monest appearance which depends upon the laws of
that science ; as, for instance, to represent the effect of
two walls standing at right angles to each other, or
the appearance of the houses on each side of a street,
as seen by a person looking down the street from one
extremity. Now, in all cases, unless the person has
happened to observe in pictures how it is that artists
produce these effects, he will be utterly unable to make
the smallest approximation to it. Yet why ? For he
has actually seen the effect every day of his life. The
reason is — that he allows his understanding to overrule his eyes. His understanding, which includes no
intuitive knowledge of the laws of vision, can furnish
him with no reason why a line which is known and can
be proved to be a horizontal line, should not *appear* a
horizontal line ; a line that made any angle with the
perpendicular, less than a right angle, would seem to
him to indicate that his houses were all tumbling down
together. Accordingly, he makes the line of his houses
a horizontal line, and fails, of course, to produce the
effect demanded. Here, then, is one instance out of
many, in which not only the understanding is allowed
to overrule the eyes, but where the understanding is
positively allowed to obliterate the eyes, as it were, for
not only does the man believe the evidence of his
understanding, in opposition to that of his eyes, but,
(what is monstrous !) the idiot is not aware that his

eyes ever gave such evidence. He does not know that he has seen (and therefore *quoad* his consciousness has *not* seen) that which he *has* seen every day of his life.

But to return from this digression, my understanding could furnish no reason why the knocking at the gate in Macbeth should produce any effect direct or reflected. In fact, my understanding said positively that it could *not* produce any effect. But I knew better; I felt that it did; and I waited and clung to the problem until further knowledge should enable me to solve it. At length, in 1812, Mr. Williams made his *début* on the stage of Ratcliffe Highway, and executed those unparalleled murders which have procured for him such a brilliant and undying reputation. On which murders, by the way, I must observe, that in one respect they have had an ill effect, by making the connoisseur in murder very fastidious in his taste, and dissatisfied by anything that has since been done in that line. All other murders look pale by the deep crimson of his; and, as an amateur once said to me in a querulous tone, ' There has been absolutely nothing *doing* since his time, or nothing that's worth speaking of.' But this is wrong; for it is unreasonable to expect all men to be great artists, and born with the genius of Mr. Williams. Now it will be remembered, that in the first of these murders, (that of the Marrs,) the same incident (of a knocking at the door, soon after the work of extermination was complete) did actually occur, which the genius of Shakspeare has invented; and all good judges, and the most eminent dilettanti, acknowledged the felicity of Shakspeare's suggestion, as soon as it was actually realized. Here, then, was a

fresh proof that I was right in relying on my own feeling, in opposition to my understanding; and I again set
myself to study the problem; at length I solved it to
my own satisfaction; and my solution is this. Murder,
in ordinary cases, where the sympathy is wholly directed to the case of the murdered person, is an incident
of coarse and vulgar horror; and for this reason, that
it flings the interest exclusively upon the natural but
ignoble instinct by which we cleave to life; an instinct, which, as being indispensable to the primal
law of self-preservation, is the same in kind, (though
different in degree,) amongst all living creatures; this
instinct, therefore, because it annihilates all distinctions, and degrades the greatest of men to the level of
‘ the poor beetle that we tread on,’ exhibits human nature in its most abject and humiliating attitude. Such
an attitude would little suit the purposes of the poet.
What then must he do? He must throw the interest
on the murderer. Our sympathy must be with *him;*
(of course I mean a sympathy of comprehension, a
sympathy by which we enter into his feelings, and are
made to understand them, — not a sympathy[1] of pity
or approbation.) In the murdered person, all strife
of thought, all flux and reflux of passion and of pur-

---

[1] It seems almost ludicrous to guard and explain my use of a
word, in a situation where it would naturally explain itself.
But it has become necessary to do so, in consequence of the
unscholarlike use of the word sympathy, at present so general,
by which, instead of taking it in its proper sense, as the act of
reproducing in our minds the feelings of another, whether for
hatred, indignation, love, pity, or approbation, it is made a
mere synonyme of the word *pity;* and hence, instead of saying
‘ sympathy *with* another,’ many writers adopt the monstrous
barbarism of ‘ sympathy *for* another.’

pose, are crushed by one overwhelming panic; the fear of instant death smites him ' with its petrific mace.' But in the murderer, such a murderer as a poet will condescend to, there must be raging some great storm of passion, — jealousy, ambition, vengeance, hatred, — which will create a hell within him; and into this hell we are to look.

In Macbeth, for the sake of gratifying his own enormous and teeming faculty of creation, Shakspeare has introduced two murderers; and, as usual in his hands, they are remarkably discriminated: but, though in Macbeth the strife of mind is greater than in his wife, the tiger spirit not so awake, and his feelings caught chiefly by contagion from her, — yet, as both were finally involved in the guilt of murder, the murderous mind of necessity is finally to be presumed in both. This was to be expressed; and on its own account, as well as to make it a more proportionable antagonist to the unoffending nature of their victim, ' the gracious Duncan,' and adequately to expound ' the deep damnation of his taking off,' this was to be expressed with peculiar energy. We were to be made to feel that the human nature, i. e., the divine nature of love and mercy, spread through the hearts of all creatures, and seldom utterly withdrawn from man, — was gone, vanished, extinct; and that the fiendish nature had taken its place. And, as this effect is marvellously accomplished in the *dialogues* and *soliloquies* themselves, so it is finally consummated by the expedient under consideration; and it is to this that I now solicit the reader's attention. If the reader has ever witnessed a wife, daughter, or sister, in a fainting fit, he may chance to have observed that the most affecting moment in

such a spectacle, is *that* in which a sigh and a stirring
announce the recommencement of suspended life. Or,
if the reader has ever been present in a vast metropolis,
on the day when some great national idol was carried
in funeral pomp to his grave, and chancing to walk
near the course through which it passed, has felt pow-
erfully, in the silence and desertion of the streets, and
in the stagnation of ordinary business, the deep interest
which at that moment was possessing the heart of man,
— if all at once he should hear the death-like stillness
broken up by the sound of wheels rattling away from
the scene, and making known that the transitory vision
was dissolved, he will be aware that at no moment was
his sense of the complete suspension and pause in
ordinary human concerns so full and affecting, as at
that moment when the suspension ceases, and the goings-
on of human life are suddenly resumed. All action
in any direction is best expounded, measured, and made
apprehensible, by reaction. Now apply this to the case
in Macbeth. Here, as I have said, the retiring of the
human heart, and the entrance of the fiendish heart,
was to be expressed and made sensible. Another
world has stept in; and the murderers are taken out
of the region of human things, human purposes, human
desires. They are transfigured : Lady Macbeth is
'unsexed;' Macbeth has forgot that he was born of
woman; both are conformed to the image of devils;
and the world of devils is suddenly revealed. But how
shall this be conveyed and made palpable? In order
that a new world may step in, this world must for a
time disappear. The murderers, and the murder, must
be insulated — cut off by an immeasurable gulph from
the ordinary tide and succession of human affairs —

locked up and sequestered in some deep recess; we must be made sensible that the world of ordinary life is suddenly arrested — laid asleep — tranced — racked into a dread armistice; time must be annihilated; relation to things without abolished; and all must pass self-withdrawn into a deep syncope and suspension of earthly passion. Hence it is, that when the deed is done, when the work of darkness is perfect, then the world of darkness passes away like a pageantry in the clouds; the knocking at the gate is heard; and it makes known audibly that the reaction has commenced: the human has made its reflux upon the fiendish; the pulses of life are beginning to beat again; and the re-establishment of the goings-on of the world in which we live, first makes us profoundly sensible of the awful parenthesis that had suspended them.

O, mighty poet! Thy works are not as those of other men, simply and merely great works of art; but are also like the phenomena of nature, like the sun and the sea, the stars and the flowers, — like frost and snow, rain and dew, hail-storm and thunder, which are to be studied with entire submission of our own faculties, and in the perfect faith that in them there can be no too much or too little, nothing useless or inert, — but that, the further we press in our discoveries, the more we shall see proofs of design and self-supporting arrangement where the careless eye had seen nothing but accident!

ON MURDER,

CONSIDERED AS ONE OF THE FINE ARTS.

ADVERTISEMENT OF A MAN MORBIDLY VIRTUOUS.

MOST of us, who read books, have probably heard
of a Society for the Promotion of Vice, of the Hell-
Fire Club, founded in the last century by Sir Francis
D —, &c. At Brighton I think it was, that a Society was formed for the Suppression of Virtue. That
society was itself suppressed; but I am sorry to say
that another exists in London, of a character still more
atrocious. In tendency, it may be denominated a Society for the Encouragement of Murder; but, according to their own delicate ευφημισμός, it is styled, The
Society of Connoisseurs in Murder. They profess to
be curious in homicide; amateurs and dilettanti in the
various modes of bloodshed; and, in short, Murder-
Fanciers. Every fresh atrocity of that class which the
police annals of Europe bring up, they meet and criticize as they would a picture, statue, or other work of
art. But I need not trouble myself with any attempt
to describe the spirit of their proceedings, as the
reader will collect *that* much better from one of the
Monthly Lectures read before the society last year.
This has fallen into my hands accidentally, in spite of

2   [17]

all the vigilance exercised to keep their transactions
from the public eye. The publication of it will alarm
them; and my purpose is, that it should. For I
would much rather put them down quietly, by an appeal to public opinion, than by such an exposure of
names as would follow an appeal to Bow Street;
which last appeal, however, if this should fail, I must
really resort to. For my intense virtue will not put
up with such things in a Christian land. Even in a
heathen land, the toleration of murder — viz., in the
dreadful shows of the amphitheatre — was felt by a
Christian writer to be the most crying reproach of the
public morals. This writer was Lactantius; and with
his words, as singularly applicable to the present occasion, I shall conclude: — 'Quid tam horribile,' says
he, ' tam tetrum, quam hominis trucidatio? Ideo
severissimis legibus vita nostra munitur; ideo bella
execrabilia sunt. Invenit tamen consuetudo quatenus
homicidium sine bello ac sine legibus faciat: et hoc
sibi voluptas quod scelus vindicavit. Quod si interesse
homicidio sceleris conscientia est, — et eidem facinori
spectator obstrictus est cui et admissor; ergo et in his
gladiatorum cædibus non minus cruore profunditur
qui spectat, quam ille qui facit: nec potest esse im-
munis à sanguine qui voluit effundi; aut videri non
interfecisse, qui interfectori et favit et prœmium postulavit.' 'What is so dreadful,' says Lactantius,
'what so dismal and revolting, as the murder of a
human creature? Therefore it is, that life for us is
protected by laws the most rigorous: therefore it is,
that wars are objects of execration. And yet the traditional usage of Rome has devised a mode of author-
izing murder apart from war, and in defiance of law;

and the demands of taste (voluptas) are now become the same as those of abandoned guilt.' Let the Society of Gentlemen Amateurs consider this; and let me call their especial attention to the last sentence, which is so weighty, that I shall attempt to convey it in English: 'Now, if merely to be present at a murder fastens on a man the character of an accomplice; if barely to be a spectator involves us in one common guilt with the perpetrator, it follows, of necessity, that, in these murders of the amphitheatre, the hand which inflicts the fatal blow is not more deeply imbrued in blood than his who passively looks on; neither can *he* be clear of blood who has countenanced its shedding; nor that man seem other than a participator in murder, who gives his applause to the murderer, and calls for prizes on his behalf.' The '*præmia postulavit*' I have not yet heard charged upon the Gentlemen Amateurs of London, though undoubtedly their proceedings tend to that; but the '*interfectori favit*' is implied in the very title of this association, and expressed in every line of the lecture which follows. . . X. Y. Z.

LECTURE.

GENTLEMEN, — I have had the honor to be appointed by your committee to the trying task of reading the Williams' Lecture on Murder, considered as one of the Fine Arts; a task which might be easy enough three or four centuries ago, when the art was little understood, and few great models had been exhibited; but in this age, when masterpieces of excellence have been executed by professional men, it must be evident, that in the style of criticism applied to them, the public will look for something of a corresponding improvement. Practice and theory must advance *pari passu.* People begin to see that something more goes to the composition of a fine murder than two blockheads to kill and be killed——a knife —— 'a purse—and a dark lane. Design, gentlemen, grouping, light and shade, poetry, sentiment, are now deemed indispensable to attempts of this nature. Mr. Williams has exalted the ideal of murder to all of us; and to me, therefore, in particular, has deepened the arduousness of my task. Like Æschylus or Milton in poetry, like Michael Angelo in painting, he has carried his art to a point of colossal sublimity; and, as Mr. Wordsworth observes, has in a manner 'created the taste by which he is to be enjoyed.' To sketch the history of the art, and to examine its principles critically, now remains as a duty for the connoisseur, and for judges of quite another stamp from his Majesty's Judges of Assize.

Before I begin, let me say a word or two to certain prigs, who affect to speak of our society as if it were in some degree immoral in its tendency. Immoral! Jupiter protect me, gentlemen, what is it that people mean? I am for morality, and always shall be, and for virtue, and all that; and I do affirm, and always shall (let what will come of it), that murder is an improper line of conduct, highly improper; and I do not stick to assert, that any man who deals in murder, must have very incorrect ways of thinking, and truly inaccurate principles; and so far from aiding and abetting him by pointing out his victim's hiding-place, as a great moralist [1] of Germany declared it to be every good man's duty to do, I would subscribe one shilling and sixpence to have him apprehended, which is more by eighteenpence than the most eminent moralists have hitherto subscribed for that purpose. But what then? Everything in this world has two handles. Murder, for instance, may be laid hold of by its moral handle (as it generally is in the pulpit, and at the Old Bailey); and *that*, I confess, is its weak side ; or it may also be treated *æsthetically*, as the Germans call it — that is, in relation to good taste.

To illustrate this, I will urge the authority of three eminent persons; viz., S. T. Coleridge, Aristotle, and Mr. Howship the surgeon. To begin with S. T. C. One night, many years ago, I was drinking tea with him in Berners Street (which, by the way, for a short street, has been uncommonly fruitful in men of genius). Others were there besides myself; and, amidst some carnal considerations of tea and toast, we were all imbibing a dissertation on Plotinus from the attic lips of S. T. C. Suddenly a cry arose of, " *Fire — fire !* " upon which all of us, master and disciples, Plato and ὁι πεϱί τον Πλάτωνα, rushed out, eager for the spectacle. The fire was in Oxford Street, at a pianoforte-maker's ; and, as it promised to be a conflagration of merit, I was sorry that my engagements forced me away from Mr. Coleridge's party, before matters had come to a crisis. Some days after, meeting with my Platonic host, I reminded him of the case, and begged to know how that very promising exhibition had terminated. ' Oh, sir,' said he, ' it turned out so ill that we damned it unanimously.' Now, does any man suppose that Mr. Coleridge — who, for all he is too fat to be a person of active virtue, is undoubtedly a worthy

Christian — that this good S. T. C., I say, was an incendiary, or capable of wishing any ill to the poor man and his pianofortes (many of them, doubtless, with the additional keys)? On the contrary, I know him to be that sort of man, that I durst stake my life upon it, he would have worked an engine in a case of necessity, although rather of the fattest for such fiery trials of his virtue. But how stood the case? Virtue was in no request. On the arrival of the fire-engines, morality had devolved wholly on the insurance office. This being the case, he had a right to gratify his taste. He had left his tea. Was he to have nothing in return?

I contend that the most virtuous man, under the premises stated, was entitled to make a luxury of the fire, and to hiss it, as he would any other performance that raised expectations in the public mind which afterwards it disappointed. Again, to cite another great authority, what says the Stagirite? He (in the Fifth Book, I think it is, of his Metaphysics) describes what he calls κλεπτὶν τέλειον — i. e., *a perfect thief;* and as to Mr. Howship, in a work of his on Indigestion, he makes no scruple to talk with admiration of a certain ulcer which he had seen, and which he styles ' a beautiful ulcer.' Now, will any man pretend, that, abstractedly considered, a thief could appear to Aristotle a perfect character, or that Mr. Howship could be enamored of an ulcer? Aristotle, it is well known, was himself so very moral a character, that, not content with writing his Nichomachéan Ethics, in one volume octavo, he also wrote another system, called *Magna Moralia,* or Big Ethics. Now, it is impossible that a man who composes any ethics at all,

big or little, should admire a thief *per se ;* and as to
Mr. Howship, it well known that he makes war upon
all ulcers, and, without suffering himself to be seduced
by their charms, endeavors to banish them from the
County of Middlesex. But the truth is, that, however objectionable *per se,* yet, relatively to others of
their class, both a thief and an ulcer may have infinite
degrees of merit. They are both imperfections, it is
true ; but, to be imperfect being their essence, the very
greatness of their imperfection becomes their perfection. *Spartam nactus es, hanc exorna.* A thief like
Autolycus, or the once famous George Barrington, and
a grim phagedænic ulcer, superbly defined, and running
regularly through all its natural stages, may no less
justly be regarded as ideals after *their* kind, than the
most faultless moss-rose amongst flowers, in its progress
from bud to ' bright consummate flower ; ' or, amongst
human flowers, the most magnificent young female,
apparelled in the pomp of womanhood. And thus not
only the ideal of an inkstand may be imagined (as Mr.
Coleridge illustrated in his celebrated correspondence
with Mr. Blackwood), in which, by the way, there is
not so much, because an inkstand is a laudable
sort of thing, and a valuable member of society ;
but even imperfection itself may have its ideal or perfect state.

Really, gentlemen, I beg pardon for so much philosophy at one time ; and now let me apply it. When
a murder is in the paulo-post-futurum tense — not
done, not even (according to modern purism) *being*
done, but only going to be done — and a rumor of it
comes to our ears, by all means let us treat it morally.
But suppose it over and done, and that you can say of

it, Τετλεςαι, It is finished, or (in that adamantine mo-
lussus of Medea) ειγαςαι, Done it is : it is *fait accom-
pli ;* suppose the poor murdered man to be out of his
pain, and the rascal that did it off like a shot, nobody
knows whither; suppose, lastly, that we have done
our best, by putting out our legs, to trip up the fellow
in his flight, but all to no purpose — 'abiit, evasit,
excessit, erupit," &c.— why, then, I say, what's the use
of any more virtue ? Enough has been given to morality; now comes the turn of Taste and the Fine Arts.
A sad thing it was, no doubt, very sad; but *we* can't
mend it. Therefore let us make the best of a bad matter; and, as it is impossible to hammer anything out
of it for moral purposes, let us treat it æsthetically,
and see if it will turn to account in that way. Such
is the logic of a sensible man, and what follows? We
dry up our tears, and have the satisfaction, perhaps, to
discover that a transaction, which, morally considered,
was shocking, and without a leg to stand upon, when
tried by principles of Taste, turns out to be a very
meritorious performance. Thus all the world is pleased;
the old proverb is justified, that it is an ill wind which
blows nobody good ; the amateur, from looking bilious
and sulky, by too close attention to virtue, begins to
pick up his crumbs ; and general hilarity prevails.
Virtue has had her day ; and henceforward, *Virtu,* so
nearly the same thing as to differ only by a single letter
— (which surely is not worth haggling or higgling
about) — *Virtu,* I repeat, and Connoisseurship, have
leave to provide for themselves. Upon this principle,
gentlemen I propose to guide your studies, from Cain to
Mr. Thurtell. Through this great gallery of murder,
therefore, together let us wander hand in hand, in de-

lighted admiration; while I endeavor to point your attention to the objects of profitable criticism.

The first murder is familiar to you all. As the inventor of murder, and the father of the art, Cain must have been a man of first-rate genius. All the Cains were men of genius. Tubal Cain invented tubes, I think, or some such thing. But, whatever might be the originality and genius of the artist, every art was then in its infancy, and the works must be criticized with a recollection of that fact. Even Tubal's work would probably be little approved at this day in Sheffield; and therefore of Cain (Cain senior, I mean) it is no disparagement to say, that his performance was but so-so. Milton, however, is supposed to have thought differently. By his way of relating the case, it should seem to have been rather a pet murder with him, for he retouches it with an apparent anxiety for its picturesque effect : —

> ' Whereat he inly raged; and, as they talk'd,
> Smote him into the midriff with a stone
> That beat out life: he fell; and, deadly pale,
> Groan'd out his soul *with gushing blood effused.*'
>
> *Par. Lost*, B. xi.

Upon this, Richardson the painter, who had an eye for effect, remarks as follows, in his 'Notes on Paradise Lost,' p. 497: — 'It has been thought,' says he, 'that Cain beat (as the common saying is) the breath out of his brother's body with a great stone; Milton gives in to this, with the addition, however, of a large wound.' In this place it was a judicious addition; for the rudeness of the weapon, unless raised and enriched by a warm, sanguinary coloring, has too much

3

of the naked air of the savage school; as if the deed
were perpetrated by a Polypheme without science, pre-
meditation, or anything but a mutton bone. However, I am chiefly pleased with the improvement, as it
implies that Milton was an amateur. As to Shakspeare, there never was a better; witness his description of the murdered Duncan, Banquo, &c.; and,
above all, witness his incomparable miniature, in
'Henry VI.,' of the murdered Gloucester.[2]

The foundation of the art having been once laid, it
is pitiable to see how it slumbered without improvement for ages. In fact, I shall now be obliged to leap
over all murders, sacred and profane, as utterly un-
worthy of notice, until long after the Christian era.
Greece, even in the age of Pericles, produced no murder, or at least none is recorded, of the slightest merit;
and Rome had too little originality of genius in any of
the arts to succeed where her model failed her.[3] In
fact, the Latin language sinks under the very idea of
murder. 'The man was murdered;' — how will this
sound in Latin? *Interfectus est, interemptus est* —
which simply expresses a homicide; and hence the
Christian Latinity of the middle ages was obliged to
introduce a new word, such as the feebleness of classic
conceptions never ascended to. *Murdratus est*, says
the sublimer dialect of the Gothic ages. Meantime, the
Jewish school of murder kept alive whatever was yet
known in the art, and gradually transferred it to the
Western World. Indeed, the Jewish school was always respectable, even in its medieval stages, as the
case of Hugh of Lincoln shows, which was honored
with the approbation of Chaucer, on occasion of another
performance from the same school, which he puts into
the mouth of the Lady Abbess.

Recurring, however, for one moment, to classical antiquity, I cannot but think that Catiline, Clodius, and some of that coterie, would have made first-rate artists ; and it is on all accounts to be regretted, that the priggism of Cicero robbed his country of the only chance she had for distinction in this line. As the *subject* of a murder, no person could have answered better than himself. Oh Gemini ! how he would have howled with panic, if he had heard Cethegus under his bed. It would have been truly diverting to have listened to him ; and satisfied I am, gentlemen, that he would have preferred the *utile* of creeping into a closet, or even into a *cloaca,* to the *honestum* of facing the bold artist.

To come now to the dark ages — (by which we that speak with precision mean, *par excellence,* the tenth century as a meridian line, and the two centuries immediately before and after, full midnight being from A. D. 888 to A. D. 1111) — these ages ought naturally to be favorable to the art of murder, as they were to church architecture, to stained glass, &c.; and, accordingly, about the latter end of this period, there arose a great character in our art, I mean the Old Man of the Mountains. He was a shining light, indeed, and I need not tell you, that the very word ' assassin ' is deduced from him. So keen an amateur was he, that on one occasion, when his own life was attempted by a favorite assassin, he was so much pleased with the talent shown, that, notwithstanding the failure of the artist, he created him a duke upon the spot, with remainder to the female line, and settled a pension on him for three lives. Assassination is a branch of the art which demands a separate notice ; and it is possible that I may devote an entire lecture to it. Meantime, I shall only observe how odd it is, that this branch of the art has flourished by intermitting fits. It never rains, but it pours. Our own age can boast of some fine specimens, such, for instance, as Bellingham's affair with the prime minister Percival, the Duc de Berri's case at the Parisian Opera House, the Maréchal Bessieres' case at Avignon; and about two and a half centuries ago, there was a most brilliant constellation·of murders in this class. I need hardly say, that I allude especially to those seven splendid works — the assassinations of William I., of Orange; of the three French Henries, viz., — Henri, Duke of Guise, that had a fancy for the throne of France; of Henry III., last prince in the line of Valois, who then occupied that throne; and finally of Henri IV., his brother-in-law, who succeeded to that throne as first prince in the line of Bourbon; not eighteen years later came the 5th on that roll, viz., that of our Duke of Buckingham, (which you will find excellently described in the letters published by Sir Henry Ellis, of the British Museum), 6thly, of Gustavus Adolphus, and 7thly, of Wallenstein. What a glorious Pleiad of murders! And it increases one's admiration — that this bright constellation of artistic displays, comprehending 3 Majesties, 3 Serene Highnesses, and 1 Excellency, all lay within so narrow a field of time as between A. D. 1588 and 1635. The King of Sweden's assassination, by the by, is doubted by many writers, Harte amongst others; but they are wrong. He was murdered; and I consider his murder unique in its excellence; for he was murdered at noon-day, and on the field of battle — a feature of original conception, which occurs in no other

work of art that I remember. To conceive the idea of
a secret murder on private account, as enclosed within
a little parenthesis on a vast stage of public battle-
carnage, is like Hamlet's subtle device of a tragedy
within a tragedy. Indeed, all of these assassinations
may be studied with profit by the advanced connoisseur. They are all of them *exemplaria* model murders,
pattern murders, of which one may say, —

'Nocturnâ versate manu, versate diurna;'

especially *nocturnâ*.

In these assassinations of princes and statesmen,
there is nothing to excite our wonder; important
changes often depend on their deaths; and, from the
eminence on which they stand, they are peculiarly exposed to the aim of every artist who happens to be
possessed by the craving for scenical effect. But there
is another class of assassinations, which has prevailed
from an early period of the seventeenth century, that
really *does* surprise me: I mean the assassination of
philosophers. For, gentlemen, it is a fact, that every
philosopher of eminence for the two last centuries has
either been murdered, or, at the least, been very near
it; insomuch, that if a man calls himself a philosopher,
and never had his life attempted, rest assured there is
nothing in him; and against Locke's philosophy in
particular, I think it an unanswerable objection (if we
needed any), that, although he carried his throat about
with him in this world for seventy-two years, no man
ever condescended to cut it. As these cases of philosophers are not much known, and are generally good
and well composed in their circumstances, I shall here
read an excursus on that subject, chiefly by way of
showing my own learning.

The first great philosopher of the seventeenth century (if we except Bacon and Galileo) was Des Cartes; and if ever one could say of a man that he was all *but* murdered — murdered within an inch — one must say it of him. The case was this, as reported by Baillet in his ' Vie De M. Des Cartes,' tom. I. p. 102 – 3. In the year 1621, when Des Cartes might be about twenty-six years old, he was touring about as usual (for he was as restless as a hyena); and, coming to the Elbe, either at Gluckstadt or at Hamburg, he took shipping for East Friezland. What he could want in East Friezland no man has ever discovered; and perhaps he took this into consideration himself; for, on reaching Embden, he resolved to sail instantly for *West* Friezland; and being very impatient of delay, he hired a bark, with a few mariners to navigate it. No sooner had he got out to sea, than he made a pleasing discovery, viz., that he had shut himself up in a den of murderers. His crew, says M. Baillet, he soon found out to be ' des scélérats ' — not *amateurs*, gentlemen, as we are, but professional men — the height of whose ambition at that moment was to cut his individual throat. But the story is too pleasing to be abridged; I shall give it, therefore, accurately, from the French of his biographer: " M. Des Cartes had no company but that of his servant, with whom he was conversing in French. The sailors, who took him for a foreign merchant, rather than a cavalier, concluded that he must have money about him. Accordingly, they came to a resolution by no means advantageous to his purse. There is this difference, however, between sea-robbers and the robbers in forests, that the latter may, without hazard, spare the lives of their victims; whereas the others cannot put a passenger on shore in such a case without running the risk of being apprehended. The crew of M. Des Cartes arranged their measures with a view to evade any danger of that sort. They observed that he was a stranger from a distance, without acquaintance in the country, and that nobody would take any trouble to inquire about him, in case he should never come to hand (*quand il viendroit à manquer*).' Think, gentlemen, of these Friezland dogs discussing a philosopher as if he were a puncheon of rum consigned to some ship-broker. 'His temper, they remarked, was very mild and patient; and, judging from the gentleness of his deportment, and the courtesy with which he treated themselves, that he could be nothing more than some green young man, without station or root in the world, they concluded that they should have all the easier task in disposing of his life. They made no scruple to discuss the whole matter in his presence, as not supposing that he understood any other language than that in which he conversed with his servant; and the amount of their deliberation was — to murder him, then to throw him into the sea, and to divide his spoils.'

Excuse my laughing, gentlemen; but the fact is, I always *do* laugh when I think of this case — two things about it seem so droll. One is, the horrid panic or 'funk' (as the men of Eton call it) in which Des Cartes must have found himself, upon hearing this regular drama sketched for his own death — funeral — succession and administration to his effects. But another thing which seems to me still more funny about this affair is, that if these Friezland hounds had

been 'game,' we should have no Cartesian philosophy; and how we could have done without *that*, considering the world of books it has produced, I leave
to any respectable trunk-maker to declare.

However, to go on: spite of his enormous funk,
Des Cartes showed fight, and by that means awed
these Anti-Cartesian rascals. 'Finding,' says M.
.Baillet, 'that the matter was no joke, M. Des Cartes
leaped upon his feet in a trice, assumed a stern countenance that these cravens had never looked for, and,
addressing them in their own language, threatened to
run them through on the spot if they dared to give
him any insult.' Certainly, gentlemen, this would
have been an honor far above the merits of such in-
considerable rascals — to be spitted like larks upon a
Cartesian sword; and therefore I am glad M. Des
Cartes did not rob the gallows by executing his threat,
especially as he could not possibly have brought his
vessel to port, after he had murdered his crew; so
that he must have continued to cruise for ever in the
Zuyder Zee, and would probably have been mistaken
by sailors for the *Flying Dutchman*, homeward bound.
'The spirit which M. Des Cartes manifested,' says
his biographer, 'had the effect of magic on these
wretches. The suddenness of their consternation
struck their minds with a confusion which blinded
them to their advantage, and they conveyed him to his
destination as peaceably as he could desire.'

Possibly, gentlemen, you may fancy that, on the
model of Cæsar's address to his poor ferryman — '*Cæ-
sarem vehis et fortunas ejus*' — M. Des Cartes needed
only to have said, 'Dogs, you cannot cut my throat,
for you carry Des Cartes and his philosophy,' and

might safely have defied them to do their worst. A German emperor had the same notion, when, being cautioned to keep out of the way of a cannonading, he replied, 'Tut! man. Did you ever hear of a cannon-ball that killed an emperor?'[4] As to an emperor I cannot say, but a less thing has sufficed to smash a philosopher; and the next great philosopher of Europe undoubtedly *was* murdered. This was Spinosa.

I know very well the common opinion about him is, that he died in his bed. Perhaps he did, but he was murdered for all that; and this I shall prove by a book published at Brussels in the year 1731, entitled 'La Vie de Spinosa, par M. Jean Colerus,' with many additions, from a MS. life, by one of his friends. Spinosa died on the 21st February, 1677, being then little more than forty-four years old. This, of itself, looks suspicious; and M. Jean admits, that a certain expression in the MS. life of him would warrant the conclusion, 'que sa mort n'a pas été-à-fait naturelle.' Living in a damp country, and a sailor's country, like Holland, he may be thought to have indulged a good deal in grog, especially in punch,[5] which was then newly discovered. Undoubtedly he might have done so; but the fact is, that he did not. M. Jean calls him ' extrêmement sobre en son boire et en son manger.' And though some wild stories were afloat about his using the juice of mandragora (p. 140) and opium (p. 144), yet neither of these articles is found in his druggist's bill. Living, therefore, with such sobriety, how was it possible that he should die a natural death at forty-four? Hear his biographer's account: — 'Sunday morning, the 21st of February, before it was church time, Spinosa came down stairs, and conversed

with the master and mistress of the house. At this
time, therefore, perhaps ten o'clock on Sunday morning, you see that Spinosa was alive, and pretty well.
But it seems 'he had summoned from Amsterdam a
certain physician, whom,' says the biographer, ' I shall
not otherwise point out to notice than by these two
letters, L. M.' This L. M. had directed the people of
the house to purchase ' an ancient cock,' and to have
him boiled forthwith, in order that Spinosa might take
some broth about noon ; which in fact he did ; and ate
some of the *old cock* with a good appetite, after the
landlord and his wife had returned from church.

' In the afternoon, L. M. staid alone with Spinosa,
the people of the house having returned to church ; on
coming out from which, they learned, with much surprise, that Spinosa had died about three o'clock, in the
presence of L. M., who took his departure for Amsterdam that same evening, by the night-boat, without
paying the least attention to the deceased,' and probably without paying very much attention to the payment of his own little account. ' No doubt he was
the readier to dispense with these duties, as he had
possessed himself of a ducatoon, and a small quantity
of silver, together with a silver-hafted knife, and had
absconded with his pillage.' Here you see, gentlemen, the murder is plain, and the manner of it. It
was L. M. who murdered Spinosa for his money. Poor
Spinosa was an invalid, meagre and weak: as no blood
was observed, L. M. no doubt threw him down, and
smothered him with pillows — the poor man being
already half suffocated by his infernal dinner. After
masticating that ' ancient cock,' which I take to mean
a cock of the preceding century, in what condition

could the poor invalid find nimself for a stand-up fight
with L. M.? But who was L. M.? It surely never
could be Lindley Murray, for I saw him at York in
1825; and, besides, I do not think he would do such
a thing — at least, not to a brother grammarian.: for you
know, gentlemen, that Spinosa wrote a very respectable
Hebrew grammar.

Hobbes — but why, or on what principle, I never
could understand — was not murdered. This was a
capital oversight of the professional men of the seventeenth century; because in every light he was a fine
subject for murder, except, indeed, that he was lean
and skinny; for I can prove that he had money, and
(what is very funny) he had no right to make the least
resistance; since, according to himself, irresistible
power creates the very highest species of right; so
that it is rebellion of the blackest dye to refuse to be
murdered, when a competent force appears to murder
you. However, gentlemen, though he was not murdered, I am happy to assure you that (by his own account) he was three times very near being murdered,
which is consolatory. The first time was in the spring
of 1640, when he pretends to have circulated a little
MS. on the king's behalf against the Parliament; he
never could produce this MS., by the by; but he says,
that, ' Had not His Majesty dissolved the Parliament '
(in May), ' it had brought him into danger of his life.'
Dissolving the Parliament, however, was of no use;
for in November of the same year the Long Parliament
assembled, and Hobbes, a second time fearing he should
be murdered, ran away to France. This looks like the
madness of John Dennis, who thought that Louis XIV.
would never make peace with Queen Anne, unless he

(Dennis, to wit) were given up to French vengeance; and actually ran away from the sea-coast under that belief. In France, Hobbes managed to take care of his throat pretty well for ten years; but at the end of that time, by way of paying court to Cromwell, he published his 'Leviathan.' The old coward now began to 'funk' horribly for the third time; he fancied the swords of the cavaliers were constantly at his throat, recollecting how they had served the Parliament ambassadors at the Hague and Madrid. 'Tum,' says he, in his dog-Latin life of himself,

'Tum venit in mentem mihi Dorislaus et Ascham;
Tanquam proscripto terror ubique aderat.'

And accordingly he ran home to England. Now, certainly, it is very true that a man deserved a cudgelling for writing 'Leviathan;' and two or three cudgellings for writing a pentameter ending so villanously as 'terror ubique aderat!' But no man ever thought him worthy of anything beyond cudgelling. And, in fact, the whole story is a bounce of his own. For, in a most abusive letter which he wrote 'to a learned person' (meaning Wallis the mathematician), he gives quite another account of the matter, and says (p. 8), he ran home 'because he would not trust his safety with the French clergy;' insinuating that he was likely to be murdered for his religion, which would have been a high joke indeed — Tom's being brought to the stake for religion.

Bounce or not bounce, however, certain it is that Hobbes, to the end of his life, feared that somebody would murder him. This is proved by the story I am going to tell you: it is not from a manuscript, but (as Mr. Coleridge says) it is as good as manuscript; for it

comes from a book now entirely forgotten, viz., 'The
Creed of Mr. Hobbes Examined : in a Conference between him and a Student in Divinity' (published
about ten years before Hobbes's death). The book is
anonymous, but it was written by Tennison, the same
who, about thirty years after, succeeded Tillotson as
Archbishop of Canterbury. The introductory anecdote
is as follows : — 'A certain divine' (no doubt Tennison himself) ' took an annual tour of one month to
different parts of the island." In one of these excursions (1670), he visited the Peak in Derbyshire, partly
in consequence of Hobbes's description of it. Being
in that neighborhood, he could not but pay a visit to
Buxton ; and at the very moment of his arrival, he was
fortunate enough to find a party of gentlemen dis-
mounting at the inn-door, amongst whom was a long
thin fellow, who turned out to be no less a person than
Mr. Hobbes, who probably had ridden over from Chatsworth.[6] Meeting so great a lion, a tourist, in search
of the picturesque, could do no less than present himself in the character of bore. And luckily for this
scheme, two of Mr. Hobbes's companions were suddenly
summoned away by express ; so that, for the rest of his
stay at Buxton, he had Leviathan entirely to himself,
and had the honor of bowsing with him in the evening. Hobbes, it seems, at first showed a good deal of
stiffness, for he was shy of divines ; but this wore off,
and he became very sociable and funny, and they
agreed to go into the bath together. How Tennison
could venture to gambol in the same water with Leviathan, I cannot explain ;. but so it was : they frolicked
about like two dolphins, though Hobbes must have
been as old as the hills ; and ' in those intervals

wherein they abstained from swimming and plunging
themselves' (*i. e.*, diving), 'they discoursed of many
things relating to the Baths of the Ancients, and the
Origine of Springs.   When they had in this manner
passed away an hour, they stepped out of the bath;
and, having dried and cloathed themselves, they sate
down in expectation of such a supper as the place af-
forded; designing to refresh themselves like the
Deipnosophistæ, and rather to reason than to drink
profoundly.   But in this innocent intention they were
interrupted by the disturbance arising from a little
quarrel, in which some of the ruder people in the house
were for a short time engaged.   At this Mr. Hobbes
seemed much concerned, though he was at some distance from the persons.'   And why was he concerned,
gentlemen?   No doubt, you fancy, from some benign
and disinterested love of peace worthy of an old man
and a philosopher.   But listen — ' For a while he was
not composed, but related it once or twice as to himself, with a low and careful, *i. e.* anxious, tone, how
Sextus Roscius was murthered after supper by the
Balneæ Palatinæ.   Of such general extent is that remark of Cicero, in relation to Epicurus the Atheist, of
whom he observed, that he of all men dreaded most
those things which he contemned — Death and the
Gods.'   Merely because it was supper time, and in the
neighborhood of a bath, Mr. Hobbes must have the
fate of Sextus Roscius.   He must be mur*th*ered, because Sextus Roscius was mur*th*ered.   What logic was
there in this, unless to a man who was always dream-
ing of murder?   Here was Leviathan, no longer afraid
of the daggers of English cavaliers or French clergy,
but ' frightened from his propriety ' by a row in an ale-

house between some honest clodhoppers of Derbyshire, whom his own gaunt scarecrow of a person, that
belonged to quite another century, would have frightened out of their wits.

Malebranche, it will give you pleasure to hear, was
murdered. The man who murdered him is well
known: it was Bishop Berkeley. The story is familiar, though hitherto not put in a proper light.
Berkeley, when a young man, went to Paris, and
called on Père Malebranche. He found him in his
cell cooking. Cooks have ever been a *genus irrita-
bile ;* authors still more so. Malebranche was both. A
dispute arose; the old father, warm already, became
warmer; culinary and metaphysical irritations united
to derange his liver: he took to his bed and died.
Such is the common version of the story. ' So the
whole ear of Denmark is abused.' The fact is, that
the matter was hushed up, out of consideration for
Berkeley, who (as Pope justly observes) had ' every
virtue under heaven : ' else it was well known that
Berkeley, feeling himself nettled by the waspishness of
the old Frenchman, squared at him; a *turn-up* was
the consequence ; Malebranche was floored in the first
round ; the conceit was wholly taken out of him ; and
he would perhaps have given in ; but Berkeley's blood
was now up, and he insisted on the old Frenchman's
retracting his doctrine of Occasional Causes. The
vanity of the man was too great for this ; and he fell
a sacrifice to the impetuosity of Irish youth, combined
with his own absurd obstinacy.

Leibnitz, being every way superior to Malebranche,
one might, *a fortiori*, have counted on *his* being murdered ; which, however, was not the case. I believe

he was nettled at this neglect, and felt himself insulted
by the security in which he passed his days. In no
other way can I explain his conduct at the latter end
of his life, when he chose to grow very avaricious,
and to hoard up large sums of gold, which he kept in
his own house. This was at Vienna, where he died;
and letters are still in existence, describing the immeasurable anxiety which he entertained for his throat.
Still his ambition, for being *attempted* at least, was so
great, that he would not forego the danger. A late
English pedagogue, of Birmingham manufacture — viz.,
Dr. Parr — took a more selfish course under the same
circumstance. He had amassed a considerable quantity of gold and silver plate, which was for some time
deposited in his bedroom at his parsonage house, Hatton. But growing every day more afraid of being
murdered, which he knew that he could not stand
(and to which, indeed, he never had the slightest pretensions), he transferred the whole to the Hatton
blacksmith; conceiving, no doubt, that the murder of
a blacksmith would fall more lightly on the *salus
reipublicæ*, than that of a pedagogue. But I have
heard this greatly disputed; and it seems now generally agreed, that one good horseshoe is worth about
two and a quarter Spital sermons.[7]

As Leibnitz, though not murdered, may be said to
have died, partly of the fear that he should be murdered, and partly of vexation that he was not, Kant,
on the other hand — who manifested no ambition in
that way — had a narrower escape from a murderer
than any man we read of, except Des Cartes. So ab-
surdly does fortune throw about her favors! The
case is told, I think, in an anonymous life of this very

great man. For health's sake, Kant imposed upon himself, at one time, a walk of six miles every day along a high-road. This fact becoming known to a man who had his private reasons for committing murder, at the third milestone from Kònigsberg, he waited for his 'intended,' who came up to time as duly as a mail-coach.

But for an accident, Kant was a dead man. This accident lay in the scrupulous, or what Mrs. Quickly would have called the *peevish*, morality of the murderer. An old professor, he fancied, might be laden with sins. Not so a young child. On this consideration, he turned away from Kant at the critical moment, and soon after murdered a child of five years old. Such is the German account of the matter ; but my opinion is, that the murderer was an amateur, who felt how little would be gained to the cause of good taste by murdering an old, arid, and adust metaphysician ; there was no room for display, as the man could not possibly look more like a mummy when dead, than he had done alive.

Thus, gentlemen, I have traced the connection between philosophy and our art, until insensibly I find that I have wandered into our own era. This I shall not take any pains to characterize apart from that which preceded it, for, in fact, they have no distinct character. The seventeenth and eighteenth centuries, together with so much of the nineteenth as we have yet seen, jointly compose the Augustan age of murder. The finest work of the seventeenth century is, unquestionably, the murder of Sir Edmondbury Godfrey, which has my entire approbation. In the grand feature of *mystery*, which in some shape or other ought to color every judicious attempt at murder, it is excellent; for the mystery is not yet dispersed. The attempt to fasten the murder upon the Papists, which would injure it as much as some well-known Correggios have been injured by the professional picture-cleaners, or would even ruin it by translating it into the spurious class of mere political or partisan murders, thoroughly wanting in the murderous *animus*, I exhort the society to discountenance. In fact, this notion is altogether baseless, and arose in pure Protestant fanaticism. Sir Edmondbury had not distinguished himself amongst the London magistrates by any severity against the Papists, or in favoring the attempts of zealots to enforce the penal laws against individuals. He had not armed against himself the animosities of any religious sect whatever. And as to the droppings of wax lights upon the dress of the corpse when first discovered in a ditch, from which it was inferred at the time that the priests attached to the Popish Queen's Chapel had been concerned in the murder, either these were mere fraudulent artifices devised by those who wished to fix the suspicion upon the Papists, or else the whole allegation — wax-droppings, and the suggested cause of the droppings — might be a bounce or fib of Bishop Burnet; who, as the Duchess of Portsmouth used to say, was the one great master of fibbing and romancing in the seventeenth century. At the same time, it must be observed that the quantity of murder was not great in Sir Edmondbury's century, at least amongst our own artists; which, perhaps, is attributable to the want of enlightened patronage. *Sint Mæcenates, non deerunt, Flacce, Marones.*

Consulting Grant's ' Observations on the Bills of Mortality ' (4th edition, Oxford, 1665), I find, that, out of 229,250, who died in London during one period of twenty years in the seventeenth century, not more than eighty-six were murdered; that is, about four three-tenths per annum. A small number this, gentlemen, to found an academy upon; and certainly, where the quantity is so small, we have a right to expect that the quality should be first-rate. Perhaps it was; yet still I am of opinion that the best artist in this century was not equal to the best in that which followed. For instance, however praiseworthy the case of Sir Edmondbury Godfrey may be (and nobody can be more sensible of its merits than I am), still, I cannot consent to place it on a level with that of Mrs. Ruscombe of Bristol, either as to originality of design, or boldness and breadth of style. This good lady's murder took place early in the reign of Geoige III. — a reign which was notoriously favorable to the arts generally. She lived in College Green, with a single maid-servant, neither of them having any pretension to the notice of history but what they derived from the great artist whose workmanship I am recording. One fine morning, when all Bristol was alive and in motion, some suspicion arising, the neighbors forced an entrance into the house, and found Mrs. Ruscombe murdered in her bedroom, and the servant murdered on the stairs. This was at noon; and, not more than two hours before, both mistress and servant had been seen alive. To the best of my remembrance, this was in 1764; upwards of sixty years, therefore, have now elapsed, and yet the artist is still undiscovered. The suspicions of posterity have settled upon two pretend-

ers — a baker and a chimney-sweeper. But posterity
is wrong; no unpractised artist could have conceived
so bold an idea as that of a noonday murder in the
heart of a great city. It was no obscure baker, gentlemen, or anonymous chimney-sweeper, be assured, that
executed this work. I know who it was. (*Here there
was a general buzz, which at length broke out into
open applause; upon which the lecturer blushed, and
went on with much earnestness.*) For Heaven's sake,
gentlemen, do not mistake me; it was not I that did
it. I have not the vanity to think myself equal to any
such achievement; be assured that you greatly over-
rate my poor talents; Mrs. Ruscombe's affair was far
beyond my slender abilities. But I came to know
who the artist was, from a celebrated surgeon who
assisted at his dissection. This gentleman had a private museum in the way of his profession, one corner
of which was occupied by a cast from a man of remarkably fine proportions.

'That,' said the surgeon, 'is a cast from the celebrated Lancashire highwayman, who concealed his profession for some time from his neighbors, by drawing
woollen stockings over his horse's legs, and in that
way muffling the clatter which he must else have made
in riding up a flagged alley that led to his stable. At
the time of his execution for highway robbery, I was
studying under Cruickshank: and the man's figure
was so uncommonly fine, that no money or exertion
was spared to get into possession of him with the least
possible delay. By the connivance of the under-
sheriff, he was cut down within the legal time, and
instantly put into a chaise-and-four; so that, when he
reached Cruickshank's, he was positively not dead.

Mr. ——, a young student at that time, had the honor
of giving him the *coup de grace*, and finishing the sentence of the law.' This remarkable anecdote, which
seemed to imply that all the gentlemen in the dissect-
ing-room were amateurs of our class, struck me a good
deal ; and I was repeating it one day to a Lancashire
lady, who thereupon informed me, that she had herself
lived in the neighborhood of that highwayman, and
well remembered two circumstances, which combined,
in the opinion of all his neighbors, to fix upon him the
credit of Mrs. Ruscombe's affair. One was, the fact
of his absence for a whole fortnight at the period of
that murder ; the other, that, within a very little time
after, the neighborhood of this highwayman was del-
uged with dollars. Now, Mrs. Ruscombe was known
to have hoarded about two thousand of that coin. Be
the artist, however, who he might, the affair remains a
durable monument of his genius ; for such was the impression of awe, and the sense of power left behind, by
the strength of conception manifested in this murder,
that no tenant (as I was told in 1810) had been found
up to that time for Mrs. Ruscombe's house.

But, whilst I thus eulogize the Ruscombian case, let
me not be supposed to overlook the many other specimens of extraordinary merit spread over the face of this
century. Such cases, indeed, as that of Miss Bland, or
of Captain Donnellan, and Sir Theophilus Boughton,
shall never have any countenance from me. Fie on
these dealers in poison, say I : can they not keep to
the old honest way of cutting throats, without introducing such abominable innovations from Italy ? I
consider all these poisoning cases, compared with the
legitimate style, as no better than waxwork by the

side of sculpture, or a lithographic print by the side of
a fine Volpato. But, dismissing these, there remain
many excellent works of art in a pure style, such as
nobody need be ashamed to own ; and this every candid connoisseur will admit. *Candid*, observe, I say ;
for great allowances must be made in these cases ; no
artist can ever be sure of carrying through his own fine
preconception. Awkward disturbances will arise ;
people will not submit to have their throats cut
quietly ; they will run, they will kick, they will bite ;
and whilst the portrait painter often has to complain
of too much torpor in his subject, the artist in our line
is generally embarrassed by too much animation. At
the same time, however disagreeable to the artist, this
tendency in murder to excite and irritate the subject is
certainly one of its advantages to the world in general,
which we ought not to overlook, since it favors the
development of latent talent. Jeremy Taylor notices
with admiration the extraordinary leaps which people
will take under the influence of fear. There was a
striking instance of this in the recent case of the
M'Keans : the boy cleared a height, such as he will
never clear again to his dying day. Talents also of
the most brilliant description for thumping, and, indeed, for all the gymnastic exercises, have sometimes
been developed by the panic which accompanies our
artists ; talents else buried and hid under a bushel, to
the possessors as much as to their friends. I remember an interesting illustration of this fact, in a case
which I learned in Germany.

Riding one day in the neighborhood of Munich, I
overtook a distinguished amateur of our society, whose
name, for obvious reasons, I shall conceal. This gen-

tleman informed me that, finding himself wearied with
the frigid pleasures (such he esteemed them) of mere
amateurship, he had quitted England for the Continent
— meaning to practise a little professionally. For this
purpose he resorted to Germany, conceiving the police
in that part of Europe to be more heavy and drowsy
than elsewhere. His *debut* as a practitioner took place
at Mannheim ; and, knowing me to be a brother amateur, he freely communicated the whole of his maiden
adventure. ' Opposite to my lodging,' said he, ' lived
a baker ; he was somewhat of a miser, and lived quite
alone. Whether it were his great expanse of chalky
face, or what else, I know not, but the fact was, I
" fancied " him, and resolved to commence business
upon his throat, which, by the way, he always carried
bare — a fashion which is very irritating to my desires.
Precisely at eight o'clock in the evening, I observed
that he regularly shut up his windows. One night I
watched him when thus engaged — bolted in after him
— locked the door — and, addressing him with great
suavity, acquainted him with the nature of my errand ;
at the same time advising him to make no resistance,
which would be mutually unpleasant. So saying, I
drew out my tools ; and was proceeding to operate
But at this spectacle the baker, who seemed to have
been struck by catalepsy at my first announcement,
awoke into tremendous agitation. ' I will *not* be murdered !' he shrieked aloud ; ' what for will I' (meaning
shall I) ' lose my precious throat ? ' ' What for ? ' said
I ; ' if for no other reason, for this — that you put
alum into your bread. But no matter, alum or no
alum' (for I was resolved to forestall any argument on
that point), ' know that I am a virtuoso in the art of

murder — am desirous of improving myself in its
details — and am enamored of your vast surface of
throat, to which I am determined to be a customer.'
' Is it so?' said he, ' but I'll find you a customer in
another line ; ' and so saying, he threw himself into a
boxing attitude. The very idea of his boxing struck
me as ludicrous. It is true, a London baker had distinguished himself in the ring, and became known to
fame under the title of the Master of the Rolls ; but
he was young and unspoiled ; whereas, this man was
a monstrous feather-bed in person, fifty years old, and
totally out of condition. Spite of all this, however,
and contending against me, who am a master in the
art, he made so desperate a defence, that many times I
feared he might turn the tables upon me ; and that I,
an amateur, might be murdered by a rascally baker.
What a situation ! Minds of sensibility will sympa-
thize with my anxiety. How severe it was, you may
understand by this, that for the first thirteen rounds
the baker positively had the advantage. Round the
14th, I received a blow on the right eye, which closed
it up ; in the end, I believe, this was my salvation ;
for the anger it roused in me was so great, that, in the
next, and every one of the three following rounds, I
floored the baker.

' Round 19th. The baker came up piping, and
manifestly the worse for wear. His geometrical ex-
ploits in the four last rounds had done him no good.
However, he showed some skill in stopping a message which I was sending to his cadaverous mug ; in
delivering which, my foot slipped, and I went down.

' Round 20th. Surveying the baker, I became
ashamed of having been so much bothered by a shape-

'less mass of dough; and I went in fiercely, and administered some severe punishment. A rally took place — both went down — baker undermost — ten to three on amateur.

'Round 21st. The baker jumped up with surprising agility; indeed, he managed his pins capitally, and fought wonderfully, considering that he was drenched in perspiration; but the shine was now taken out of him, and his game was the mere effect of panic. It was now clear that he could not last much longer. In the course of this round we tried the weaving system, in which I had greatly the advantage, and hit him repeatedly on the conk. My reason for this was, that his conk was covered with carbuncles; and I thought I should vex him by taking such liberties with his conk, which in fact I did.

'The three next rounds, the master of the rolls staggered about like a cow on the ice. Seeing how matters stood, in round 24th I whispered something into his ear, which sent him down like a shot. It was nothing more than my private opinion of the value of his throat at an annuity office. This little confidential whisper affected him greatly; the very perspiration was frozen on his face, and for the next two rounds I had it all my own way. And when I called *time* for the 27th round, he lay like a log on the floor.'

After which, said I to the amateur, 'It may be presumed that you accomplished your purpose.' 'You are right,' said he mildly, 'I did; and a great satisfaction, you know, it was to my mind, for by this means I killed two birds with one stone;' meaning that he had both thumped the baker and murdered him. Now, for the life of me, I could not see *that*; for, on the contrary, to my mind it appeared that he had taken two stones to kill one bird, having been obliged to take the conceit out of him first with his fist, and then with his tools. But no matter for his logic. The moral of his story was good, for it showed what an astonishing stimulus to latent talent is contained in any reasonable prospect of being murdered. A pursy, unwieldy, half cataleptic baker of Mannheim had absolutely fought seven-and-twenty rounds with an accomplished English boxer, merely upon this inspiration; so great was natural genius exalted and sublimed by the genial presence of his murderer.

: Really, gentlemen, when one hears of such things as these, it becomes a duty, perhaps, a little to soften that extreme asperity with which most men speak of murder. To hear people talk, you would suppose that all the disadvantages and inconveniences were on the side of being murdered, and that there were none at all in *not* being murdered. But considerate men think otherwise. 'Certainly,' says Jeremy Taylor, 'it is a less temporal evil to fall by the rudeness of a sword than the violence of a fever: and the axe' (to which he might have added the ship-carpenter's mallet and the crowbar), 'a much less affliction than a strangury.' Very true; the bishop talks like a wise man and an amateur, as I am sure he was; and another great philosopher, Marcus Aurelius, was equally above the vulgar prejudices on this subject. He declares it to be one of 'the noblest functions of reason to know whether it is time to walk out of the world or not.' (Book iii., Collers' Translation.) No sort of knowledge being rarer than this, surely *that* man must be a most philanthropic character, who undertakes to instruct people in this branch of knowledge gratis, and at no little hazard to himself. All this, however, I throw out only in the way of speculation to future moralists; declaring in the meantime my own private conviction, that very few men commit murder upon philanthropic or patriotic principles, and repeating what I have already said once at least — that, as to the majority of murderers, they are very incorrect characters.

With respect to the Williams' murders, the sublimest and most entire in their excellence that ever were committed, I shall not allow myself to speak incidentally. Nothing less than an entire lecture, or even an entire course of lectures, would suffice to expound their merits. But one curious fact connected with his case I shall mention, because it seems to imply that the blaze of his genius absolutely dazzled the eye of criminal justice. You all remember, I doubt not, that the instruments with which he executed his first great work (the murder of the Marrs) were a ship-carpenter's mallet and a knife. Now, the mallet belonged to an old Swede, one John Peterson, and bore his initials. This instrument Williams left behind him in Marr's house, and it fell into the hands of the magistrates. But, gentlemen, it is a fact that the publication of this circumstance of the initials led immediately to the apprehension of Williams, and, if made earlier, would have prevented his second great work (the murder of the Williamsons), which took place precisely twelve days after. Yet the magistrates kept back this fact from the public for the entire twelve days, and until that second work was accomplished. That finished, they published it, apparently feeling that Williams had now done enough for his fame, and that his glory was at length placed beyond the reach of accident.

As to Mr. Thurtell's case, I know not what to say. Naturally, I have every disposition to think highly of my predecessor in the chair of this society; and I acknowledge that his lectures were unexceptionable. But, speaking ingenuously, I do really think that his principal performance, as an artist, has been much overrated. I admit, that at first, I was myself carried away by the general enthusiasm. On the morning when the murder was made known in London, there was the fullest meeting of amateurs that I have ever known since the days of Williams; old bedridden connoisseurs, who had got into a peevish way of sneering and complaining ' that there was nothing doing,' now hobbled down to our club-room: such hilarity, such benign expression of general satisfaction, I have rarely witnessed. On every side you saw people shaking hands, congratulating each other, and forming dinner parties for the evening; and nothing was to be heard but triumphant challenges of — ' Well! will *this* do ? ' ' Is *this* the right thing ? ' ' Are you satisfied at last ? ' But in the middle of the row, I remember, we all grew silent, on hearing the old cynical amateur L. S—— stumping along with his wooden leg; he entered the room with his usual scowl; and, as he advanced, he continued to growl and stutter the whole way — ' Mere plagiarism — base plagiarism from hints that I threw out! Besides, his style is as harsh as Albert Durer, and as coarse as Fuseli.' Many thought that this was mere jealousy, and general waspishness; but I confess that, when the first glow of enthusiasm had subsided, I have found most judicious critics to agree that there was something *falsetto* in the style of Thurtell. The fact is, he was a member of our society, which naturally gave a friendly bias to our judgments; and his person was universally familiar to the ' fancy,' which gave him, with the whole London public, a temporary popularity, that his pretensions are not capable of supporting ; for *opinionum commenta delet dies, naturæ judicia confirmat.* There was, however, an unfinished design of Thurtell's for the murder of a man with a pair of dumb-bells, which I admired greatly; it was a mere outline, that he never filled in; but to my mind it seemed every way superior to his chief work. I remember that there was great regret expressed by some amateurs that this sketch should have been left in an unfinished state : but there I cannot agree with them ; for the fragments and first bold outlines of original artists have often a felicity about them which is apt to vanish in the management of the details.

The case of the M'Keans I consider far beyond the vaunted performance of Thurtell — indeed, above all praise ; and bearing that relation, in fact, to the immortal works of Williams, which the ' Æneid ' bears to the ' Iliad.'

But it is now time that I should say a few words about the principles of murder, not with a view to regulate your practice, but your judgment : as to old women, and the mob of newspaper readers, they are pleased with anything, provided it is bloody enough. But the mind of sensibility requires something more. *First,* then, let us speak of the kind of person who is adapted to the purpose of the murderer; *secondly,* of the place where; *thirdly*, of the time when, and other little circumstances.

As to the person, I suppose that it is evident that he ought to be a good man; because, if he were not, he might himself, by possibility, be contemplating murder at the very time; and such 'diamond-cut-diamond' tussles, though pleasant enough where nothing better is stirring, are really not what a critic can allow himself to call murders. I could mention some people (I name no names) who have been murdered by other people in a dark lane; and so far all seemed correct enough; but, on looking farther into the matter, the public have become aware that the murdered party was himself, at the moment, planning to rob his murderer, at the least, and possibly to murder him, if he had been strong enough. Whenever that is the case, or may be thought to be the case, farewell to all the genuine effects of the art. For the final purpose of murder, considered as a fine art, is precisely the same as that of tragedy, in Aristotle's account of it; viz., 'to cleanse the heart by means of pity and terror.' Now, terror there may be, but how can there be any pity for one tiger destroyed by another tiger?

It is also evident that the person selected ought not to be a public character. For instance, no judicious artist would have attempted to murder Abraham Newland.[8] For the case was this: everybody read so much about Abraham Newland, and so few people ever saw him, that to the general belief he was a mere abstract idea. And I remember, that once, when I happened to mention that I had dined at a coffee-house in company with Abraham Newland, everybody looked scornfully at me, as though I had pretended to

have played at billiards with Prester John, or to have
had an affair of honor with the Pope. And, by the
way, the Pope would be a very improper person to
murder: for he has such a virtual ubiquity as the
father of Christendom, and, like the cuckoo, is so
often heard but never seen, that I suspect most people
regard *him* also as an abstract idea. Where, indeed,
a public man is in the habit of giving dinners, ' with
every delicacy of the season,' the case is very different: every person is satisfied that *he* is no abstract
idea; and, therefore, there can be no impropriety in
murdering him, only that his murder will fall into the
class of assassinations, which I have not yet treated.

Thirdly. The subject chosen ought to be in good
health: for it is absolutely barbarous to murder a sick
person, who is usually quite unable to bear it. On
this principle, no tailor ought to be chosen who is
above twenty-five, for after that age he is sure to be
dyspeptic. Or at least, if a man will hunt in that
warren, he will of course think it his duty, on the old
established equation, to murder some multiple of 9 —
say 18, 27, or 36. And here, in this benign attention
to the comfort of sick people, you will observe the
usual effect of a fine art to soften and refine the feelings. The world in general, gentlemen, are very
bloody-minded; and all they want in a murder is a
copious effusion of blood; gaudy display in this point
is enough for *them*. But the enlightened connoisseur
is more refined in his taste; and from our art, as from
all the other liberal arts when thoroughly mastered,
the result is, to humanize the heart; so true is it, that

' Ingenuas didicisse fideliter artes,
Emollit mores, nec sinit esse feros.'

A philosophic friend, well known for his philan-
thropy and general benignity, suggests that the subject
chosen ought also to have a family of young children wholly dependent upon his exertions, by way of
deepening the pathos. And, undoubtedly, this is a
judicious caution. Yet I would not insist too keenly
on such a condition. Severe good taste unquestionably suggests it; but still, where the man was otherwise unobjectionable in point of morals and health, I
would not look with too curious a jealousy to a re-
striction which might have the effect of narrowing the
artist's sphere.

So much for the person. As to the time, the place,
and the tools, I have many things to say, which at
present I have no room for. The good sense of the
practitioner has usually directed him to night and
privacy. Yet there have not been wanting cases
where this rule was departed from with excellent
effect. In respect to time, Mrs. Ruscombe's case is a
beautiful exception, which I have already noticed; and
in respect both to time and place, there is a fine exception in the annals of Edinburgh (year 1805), familiar
to every child in Edinburgh, but which has unaccountably been defrauded of its due portion of fame
amongst English amateurs. The case I mean is that
of a porter to one of the banks, who was murdered,
whilst carrying a bag of money, in broad daylight, on
turning out of the High Street, one of the most public
streets in Europe; and the murderer is to this hour
undiscovered.

> ' Sed fugit interea, fugit irreparabile tempus,
> Singula dum capti circumvectamur amore.'

And now, gentlemen, in conclusion, let me again

solemnly disclaim all pretensions on my own part to
the character of a professional man. I never attempted
any murder in my life, except in the year 1801, upon
the body of a tom-cat; and *that* turned out differently
from my intention. My purpose, I own, was downright murder. 'Semper. ego auditor tantum?' said I,
'nunquamne reponam?' And I went down stairs in
search of Tom at one o'clock on a dark night, with
the 'animus,' and no doubt with the fiendish looks, of
a murderer. But when I found him, he was in the
act of plundering the pantry of bread and other
things. Now this gave a new turn to the affair; for
the time being one of general scarcity, when even
Christians were reduced to the use of potato-bread,
rice-bread, and all sorts of things, it was downright
treason in a tom-cat to be wasting good wheaten-
bread in the way he was doing. It instantly became
a patriotic duty to put him to death; and, as I raised
aloft and shook the glittering steel, I fancied myself
rising, like Brutus, effulgent from a crowd of patriots,
and, as I stabbed him, I

> 'Call'd aloud on Tully's name,
> And bade the father of his country hail!'

Since then, what wandering thoughts I may have
had of attempting the life of an ancient ewe, of a
superannuated hen, and such 'small deer,' are locked
up in the secrets of my own breast; but, for the
higher departments of the art, I confess myself to be
utterly unfit. My ambition does not rise so high.
No, gentlemen, in the words of Horace,

> 'Fungar vice cotis, acutum
> Reddere quæ ferrum valet, exsors ipsa secandi.'

SUPPLEMENTARY PAPER ON MURDER,

CONSIDERED AS ONE OF THE FINE ARTS.

A GOOD many years ago, the reader may remember
that I came forward in the character of a *dilettante* in
murder. Perhaps *dilettante* is too strong a word.
Connoisseur is better suited to the scruples and infirmity of public taste. ·I suppose there is no harm in
that, at least. A man is not bound to put his eyes,
ears, and understanding into his breeches-pocket when
he meets with a murder. If he is not in a downright
comatose state, I suppose he must see that one murder
is better or worse than another, in point of good taste.
Murders have their little differences and shades of
merit, as well as statues, pictures, oratorios, cameos,
intaglios, or what not. You may be angry with the
man for talking too much, or too publicly (as to the
too much, that I deny — a man can never cultivate his
taste too highly); but you must allow him to think, at
any rate. Well, would you believe it? all my neighbors came to hear of that little æsthetic essay which I
had published ; and, unfortunately, hearing at the very ˎ
same time of a club that I was connected with, and a
dinner at which I presided — both tending to the same
little object as the essay, viz., the diffusion of a just
taste among Her [9] Majesty's subjects, they got up the
most barbarous calumnies against me. In particular,
they said that I, or that the club (which comes to the

[58]

same thing), had offered bounties on well-conducted homicides — with a scale of drawbacks, in case of any one defect or flaw, according to a table issued to private friends. Now, let me tell the whole truth about the dinner and the club, and it will be seen how malicious the world is. But first, confidentially, allow me to say what my real principles are upon the matter in question.

As to murder, I never committed one in my life. It's a well-known thing amongst all my friends. I can get a paper to certify as much, signed by lots of people. Indeed, if you come to that, I doubt whether many people could produce as strong a certificate. Mine would be as big as a breakfast tablecloth. There is indeed one member of the club, who pretends to say he caught me once making too free with his throat on a club night, after everybody else had retired. But, observe, he shuffles in his story according to his state of civilation. When not far gone, he contents himself with saying that he caught me ogling his throat; and that I was melancholy for some weeks after, and that my voice sounded in a way expressing, to the nice ear of a connoisseur, *the sense of opportunities lost;* but the club all know that he is a disappointed man himself, and that he speaks querulously at times about the fatal neglect of a man's coming abroad without his tools. Besides, all this is an affair between two amateurs, and everybody makes allowances for little asperities and fibs in such a case. 'But,' say you, 'if no murderer, you may have encouraged, or even have bespoken a murder.' No, upon my honor — no. And that was the very point I wished to argue for your satisfaction. The truth is, I am a very particular man in everything

relating to murder; and perhaps I carry my delicacy
too far. The Stagirite most justly, and possibly with
a view to my case, placed virtue in the τὸ μέσον, or middle point between two extremes. A golden mean is
certainly what every man should aim at. But it is
easier talking than doing; and, my infirmity being notoriously too much milkiness of heart, I find it difficult
to maintain that steady equatorial line between the
two poles of too much murder on the one hand, and
too little on the other. I am too soft — and people
get excused through me — nay, go through life without an attempt made upon them, that ought *not* to be
excused. I believe, if I had the management of things,
there would hardly be a murder from year's end to
year's end. In fact, I'm for peace, and quietness, and
fawningness, and what may be styled *knocking-under-
ness*. A man came to me as a candidate for the place
of my servant, just then vacant. He had the reputation of having dabbled a little in our art; some said,
not without merit. What startled me, however, was,
that he supposed this art to be part of his regular duties in my service, and talked of having it considered
in his wages. Now, that was a thing I would not
allow; so I said at once, ' Richard (or James, as the
case might be), you misunderstand my character. If a
man will and must practise this difficult (and allow me
to add, dangerous) branch of art — if he has an over-
ruling genius for it, why, in that case, all I say is, that
he might as well pursue his studies whilst living in my
service as in another's. And also, I may observe, that
it can do no harm either to himself or to the subject
on whom he operates, that he should be guided by
men of more taste than himself. Genius may do

much, but long study of the art must always entitle a
man to offer advice. So far I will go — general principles I will suggest. But as to any particular case,
once for all I will have nothing to do with it. Never
tell me of any special work of art you are meditating
— I set my face against it *in toto*. For, if once a man
indulges himself in murder, very soon he comes to
think little of robbing ; and from robbing he comes
next to drinking and Sabbath-breaking, and from that
to incivility and procrastination. Once begin upon
this downward path, you never know where you are
to stop. Many a man has dated his ruin from some
murder or other that perhaps he thought little of at
the time. *Principiis obsta* — that's my rule.' Such
was my speech, and I have always acted up to it ; so,
if that is not being virtuous, I should be glad to know
what is. But now about the dinner and the club.
The club was not particularly of my creation ; it arose
pretty much as other similar associations, for the prop-
agation of truth and the communication of new ideas;
rather from the necessities of things, than upon any
one man's suggestion. As to the dinner, if any man
more than another could be held responsible for that,
it was a member known amongst us by the name of
Toad-in-the-hole. He was so called from his gloomy,
misanthropical disposition, which led him into constant
disparagements of all modern murders as vicious abor-
tions, belonging to no authentic school of art. The
finest performances of our own age he snarled at cyn-
ically ; and at length this querulous humor grew upon
him so much, and he became so notorious as a *laudator
temporis acti*, that few people cared to seek his society.
This made him still more fierce and truculent. He

went about muttering and growling; wherever you
met him, he was soliloquizing, and saying, 'despicable
pretender — without grouping — without two ideas
upon handling — without' — and there you lost him.
At length existence seemed to be painful to him; he
rarely spoke, he seemed conversing with phantoms in
the air; his housekeeper informed us that his reading
was nearly confined to ' God's Revenge upon Murder,'
by Reynolds, and a more ancient book of the same
title, noticed by Sir Walter Scott in his ' Fortunes of
Nigel.' Sometimes, perhaps, he might read in the
' Newgate Calendar' down to the year 1788, but he
never looked into a book more recent. In fact, he
had a theory with regard to the French Revolution, as
having been the great cause of degeneration in murder. ' Very soon, sir,' he used to say, '·men will have
lost the art of killing poultry : the very rudiments of
the art will have perished !' In the year 1811, he
retired from general society. Toad-in-the-hole was
no more seen in any public resort. We missed him
from his wonted haunts — ' nor up the lawn, nor at
the wood was he.' By the side of the main conduit
his listless length at noontide he would stretch, and
pore upon the filth that muddled by. ' Even dogs,'
this pensive moralist would say, ' are not what they
were, sir — not what they should be. I remember in
my grandfather's time that some dogs had an idea of
murder. I have known a mastiff, sir, that lay in am-
bush for a rival, yes, sir, and finally murdered him,
with pleasing circumstances of good taste. I also was
on intimate terms of acquaintance with a tom-cat that
was an assassin. But now' —— and then, the subject growing too painful, he dashed his hand to his

forehead, and went off abruptly in a homeward direction towards his favorite conduit, where he was seen by an amateur in such a state, that he thought it dangerous to address him. Soon after Toad shut himself entirely up; it was understood that he had resigned himself to melancholy; and at length the prevailing notion was, that Toad-in-the-hole had hanged himself.

The world was wrong *there*, as it had been on some other questions. Toad-in-the-hole might be sleeping, but dead he was not; and of that we soon had ocular proof. One morning in 1812, an amateur surprised us with the news that he had seen Toad-in-the-hole brushing with hasty steps the dews away, to meet the postman by the conduit side. Even that was something: how much more, to hear that he had shaved his beard — had laid aside his sad-colored clothes, and was adorned like a bridegroom of ancient days. What could be the meaning of all this? Was Toad-in-the-hole mad? or how? Soon after the secret was explained — in more than a figurative sense 'the murder was out.' For in came the London morning papers, by which it appeared that but three days before a murder, the most superb of the century by many degrees, had occurred in the heart of London. I need hardly say, that this was the great exterminating *chef-d'œuvre* of Williams at Mr. Marr's, No. 29 Ratcliffe Highway. That was the *début* of the artist; at least for anything the public knew. What occurred at Mr. Williamson's twelve nights afterwards — the second work turned out from the same chisel — some people pronounced even superior. But Toad-in-the-hole always 'reclaimed,' he was even angry, at such comparisons. 'This vulgar *gout de comparaison*, as La Bruyère calls it,' he would often remark, "will be our ruin ; each work has its own separate characteristics — each in and for itself is incomparable. One perhaps might suggest the ' Iliad ' — the other the ' Odyssey : ' but what do you get by such comparisons ? Neither ever was, or will be surpassed ; and when you've talked for hours, you must still come back to that.' Vain, however, as all criticism might be, he often said that volumes might be written on each case for itself; and he even proposed to publish in quarto on the subject.

Meantime, how had Toad-in-the-hole happened to hear of this great work of art so early in the morning? He had received an account by express, despatched by a correspondent in London, who watched the progress of art on *Toad's* behalf, with a general commission to send off a special express, at whatever cost, in the event of any estimable works appearing. The express arrived in the night-time ; Toad-in-the-hole was then gone to bed ; he had been muttering and grumbling for hours, but of course he was called up. On reading the account, he threw his arms round the express, declared him his brother and his preserver, and expressed his regret at not having it in his power to knight him. We, amateurs, having heard that he was abroad, and therefore had *not* hanged himself, made sure of soon seeing him amongst us. Accordingly he soon arrived ; seized every man's hand as he passed him — wrung it almost frantically, and kept ejaculating, ' Why, now, here's something like a murder ! — this is the real thing — this is genuine — this is what you can approve, can recommend to a friend : this — says every man, on reflection — this is the thing that ought to be ! Such works are enough to make us all young.' And in fact the general opinion is, that Toad-in-the-hole would have died but for this regeneration of art, which he called a second age of Leo the Tenth; and it was our duty, he said, solemnly to commemorate it. At present, and *en attendant*, he proposed that the club should meet and dine together. A dinner, therefore, was given by the club; to which all amateurs were invited from a distance of one hundred miles.

Of this dinner, there are ample short-hand notes amongst the archives of the club. But they are not 'extended,' to speak diplomatically; and the reporter, who only could give the whole report *in extenso*, is missing — I believe murdered. Meantime, in years long after that day, and on an occasion perhaps equally interesting, viz., the turning up of Thugs and Thuggism, another dinner was given. Of this I myself kept notes, for fear of another accident to the short-hand reporter. And I here subjoin them. Toad-in-the-hole, I must mention, was present at this dinner. In fact, it was one of its sentimental incidents. Being as old as the valleys at the dinner of 1812, naturally he was as old as the hills at the Thug dinner of 1838. He had taken to wearing his beard again; why, or with what view, it passes my persimmon to tell you. But so it was. And his appearance was most benign and venerable. Nothing could equal the angelic radiance of his smile, as he inquired after the unfortunate reporter (whom, as a piece of private scandal, I should tell you that he was himself supposed to have murdered, in a rapture of creative art): the answer was, with roars of laughter, from the under-sheriff of our county — '*Non est inventus.*' Toad-in-the-hole laughed outrageously at this : in fact, we all thought he was

6

choking; and, at the earnest request of the company, a musical composer furnished a most beautiful glee upon the occasion, which was sung five times after dinner, with universal applause and inextinguishable laughter, the words being these (and the chorus so contrived, as most beautifully to mimic the peculiar laughter of Toad-in-the-hole) :—

' Et interrogatum est à Toad-in-the-hole — Ubi est ille reporter ? Et responsum est cum cachinno — *Non est inventus.*'

Chorus.

' Deinde iteratum est ab omnibus, cum cachinnatione undulante trepidante — *Non est inventus.*'

Toad-in-the-hole, I ought to mention, about nine years before, when an express from Edinburgh brought him the earliest intelligence of the Burke-and-Hare revolution in the art, went mad upon the spot; and, instead of a pension to the express for even one life, or a knighthood, endeavored to Burke him; in consequence of which he was put into a strait-waistcoat. And that was the reason we had no dinner then. But now all of us were alive and kicking, strait-wasitcoaters and others; in fact, not one absentee was reported upon the entire roll. There were also many foreign amateurs present.

Dinner being over, and the cloth drawn, there was a general call made for the new glee of *Non est inventus ;* but, as this would have interfered with the requisite gravity of the company during the earlier toasts, I overruled the call. After the national toasts had been given, the first official toast of the day was, *The Old Man of the Mountains* — drunk in solemn silence. Toad-in-the-hole returned thanks in a neat speech.

He likened himself to the Old Man of the Mountains, in a few brief allusions, that made the company yell with laughter; and he concluded with giving the health of

Mr. Von Hammer, with many thanks to him for his learned History of the Old Man and his subjects the assassins.

Upon this I rose and said, that doubtless most of the company were aware of the distinguished place assigned by orientalists to the very learned Turkish scholar, Von Hammer the Austrian; that he had made the profoundest researches into our art, as connected with those early and eminent artists, the Syrian assassins in the period of the Crusaders; that his work had been for several years deposited, as a rare treasure of art, in the library of the club. Even the author's name, gentlemen, pointed him out as the historian of our art — Von Hammer ——

' Yes, yes,' interrupted Toad-in-the-hole, ' Von Hammer — he's the man for a *malleus hæreticorum*. You all know what consideration Williams bestowed on the hammer, or the ship-carpenter's mallet, which is the same thing. Gentlemen,. I give you another great hammer — Charles the Hammer, the Marteau, or, in old French, the Martel — he hammered the Saracens till they were all as dead as door-nails.'

' *Charles the Hammer*, with all the honors.'

But the explosion of Toad-in-the-hole, together with the uproarious cheers for the grandpapa of Charlemagne, had now made the company unmanageable. The orchestra was again challenged with shouts the stormiest for the new glee. I foresaw a tempestuous evening; and I ordered myself to be strengthened with three waiters on each side ; the vice-president with as many. Symptoms of unruly enthusiasm were beginning to show out; and I own that .I myself was considerably excited, as the orchestra opened with its storm of music, and the impassioned glee began — 'Et interrogatum est à Toad-in-the-hole — Ubi est ille Reporter?' And the frenzy of the passion became absolutely convulsing, as the full chorus fell in — ' Et iteratum est ab omnibus — *Non est inventus.*'

The next toast was — *The Jewish Sicarii.*

Upon which I made the following explanation to the company : — ' Gentlemen, I am sure it will interest you all to hear that the assassins, ancient as they were, had a race of predecessors in the very same country. All over Syria, but particularly in Palestine, during the early years of the Emperor Nero, there was a band of murderers, who prosecuted their studies in a very novel manner. They did not practise in the nighttime, or in lonely places ; but, justly considering that great crowds are in themselves a sort of darkness by means of the dense pressure, and the impossibility of finding out who it was that gave the blow, they mingled with mobs everywhere ; particularly at the great paschal feast in Jerusalem ; where they actually had the audacity, as Josephus assures us, to press into the temple — and whom should they choose for operating upon but Jonathan himself, the Pontifex Maximus? They murdered him, gentlemen, as beautifully as if they had had him alone on a moonless night in a dark lane. . And when it was asked, who was the murderer, and where he was ———— '

' Why then, it was answered,' interrupted Toad-in-the-hole, " *Non est inventus.*" ' And then, in spite of all I could do or say, the orchestra opened, and the whole company began — ' Et interrogatum est à Toad-in-the-hole — Ubi est ille Sicarius? Et responsum est ab omnibus — *Non est inventus.*'

When the tempestuous chorus had subsided, I began again: — ',Gentlemen, you will find a very circumstantial account of the Sicarii in at least three different parts of Josephus; once in Book XX., sec. v. c. 8, of his " Antiquities ; " once in Book I. of his " Wars : " but in sec. x. of the chapter first cited you will find a particular description of their tooling. This is what he says : — " They tooled with small scimitars not much different from the Persian *acinacæ,* but more curved, and for all the world most like the Roman semi-lunar *sicæ.*" It is perfectly magnificent, gentlemen, to hear the sequel of their history. Perhaps the only case on record where a regular army of murderers was assembled, a *justus exercitus,* was in the case of these *Sicarii.* They mustered in such strength in the wilderness, that Festus himself was obliged to march against them with the Roman legionary force. A pitched battle ensued; and this army of amateurs was all cut to pieces in the desert. Heavens, gentlemen, what a sublime picture ! The Roman legions — the wilderness — Jerusalem in the distance — an army of murderers in the foreground ! '

The next toast was — ' To the further improvement of Tooling, and thanks to the committee for their services.'

Mr. L., on behalf of the Committee who had reported on that subject, returned thanks. He made an interesting extract from the report, by which it appeared how very much stress had been laid formerly on

the mode of tooling by the fathers, both Greek and
Latin.   In confirmation of this pleasing fact, he made
a very striking statement in reference to the earliest
work of antediluvian art.   Father Mersenne, that
learned French Roman Catholic, in page one thousand
four hundred and thirty-one [10] of his operose Commen-
tary on Genesis, mentions, on the authority of several
rabbis, that the quarrel of Cain with Abel was about a
young woman ; that, according to the various accounts,
Cain had tooled with his teeth (Abelem fuisse *morsibus*
dilaceratum à Cain) ; according to many others, with
the jaw-bone of an ass, which is the tooling adopted
by most painters.   But it is pleasing to the mind of
sensibility to know that, as science expanded, sounder
views were adopted.   One author contends for a pitch-
fork, St. Chrysostom for a sword, Irenæus for a scythe,
and Prudentius, the Christian poet of the fourth century, for a hedging-bill.   This last writer delivers his
opinion thus : —

> ' Frater, probatæ sanctitatis æmulus,
>   Germana curvo colla frangit sarculo : '

i. e., his brother, jealous of his attested sanctity, frac-
tures his fraternal throat with a curved hedging-bill.
' All which is respectfully submitted by your committee, not so much as decisive of the question (for it
is not), but in order to impress upon the youthful mind
the importance which has ever been attached to the
quality of the tooling by such men as Chrysostom and
Irenæus.'

' Irenæus be hanged ! ' said Toad-in-the-hole, who
now rose impatientiy to give the next toast : — ' Our
Irish friends ; wishing them a speedy revolution in

their mode of tooling, as well as in everything else connected with the art!'

'Gentlemen, I'll tell you the plain truth. Every day of the year we take up a paper, we read the opening of a murder. We say, this is good, this is charming, this is excellent! But, behold you! scarcely have we read a little farther, before the word Tipperary or Ballina-something betrays the Irish manufacture. Instantly we loathe it; we call to the waiter; we say, "waiter, take away this paper; send it out of the house; it is absolutely a scandal in the nostrils of-all just taste." I appeal to every man, whether, on finding a murder (otherwise perhaps promising enough) to be Irish, he does not feel himself as much insulted as when, Madeira being ordered, he finds it to be Cape; or when, taking up what he takes to be a mushroom, it turns out what children call a toad-stool. Tithes, politics, something wrong in principle, vitiate every Irish murder. Gentlemen, this must be reformed, or Ireland will not be a land to live in; at least, if we do live there, we must import all our murders, that's clear.' Toad-in-the-hole sat down, growling with suppressed wrath; and the uproarious 'Hear, hear!' clamorously expressed the general concurrence.

The next toast was — 'The sublime epoch of Burkism and Harism!'

This was drunk with enthusiasm; and one of the members, who spoke to the question, made a very curious communication to the company: — 'Gentlemen, we fancy Burkism to be a pure invention of our own times: and in fact no Pancirollus has ever enumerated this branch of art when writing *de rebus deperditis*. Still, I have ascertained that the essential

principle of this variety in the art *was* known to the
ancients; although, like the art of painting upon glass,
of making the myrrhine cups, &c., it was lost in the
dark ages for want of encouragement.   In the famous
collection of Greek epigrams made by Planudes, is one
upon a very fascinating case of Burkism : it is a perfect little gem of art.   The epigram itself I cannot lay
my hand upon at this moment; but the following is
an abstract of it by Salmasius, as I find it in his notes
on Vopiscus : "Est et elegans epigramma Lucilii, ubi
medicus et pollinctor de compacto sic egerunt, ut
medicus ægros omnes cúræ suæ commissos occideret:
this was the basis of the contract, you see, that on the
one part the doctor, for himself and his assigns, doth
undertake and contract duly and truly to murder all
the patients committed to his charge : but why?
There lies the beauty of the case — Et ut pollinctori
amico suo traderet pollingendos."   The *pollinctor*,
you are aware, was a person whose business it was to
dress and prepare dead bodies for burial.   The orginal
ground of the transaction appears to have been sentimental : "He was my friend," says the murderous
doctor; "he was dear to me," in speaking of the pollinctor.   But the law, gentlemen, is stern and harsh :
the law will not hear of these tender motives : to sustain a contract of this nature in law, it is essential that
a " consideration " should be given.   Now what *was*
the consideration ?   For thus far all is on the side of
the pollinctor : he will be well paid for his services ;
but, meantime, the generous, the noble-minded doctor gets nothing.   What *was* the equivalent, again I
ask, which the law would insist on the doctor's taking,
in order to establish that " consideration," without

which the contract had no force? You shall hear:
" Et ut pollinctor vicissim τελαμῶνας quos furabatar de
pollinctione mortuorum medico mitteret donis ad alli-
ganda vulnera eorum quos curabat;" ·i. e., and that
reciprocally the pollinctor should transmit to the physician, as free gifts for the binding-up of wounds in
those whom he treated medically, the belts or trusses
(τελαμῶιας) which he had succeeded in purloining in
the course of his functions about the corpses.

'Now, the case is clear: the whole went on a principle of reciprocity which would have kept up .the
trade for ever. The doctor was also a surgeon: he
could not murder *all* his patients: some of the patients must be retained intact. For these he wanted
linen bandages. But, unhappily, the Romans wore
woollen, on which account it was that they bathed so
often. Meantime, there *was* linen to be had in Rome;
but it was monstrously dear; and the τελαμῶτας, or
linen swathing bandages, in which superstition obliged
them to bind up corpses, would answer capitally for
the surgeon. The doctor, therefore, contracts to furnish his friend with a constant succession of corpses,
provided, and be it understood always, that his said
friend, in return, should supply him with oné-half of
the articles he would receive from the friends of the.
parties murdered or to be murdered. The doctor
invariably recommended his invaluable friend the
pollinctor (whom let us call the undertaker); the
undertaker, with equal regard to the sacred rights of
friendship, uniformly recommended the doctor. Like
Pylades and Orestes, they were models of a perfect
friendship: in their lives they were lovely: and on
the gallows, it is to be hoped, they were not divided.

7

'Gentlemen, it makes me laugh horribly, when I think of those two friends drawing and re-drawing on each other: "Pollinctor in account with Doctor, debtor by sixteen corpses: creditor by forty-five bandages, two of which damaged." Their names unfortunately are lost; but I conceive they must have been Quintus Burkius and Publius Harius. By the way, gentlemen, has anybody heard lately of Hare? I understand he is comfortably settled in Ireland, considerably to the west, and does a little business now and then; but, as he observes with a sigh, only as a retailer — nothing like the fine thriving wholesale concern so carelessly blown up at Edinburgh. "You see what comes of neglecting business" — is the chief moral, the ἐπιμύθιον, as Æsop would say, which Hare draws from his past experience.'

At length came the toast of the day — *Thugdom in all its branches.*

The speeches *attempted* at this crisis of the dinner were past all counting. But the applause was so furious, the music so stormy, and the crashing of glasses so incessant, from the general resolution never again to drink an inferior toast from the same glass, that I am unequal to the task of reporting. Besides which, Toad-in-the-hole now became ungovernable. He kept firing pistols in every direction; sent his servant for a blunderbuss, and talked of loading with ball-cartridge. We conceived that his former madness had returned at the mention of Burke and Hare; or that, being again weary of life, he had resolved to go off in a general massacre. This we could not think of allowing; it became indispensable, therefore, to kick him out; which we did with universal consent, the whole company lending their toes *uno pede*, as I may say, though pitying his gray hairs and his angelic smile. During the operation, the orchestra poured in their old chorus. The universal company sang, and (what surprised us most of all) Toad-in-the-hole joined us furiously in singing —

'Et interrogatum est ab omnibus — Ubi est ille Toad-in-the-hole?
Et responsum est ab omnibus — *Non est inventus*.'

NOTES.

Note 1. Page 20.

Kant — who carried his demands of unconditional veracity to so extravagant a length as to affirm, that, if a man were to see an innocent person escape from a murderer, it would be his duty, on being questioned by the murderer, to tell the truth, and to point out the retreat of the innocent person, under any certainty of causing murder. Lest this doctrine should be supposed to have escaped him in any heat of dispute, on being taxed with it by a celebrated French writer, he solemnly re-affirmed it, with his reasons.

Note 2. Page 26.

The passage occurs in the *second* part (act 3) of 'Henry VI.,' and is doubly remarkable — first, for its critical fidelity to nature, were the description meant only for *poetic* effect ; but, secondly, for the *judicial* value impressed upon it when offered (as here it *is* offered) in silent corroboration legally of a dreadful whisper all at once arising, that foul play had been dealing with a great prince, clothed with an official state character. It is the Duke of Gloucester, faithful guardian and loving uncle of the simple and imbecile king, who has been found dead in his bed. How shall this event be interpreted ? Had he died under some natural visitation of Providence, or by violence from his enemies ? The two court factions read the circumstantial indications of the case into opposite constructions. The affectionate and afflicted young king, whose position almost pledges him to neutrality, cannot, nevertheless, disguise his overwhelming suspicions of hellish conspiracy in the background. Upon this, a leader of the queen's faction endeavors to break the force of this royal frankness, countersigned and echoed most impressively by

[76]

Lord Warwick. 'What *instance*,' he asks — meaning by *instance* not example or illustration, as thoughtless commentators have constantly supposed, but in the common scholastic sense;— what *instantia*, what pressure of argument, what urgent plea, can Lord Warwick put forward in support of his 'dreadful oath'.— an oath, namely, that, as surely as he hopes for the life eternal, so surely

> 'I do believe that violent hands were laid
> Upon the life of this thrice-famed duke.'

Ostensibly the challenge is to Warwick, but substantially it is meant for the king. And the reply of Warwick, the argument on which he builds, lies in a solemn array of all the changes worked in the duke's features by death, as irreconcilable with any other hypothesis than that this death had been a violent one. What argument have I that Gloucester died under the hands of murderers? Why, the following roll-call of awful changes, affecting head, face, nostrils, eyes, hands, &c., which do not belong indifferently to *any* mode of death, but exclusively to a death by violence :—

> 'But see, his face is black and full of blood;
> His eyeballs farther out than when he lived,
> Staring full ghastly, like a strangled man;
> His hair uprear'd, his nostrils stretch'd with struggling;
> His hands abroad display'd, as one that grasp'd
> And tugg'd for life, and was by strength subdued.
> Look on the sheets :— his hair, you see, is sticking;
> His well-proportion'd beard made rough and rugged,
> Like to the summer's corn by tempest lodged.
> It cannot be but he was murder'd here;
> The least of all these signs were probable.'

As the logic of the case, let us not for a moment forget, that, to be of any value, the signs and indications pleaded must be sternly *diagnostic*. The discrimination sought for is between death that is natural, and death that is violent. All indications, therefore, that belong equally and indifferently to either, are equivocal, useless, and alien from the very purpose of the signs here registered by Shakspeare.

Note 3. Page 26.

At the time of writing this, I held the common opinion upon that subject. Mere inconsideration it was that led to so erroneous a judgment. Since then, on closer reflection, I have seen ample reason to retract it: satisfied I now am, that the Romans, in every art which allowed to them any parity of advantages, had merits as racy, native, and characteristic, as the best of the Greeks. Elsewhere I shall plead this cause circumstantially, with the hope of converting the reader. In the meantime, I was anxious to lodge my protest against this ancient error; an error which commenced in the time-serving sycophancy of Virgil, the court-poet. With the base purpose of gratifying Augustus in his vindictive spite against Cicero, and by way of introducing, therefore, the little clause *orabunt Causas melius* as applying to all Athenian against all Roman orators, Virgil did not scruple to sacrifice by wholesale the just pretensions of his compatriots collectively.

Note 4. Page 33.

This same argument has been employed at least once too often. Some centuries back a dauphin of France, when admonished of his risk from small-pox, made the same demand as the emperor — 'Had any gentleman heard of a dauphin killed by small-pox?' No; not any gentleman *had* heard of such a case. And yet, for all that, this dauphin died of that same small-pox.

Note 5. Page 33.

'June 1, 1675. — Drinke part of three boules of punch (a liquor very strainge to me),' says the Rev. Mr. Henry Teonge, in his Diary published by C. Knight. In a note on this passage, a reference is made to Fryer's Travels to the East Indies, 1672, who speaks of 'that enervating liquor called *paunch* (which is Hindostanee for five), from five ingredients.' Made thus, it seems the medical men called it diapente; if with four only, diatessaron. No doubt, it was this evangelical name that recommended it to the Rev. Mr. Teonge.

Note 6.   Page 37.

Chatsworth was then, as now, the superb seat of the Cavendishes in their highest branch — in those days Earl, at present Duke, of Devonshire. It is to the honor of this family that, through two generations, they gave an asylum to Hobbes. It is noticeable that Hobbes was born in the year of the Spanish Armada, *i. e.*, in 1588 : such, at least, is my belief. And, therefore, at this meeting with Tennison in 1670, he must have been about 82 years old.

Note 7.   Page 40.

' *Spital Sermons :* ' — Dr. Parr's chief public appearances as an author, after his original appearance in the famous Latin preface to Bellendénus (don't say Bellendĕnus), occurred in certain Sermons at periodic intervals, delivered on behalf of some hospital (I really forget what) which retained for its official designation the old word *Spital ;* and thus it happened that the Sermons themselves were generally known by the title of *Spital* Sermons.

Note 8.   Page 54.

Abraham Newland is now utterly forgotten. But when this was written, his name had not ceased to ring in British ears, as the most familiar and most significant that perhaps has ever existed. It was the name which appeared on the face of all Bank of England notes, great or small; and had been, for more than a quarter of a century (especially through the whole career of the French Revolution), a short-hand expression for paper money in its safest form.

Note 9.   Page 58.

Her Majesty : — In the lecture, having occasion to refer to the reigning sovereign, I said ' *His* Majesty ; ' for at that time William IV. was on the throne : but between the lecture and this supplement had occurred the accession of our present Queen.

Note 10.   Page 70.

' Page one thousand four hundred and thirty-one:' — *literally,* good reader, and no joke at all.

JOAN OF ARC.[1]

IN REFERENCE TO M. MICHELET'S HISTORY OF FRANCE.

WHAT is to be thought of *her* ? What is to be thought of the poor shepherd girl from the hills and forests of Lorraine, that — like the Hebrew shepherd boy from the hills and forests of Judæa — rose suddenly out of the quiet, out of the safety, out of the religious inspiration, rooted in deep pastoral solitudes, to a station in the van of armies, and to the more perilous station at the right hand of kings ? The Hebrew boy inaugurated his patriotic mission by an *act*, by a victorious *act*, such as no man could deny. But so did the girl of Lorraine, if we read her story as it was read by those who saw her nearest. Adverse armies bore witness to the boy as no pretender ; but so they did to the gentle girl. Judged by the voices of all who saw them *from a station of good-will*, both were found true and loyal to any promises involved in their first acts. Enemies it was that made the difference between their subsequent fortunes. The boy rose to a splendor and a noonday prosperity, both personal and public, that rang through the records of his people, and became a by-word amongst his posterity for a thousand years, until the sceptre was departing from Judah. The poor, forsaken girl, on the contrary, drank not herself from that cup of rest which she had secured for France. She never sang together with the songs that rose in her native Domrémy, as echoes to the departing steps of invaders. She mingled not in the festal dances at Vaucouleurs which celebrated in rapture the redemption of France. No! for her voice was then silent: no! for her feet were dust. Pure, innocent, noble-hearted girl! whom, from earliest youth, ever I believed in as full of truth and self-sacrifice, this was amongst the strongest pledges for *thy* truth, that never once — no, not for a moment of weakness — didst thou revel in the vision of coronets and honor from man. Coronets for thee! O no! Honors, if they come when all is over, are for those that share thy blood.[2] Daughter of Domrémy, when the gratitude of thy king shall awaken, thou wilt be sleeping the sleep of the dead. Call her, King of France, but she will not hear thee! Cite her by thy apparitors to come and receive a robe of honor, but she will be found *en contumace*. When the thunders of universal France, as even yet may happen, shall proclaim the grandeur of the poor shepherd girl that gave up all for her country, thy ear, young shepherd girl, will have been deaf for five centuries. To suffer and to do, that was thy portion in this life; that was thy destiny; and not for a moment was it hidden from thyself. Life, thou saidst, is short: and the sleep which is in the grave is long! Let me use that life, so transitory, for the glory of those heavenly dreams destined to comfort the sleep which is so long. This pure creature — pure from every suspicion of even a visionary self-interest, even as she was pure in senses more obvious — never once did this holy child, as regarded herself, relax from her belief in the darkness that was travelling to meet her. She might not prefigure the very manner of her death; she saw not

in vision, perhaps, the aerial altitude of the fiery scaffold, the spectators without end on every road pouring
into .Rouen as to a coronation, the surging smoke, the
volleying flames, the hostile faces all around, the pitying eye that lurked but here and there, until nature
and imperishable truth broke⁻ loose from artificial
restraints ; — these might not be apparent through the
mists of the hurrying future. But the vioice that
called her to death, *that* she heard for ever.

Great was the throne of France even in those days,
and great was he that sat upon it : but well Joanna
knew that not the throne, nor he that sat upon it, was
for *her ;* but, on the contrary, that she was for *them ;*
not she by them, but they by her, should rise from the
dust. Gorgeous were the lilies of France, and for centuries had the privilege to spread their beauty over
land and sea, until, in another century, the wrath of
God and man combined to wither them ; but well
Joanna knew, early at Domrémy she had read that
bitter truth, that the lilies of France would decorate
no garland for *her.* Flower nor bud, bell nor blossom,
would ever bloom for *her.*

. . . .

But stay. What reason is there for taking up this
subject of Joanna precisely in the spring of 1847 ?
Might it not have been left till the spring of 1947 ; or,
perhaps, left till called for ? Yes, but it *is* called for ;
and clamorously. You are aware, reader, that amongst
the many original thinkers whom modern France has
produced, one of the reputed leaders is M. Michelet.
All these writers are of a revolutionary cast ; not in a
political sense merely, but in all senses ; mad, oftentimes, as March hares ; crazy with the laughing gas of

recovered liberty; drunk with the wine-cup of their mighty revolution, snorting, whinnying, throwing up their heels, like wild horses in the boundless Pampas, and running races of defiance with snipes, or with the winds, or with their own shadows, if they can find nothing else to challenge. Some time or other I, that have leisure to read, may introduce *you*, that have not, to two or three dozen of these writers; of whom I can assure you beforehand, that they are often profound, and at intervals are even as impassioned as if they were come of our best English blood. But now, confining our attention to M. Michelet, we in England — who know him best by his worst book, the book against priests, &c. — know him disadvantageously. That book is a rhapsody of incoherence. But his 'History of France' is quite another thing. A man, in whatsoever craft he sails, cannot stretch away out of sight when he is linked to the windings of the shore by towing ropes of history. Facts, and the consequences of facts, draw the writer back to the falconer's lure from the giddiest heights of speculation. Here, therefore — in his 'France' — if not always free from flightiness, if now and then off like a rocket for an airy wheel in the clouds, M. Michelet, with natural politeness, never forgets that he has left a large audience waiting for him on earth, and gazing upwards in anxiety for his return: return, therefore, he does. But history, though clear of certain temptations in one direction, has separate dangers of its own. It is impossible so to write a history of France, or of England — works becoming every hour more indispensable to the inevitably-political man of this day — without perilous openings for error. If I, for instance, on the part

of England, should happen to turn my labors in that
channel, and (on the model of Lord Percy going to
Chevy Chase)

> ' A vow to God should make
> My pleasure in the Michelet woods
> Three summer days to take,'

probably, from simple delirium, I might hunt M.
Michelet into *delirium tremens*. Two strong angels
stand by the side of history, whether French history or
English, as heraldic supporters: the angel of research
on the left hand, that must read millions of dusty
parchments, and of pages blotted with lies; the angel
of meditation on the right hand, that must cleanse these
lying records with fire, even as of old the draperies of
asbestos were cleansed, and must quicken them into
regenerated life. Willingly I acknowledge that no
man will ever avoid innumerable errors of detail; with
so vast a compass of ground to traverse, this is impossible; but such errors (though I have a bushel on
hand, at M. Michelet's service) are not the game I
chase; it is the bitter and unfair spirit in which M.
Michelet writes against England. Even *that*, after all,
is but my secondary object; the real one is Joanna,
the Pucelle d'Orleans for herself.

I am not going to write the History of *La Pucelle*:
to do this, or even circumstantially to report the history of her persecution and bitter death, of her struggle with false witnesses and with ensnaring judges, it
would be necessary to have before us *all* the documents, and therefore the collection only[3] now forthcoming in Paris. But *my* purpose is narrower. There
have been great thinkers, disdaining the careless judgments of contemporaries, who have thrown themselves

boldly on the judgment of a far posterity, that should have had time to review, to ponder, to compare. There have been great actors on the stage of tragic humanity that might with the same depth of confidence, have appealed from the levity of compatriot friends — too heartless for the sublime interest of their story, and too impatient for the labor of sifting its perplexities — to the magnanimity and justice of enemies. To this class belongs the Maid of Arc. The ancient Romans were too faithful to the ideal of grandeur in themselves not to relent, after a generation or two, before the grandeur of Hannibal. Mithridates — a more doubtful person — yet merely for the magic perseverance of his indomitable malice, won from the same Romans the only real honor that ever he received on earth. And we English have ever shown the same homage to stubborn enmity. To work unflinchingly for the ruin of England; to say through life, by word and by deed, *Delenda est Anglia Victrix!* that one purpose of malice, faithfully pursued, has quartered some people upon our national funds of homage as by a perpetual annuity. Better than an inheritance of service rendered to England herself, has sometimes proved the most insane hatred to England. Hyder Ali, even his son Tippoo, though so far inferior, and Napoleon, have all benefited by this disposition amongst ourselves to exaggerate the merit of diabolic enmity. Not one of these men was ever capable, in a solitary instance, of praising an enemy [what do you say to *that*, reader?], and yet in *their* behalf, we consent to forget, not their crimes only, but (which is worse) their hideous bigotry and anti-magnanimous egotism, for nationality it was not. Suffrein, and some half dozen of other French nautical heroes, because rightly they did us all the mischief they could (which was really great), are names justly reverenced in England. On the same principle, La Pucelle d'Orleans, the victorious enemy of England, has been destined to receive her deepest commemoration from the magnanimous justice of Englishmen.

Joanna, as we in England should call her, but, according to her own statement, Jeanne (or, as M. Michelet asserts, Jean [4]) D'Arc, was born at Domrémy, a village on the marches of Lorraine and Champagne, and dependent upon the town of Vaucouleurs. I have called her a Lorrainer, not simply because the word is prettier, but because Champagne too odiously reminds us English of what are for *us* imaginary wines, which, undoubtedly, *La Pucelle* tasted as rarely as we English; we English, because the Champagne of London is chiefly grown in Devonshire; *La Pucelle*, because the Champagne of Champagne never, by any chance, flowed into the fountain of Domrémy, from which only she drank. M. Michelet will have her to be a *Champenoise*, and for no better reason than that she 'took after her father,' who happened to be a *Champenois*.

These disputes, however, turn on refinements too nice. Domrémy stood upon the frontiers, and, like other frontiers, produced a *mixed* race representing the *cis* and the *trans*. A river (it is true) formed the boundary-line at this point — the river Meuse; and *that*, in old days, might have divided the populations; but in these days it did not : there were bridges, there were ferries, and weddings crossed from the right bank to the left. Here lay two great roads, not so much for travellers that were few, as for armies that were too many by half. These two roads, one of which was the great high road between France and Germany, *decussated* at this very point; which is a learned way of saying, that they formed a St. Andrew's cross, or letter X. I hope the compositor will choose a good large X; in which case the point of intersection, the *locus* of conflux and intersection for these four diverging arms, will finish the reader's geographical education, by showing him to a hair's-breadth where it was that Domrémy stood. Those roads, so grandly situated, as great trunk arteries between two mighty realms,[5] and haunted for ever by wars, or rumors of wars, decussated (for anything I know to the contrary) absolutely under Joanna's bedroom window; one rolling away to the right, past Monsieur D'Arc's old barn, and the other unaccountably preferring to sweep round that odious man's pigsty to the left.

On whichever side of the border chance had thrown Joanna, the same love to France would have been nurtured. For it is a strange fact, noticed by M. Michelet and others, that the Dukes of Bar and Lorraine had for generations pursued the policy of eternal warfare with France on their own account, yet also of eternal amity and league with France, in case anybody else presumed to attack her. Let peace settle upon France, and before long you might rely upon seeing the little vixen Lorraine flying at the throat of France. Let France be assailed by a formidable enemy, and instantly you saw a Duke of Lorraine insisting on having his own throat cut in support of France; which favor accordingly was cheerfully granted to him in three great successive battles — twice by the English, viz., at Crécy and Agincourt, once by the Sultan at Nicopolis.

This sympathy with France during great eclipses, in those that during ordinary seasons were always teasing her with brawls and guérilla inroads, strengthened the natural piety to France of those that were confessedly the children of her own house. The outposts of France, as one may call the great frontier provinces, were of all localities the most devoted to the Fleurs de Lys. To witness, at any great crisis, the generous devotion to these lilies of the little fiery cousin that in gentler weather was for ever tilting at the breast of France, could not but fan the zeal of France's legitimate daughters : whilst to occupy a post of honor on the frontiers against an old hereditary enemy of France, would naturally stimulate this zeal by a sentiment of martial pride, by a sense of danger always threatening, and of hatred always smouldering. That great four-headed road was a perpetual memento to patriotic ardor. To say, this way lies the road to Paris, and that other way to Aix-la-Chapelle — this to Prague, that to Vienna — nourished the warfare of the heart by daily ministrations of sense. The eye that watched for the gleams of lance or helmet from the hostile frontier, the ear that listened for the groaning of wheels, made the high road itself, with its relations to centres so remote, into a manual of patriotic duty.

The situation, therefore, *locally*, of Joanna was full of profound suggestions to a heart that listened for the stealthy steps of change and fear that too surely were in motion. But, if the place were grand, the time, the burden of the time, was far more so. The air overhead in its upper chambers was *hurtling* with the obscure sound ; was dark with sullen fermenting of storms that had been gathering for a hundred and

8

thirty years. The battle of Agincourt in Joanna's childhood had re-opened the wounds of France. Crécy and Poictiers, those withering overthrows for the chivalry of France, had, before Agincourt occurred, been tranquillized by more than half a century; but this resurrection of their trumpet wails made the whole series of battles and endless skirmishes take their stations as parts in one drama. The graves that had closed sixty years ago, seemed to fly open in sympathy with a sorrow that echoed their own. The monarchy of France labored in extremity, rocked and reeled like a ship fighting with the darkness of monsoons. The madness of the poor king (Charles VI.) falling in at such a crisis, like the case of women laboring in childbirth during the storming of a city, trebled the awfulness of the time. Even the wild story of the incident which had immediately occasioned the explosion of this madness — the case of a man unknown, gloomy, and perhaps maniacal himself, coming out of a forest at noonday, laying his hand upon the bridle of the king's horse, checking him for a moment to say, 'Oh, king, thou art betrayed,' and then vanishing, no man knew whither, as he had appeared for no man knew what — fell in with the universal prostration of mind that laid France on her knees, as before the slow unweaving of some ancient prophetic doom. The famines, the extraordinary diseases, the insurrections of the peasantry up and down Europe — these were chords struck from the same mysterious harp; but these were transitory chords. There have been others of deeper and more ominous sound. The termination of the Crusades, the destruction of the Templars, the Papal interdicts, the tragedies caused or suffered by the house of Anjou, and by the emperor — these were full of a more permanent significance. But, since then, the colossal figure of feudalism was seen standing, as it were, on tiptoe, at Crécy, for flight from earth: that was a revolution unparalleled; yet *that* was a trifle, by comparison with the more fearful revolutions that were mining below the church. By her own internal schisms, by the abominable spectacle of a double pope — so that no man, except through political bias, could even guess which was Heaven's vicegerent, and which the creature of hell — the church was rehearsing, as in still earlier forms she had already rehearsed, those vast rents in her foundations which no man should ever heal.

These were the loftiest peaks of the cloudland in the skies, that to the scientific gazer first caught the colors of the *new* morning in advance. But the whole vast range alike of sweeping glooms overhead, dwelt upon all meditative minds, even upon those that could not distinguish the tendencies nor decipher the forms. It was, therefore, not her own age alone, as affected by its immediate calamities, that lay with such weight upon Joanna's mind; but her own age, as one section in a vast mysterious drama, unweaving through a century back, and drawing nearer continually to some dreadful crisis. Cataracts and rapids were heard roaring ahead; and signs were seen far back, by help of old men's memories, which answered secretly to signs now coming forward on the eye, even as locks answer to keys. It was not wonderful that in such a haunted solitude, with such a haunted heart, Joanna should see angelic visions, and hear angelic voices. These voices whispered to her for ever the duty, self-

imposed, of delivering France. Five years she listened
to these monitory voices with internal struggles. At
length she could resist no longer. Doubt gave way;
and she left her home for ever in order to present herself at the dauphin's court.

The education of this poor girl was mean according
to the present standard: was ineffably grand, according to a purer philosophic standard: and only not good
for our age, because for us it would be unattainable.
She read nothing, for she could not read; but she had
heard others read parts of the Roman martyrology.
She wept in sympathy with the sad *Misereres* of the
Romish church; she rose to heaven with the glad triumphant *Te Deums* of Rome: she drew her comfort and
her vital strength from the rites of the same church.
But, next after these spiritual advantages, she owed most
to the advantages of her situation. The fountain of Domrémy was on the brink of a boundless forest; and it was
haunted to that degree by fairies, that the parish priest
(*curé*) was obliged to read mass there once a-year, in
order to keep them in any decent bounds. Fairies are
important, even in a statistical view: certain weeds
mark poverty in the soil, fairies mark its solitude. As
surely as the wolf retires before cities, does the fairy
sequester herself from the haunts of the licensed vict-
ualler. A village is too much for her nervous delicacy:
at most, she can tolerate a distant view of a hamlet.
We may judge, therefore, by the uneasiness and extra
trouble which they gave to the parson, in what
strength the fairies mustered at Domrémy; and, by a
satisfactory consequence, how thinly sown with men
and women must have been that region even in its
inhabited spots. But the forests of Domrémy — those

were the glories of the land: for in them abode mysterious power and ancient secrets that towered into tragic strength. 'Abbeys there were, and abbey windows,' — 'like Moorish temples of the Hindoos,' that exercised even princely power both in Lorraine and in the German Diets. These had their sweet bells that pierced the forests for many a league at matins or vespers, and each its own dreamy legend. Few enough, and scattered enough, were these abbeys, so as in no degree to disturb the deep solitude of the region; yet many enough to spread a network or awning of Christian sanctity over what else might have seemed a heathen wilderness. This sort of religious talisman being secured, a man the most afraid of ghosts (like myself, suppose, or the reader) becomes armed into courage to wander for days in their sylvan recesses. The mountains of the Vosges, on the eastern frontier of France, have never attracted much notice from Europe, except in 1813 – 14 for a few brief months, when they fell within Napoleon's line of defence against the Allies. But they are interesting for this, amongst other features, that they do not, like some loftier ranges, repel woods: the forests and the hills are on sociable terms. *Live and let live*, is their motto. For this reason, in part, these tracts in Lorraine were a favorite hunting-ground with the Carlovingian princes. About six hundred years before Joanna's childhood, Charlemagne was known to have hunted there. That, of itself, was a grand incident in the traditions of a forest or a chase. In these vast forests, also, were to be found (if anywhere to be found) those mysterious fawns that tempted solitary hunters into visionary and perilous pursuits. Here

was seen (if anywhere seen) that ancient stag who
was already nine hundred years old, but possibly a
hundred or two more, when met by Charlemagne; and
the thing was put beyond doubt by the inscription
upon his golden collar. I believe Charlemagne knight-
ed the stag; and, if ever he is met again by a king, he
ought to be made an earl — or, being upon the marches
of France, a marquis. Observe, I don't absolutely
vouch for all these things: my own opinion varies.
On a fine breezy forenoon I am audaciously sceptical;
but, as twilight sets in, my credulity grows steadily,
till it becomes equal to anything that could be desired.
And I have heard candid sportsmen declare that, outside of these very forests, they laughed loudly at all
the dim tales connected with their haunted solitudes;
but, on reaching a spot notoriously eighteen miles
deep within them, they agreed with Sir Roger de Cov-
erley, that a good deal might be said on both sides.

Such traditions, or any others that (like the stag)
connect distant generations with each other, are, for
that cause, sublime; and the sense of the shadowy,
connected with such appearances that reveal themselves
or not according to circumstances, leaves a coloring of
sanctity over ancient forests, even in those minds that
utterly reject the legend as a fact.

But, apart from all distinct stories of that order, in
any solitary frontier between two great empires, as
here, for instance, or in the desert between Syria and
the Euphrates, there is an inevitable tendency in
minds of any deep sensibility, to people the solitudes
with phantom images of powers that were of old so
vast. Joanna, therefore, in her quiet occupation of a
shepherdess, would be led continually to brood over

the political condition of her country, by the traditions
of the past no less than by the mementoes of the local
present.

M. Michelet, indeed, says that La Pucelle was *not* a
shepherdess. I beg his pardon: she *was*. What he
rests upon, I guess pretty well: it is the evidence of a
woman called Haumette, the most confidential friend
of Joanna. Now, she is a good witness; and a good
girl, and I like her; for she makes a natural and affectionate report of Joanna's ordinary life. But still,
however good she may be as a witness, Joanna is
better; and she, when speaking to the dauphin, calls
herself in the Latin report *Bergereta*. Even Haumette
confesses, that Joanna tended sheep in her girlhood.
And I believe, that if Miss Haumette were taking
coffee alone with me this very evening (February 12,
1847) — in which there would be no subject for scandal
for or maiden blushes, because I am an intense philosopher, and Miss H. would be hard upon four hundred
and fifty years old — she would admit the following
comment upon her evidence to be right. A Frenchman, about forty years ago, M. Simond, in his 'Travels,'
mentions incidently the following hideous scene as one
steadily observed and watched by himself in chivalrous
France, not very long before the French Revolution:
— A peasant was ploughing; the team that drew his
plough was a donkey and a woman. Both were regularly harnessed: both pulled alike. This is bad
enough; but the Frenchman adds, that, in distribut-
ing his lashes, the peasant was obviously desirous of
being impartial; or, if either of the yoke-fellows had
a right to complain, certainly it was not the donkey.
Now, in any country where such degradation of fe-

males could be tolerated by the state of manners, a woman of delicacy would shrink from acknowledging, either for herself or her friend, that she had ever been addicted to any mode of labor not strictly domestic; because, if once owning herself a prædial servant, she would be sensible that this confession extended by probability in the hearer's thoughts to the having incurred indignities of this horrible kind. Haumette clearly thinks it more dignified for Joanna to have been darning the stockings of her horny-hoofed father, Monsieur D'Arc, than keeping sheep, lest she might then be suspected of having ever done something worse. But, luckily, there was no danger of *that:* Joanna never was in service; and my opinion is, that her father should have mended his own stockings, since probably he was the party to make holes in them, as many a better man than D'Arc does; meaning by *that* not myself, because, though probably a better man than D'Arc, I protest against doing anything of the kind. If I lived even with Friday in Juan Fernandez, either Friday must do all the darning, or else it must go undone. The better men that I meant were the sailors in the British navy, every man of whom mends his own stockings. Who else is to do it? Do you suppose, reader, that the junior lords of the admiralty are under articles to darn for the navy?

The reason, meantime, for my systematic hatred of D'Arc is this. There was a story current in France before the Revolution, framed to ridicule the pauper aristocracy, who happened to have long pedigrees and short rent rolls, viz., that a head of such a house, dating from the Crusades, was overheard saying to his son, a Chevalier of St. Louis, '*Chevalier, as-tu donné au cochon à manger !*' Now, it is clearly made out by the surviving evidence, that D'Arc would much have preferred continuing to say, ' *Ma fille as-tu donné au cochon à manger ?* ' to saying, *Pucelle d' Orleans, as-tu sauvé los fleurs-de-lys ?* ' There is an old English copy of verses which argues thus : —

> ' If the man that turnips cries,
> Cry not when his father dies —
> Then 'tis plain the man had rather —
> Have a turnip than his father.'

I cannot say that the logic in these verses was ever *entirely* to my satisfaction. I do not see my way through it as clearly as could be wished. But I see my way most clearly through D'Arc ; and the result is — that he would greatly have preferred not merely a turnip to his father, but saving a pound or so of bacon to saving the Oriflamme of France.

It is probable (as M. Michelet suggests) that the title of Virgin, or *Pucelle*, had in itself, and apart from the miraculous stories about her, a secret power over the rude soldiery and partisan chiefs of that period ; for, in such a person, they saw a representative manifestation of the Virgin Mary, who in a course of centuries, had grown steadily upon the popular heart.

As to Joanna's supernatural detection of the dauphin (Charles VII.) amongst three hundred lords and knights, I am surprised at the credulity which could ever lend itself to that theatrical juggle. Who admires more than myself the sublime enthusiasm, the rapturous faith in herself, of this pure creature ? But I am far from admiring stage artifices, which not *La Pucelle*, but the court, must have arranged ; nor can

surrender myself to the conjurer's *legerdemain*, such
as may be seen every day for a shilling. Southey's
'Joan of Arc' was published in 1796. Twenty years
after, talking with Southey, I was surprised to find
him still owning a secret bias in favor of Joan, founded
on her detection of the dauphin. The story, for the
benefit of the reader new to the case, was this : — *La
Pucelle* was first made known to the dauphin, and presented to his court, at Chinon: and here came her
first trial. By way of testing her supernatural pretensions, she was to find out the royal personage
amongst the whole ark of clean and unclean creatures.
Failing in this *coup d'essai*, she would not simply dis-
appoint many a beating heart in the glittering crowd
that on different motives yearned for her success, but
she would ruin herself — and, as the oracle within had
told her, would, by ruining herself, ruin France. Our
own sovereign lady Victoria rehearses annually a trial
not so severe in degree, but the same in kind. She
'pricks' for sheriffs. Joanna pricked for a king. But
observe the difference: our own lady pricks for two
men out of three; Joanna for one man out of three
hundred. Happy Lady of the islands and the orient!
— she *can* go astray in her choice only by one half;
to the extent of one half she *must* have the satisfaction
of being right. And yet, even with these tight limits
to the misery of a boundless discretion, permit me,
liege Lady, with all loyalty, to submit — that now and
then you prick with your pin the wrong man. But
the poor child from Domrémy, shrinking under the
gaze of a dazzling court — not *because* dazzling (for in
visions she had seen those that were more so), but
because some of them wore a scoffing smile on their

features — how should *she* throw her line into so deep a river to angle for a king, where many a gay creature was sporting that masqueraded as kings in dress? Nay, even more than any true king would have done: for, in Southey's version of the story, the dauphin says, by way of trying the virgin's magnetic sympathy with royalty,

> 'On the throne,
> I the while mingling with the menial throng,
> Some courtier shall be seated.'

This usurper is even crowned : ' the jewelled crown shines on a menial's head.' But, really, that is ' *un peu fort ;* ' and the mob of spectators might raise a scruple whether our friend the jackdaw upon the throne, and the dauphin himself, were not grazing the shins of treason. For the dauphin could not lend more than belonged to him. According to the popular notion, he had no crown for himself; consequently none to lend, on any pretence whatever, until the consecrated Maid should take him to Rheims. This was the *popular* notion in France. But, certainly, it was the dauphin's interest to support the popular notion, as he meant to use the services of Joanna. For, if he were king already, what was it that she could do for him beyond Orleans ? That is to say, what more than a mere *military* service could she render him ? And, above all, if he were king without a coronation, and without the oil from the sacred ampulla, what advantage was yet open to him by celerity above his competitor the English boy ? Now was to be a race for a coronation : he that should win *that* race, carried the superstition of France along with him : he that should first be drawn from the ovens of Rheims, was under that superstition baked into a king.

La Pucelle, before she could be allowed to practise as a warrior, was put through her manual and platoon exercise, as a pupil in divinity, at the bar of six eminent men in wigs. According to Southey (v. 393, Book III., in the original edition of his ' Joan of Arc '), she ' appalled the doctors.' It's not easy to do *that* : but they had some reason to feel bothered, as that surgeon would assuredly feel bothered, who, upon proceeding to dissect a subject, should find the subject retaliating as a dissector upon himself, especially if Joanna ever made the speech to them which occupies v. 354–391, B. III. It is a double impossibility : 1st, because a piracy from Tindal's ' Christianity as old as the Creation ' — a piracy *à parte ante*, and by three centuries ; 2dly, it is quite contrary to the evidence on Joanna's trial. Southey's ' Joan,' of A. D. 1796 (Cottle, Bristol), tells the doctors, amongst other secrets, that she never in her life attended — 1st, Mass ; nor 2d, the Sacramental table ; nor 3d, Confession. In the meantime, all this deistical confession of Joanna's, besides being suicidal for the interest of her cause, is opposed to the depositions upon *both* trials. The very best witness called from first to last, deposes that Joanna attended these rites of her church even too often ; was taxed with doing so ; and, by blushing, owned the charge as a fact, though certainly not as a fault. Joanna was a girl of natural piety, that saw God in forests, and hills, and fountains ; but did not the less seek him in chapels and consecrated oratories.

This peasant girl was self-educated through her own natural meditativeness. If the reader turns to that

divine passage in 'Paradise Regained,' which Milton
has put into the mouth of our Saviour when first entering the wilderness, and musing upon the tendency
of those great impulses growing within himself—

> ' Oh, what a multitude of thoughts at once
> Awaken'd in me swarm, while I consider
> What from within I feel myself, and hear
> What from without comes often to my ears,
> Ill sorting with my present state compared!
> When I was yet a child, no childish play
> To me was pleasing; all my mind was set
> Serious to learn and know, and thence to do
> What might be public good; myself I thought
> Born to that end ' —

he will have some notion of the vast reveries which
brooded over the heart of Joanna in early girlhood,
when the wings were budding that should carry her
from Orleans to Rheims ; when the golden chariot was
dimly revealing itself, that should carry her from the
kingdom of *France Delivered* to the eternal kingdom.

It is not requisite, for the honor of Joanna, nor is
there, in this place, room to pursue her brief career of
action. That, though wonderful, forms the earthly
part of her story : the spiritual part is the saintly passion of her imprisonment, trial, and execution. It is
unfortunate, therefore, for Southey's 'Joan of Arc '
(which, however, should always be regarded as a
juvenile effort), that, precisely when her real glory
begins, the poem ends. But this limitation of the
interest grew, no doubt, from the constraint inseparably
attached to the 'law of epic unity. Joanna's history
bisects into two opposite hemispheres, and both could
not have been presented to the eye in one poem, unless by sacrificing all unity of theme, or else by involv

ing the earlier half,' as a narrative episode, in the
latter; which, however, might have been done, for it
might have been communicated to a fellow-prisoner,
or a confessor, by Joanna herself. It is sufficient, as
concerns *this* section of Joanna's life, to say that she
fulfilled, to the height of her promises, the restoration
of the prostrate throne. France had become a prov-
ince of England; and for the ruin of both, if such a
yoke could be maintained. Dreadful pecuniary exhaustion caused the English energy to droop; and
that critical opening *La Pucelle* used with a corresponding felicity of audacity and suddenness (that were
in themselves portentous) for introducing the wedge
of French native resources, for rekindling the national
pride, and for planting the dauphin once more upon
his feet. When Joanna appeared, he had been on the
point of giving up the struggle with the English, dis-
tressed as they were, and of flying to the south of
France. She taught him to blush for such abject
counsels. She liberated Orleans, that great city, so
decisive by its fate for the issue of the war, and then
beleagured by the English with an elaborate application of engineering skill unprecedented in Europe.
·Entering the city after sunset, on the 29th of April,
she sang mass on Sunday, May 8, for the entire dis-
appearance of the besieging force. On the 29th of
June, she fought and gained over the English the
decisive battle of Patay; on the 9th of July, she took
Troyes by a coup-de-main from a mixed garrison of
English and Burgundians; on the 15th of that month,
she carried the dauphin into Rheims; on Sunday
the 17th, she crowned him; and there she rested
from her labor of triumph. All that was to be *done,*

she had now accomplished: what remained was — to *suffer.*

All this forward movement was her own: excepting one man, the whole council was against her. Her enemies were all that drew power from earth. Her supporters were her own strong enthusiasm, and the headlong contagion by which she carried this sublime frenzy into the hearts of women, of soldiers, and of all who lived by labor. Henceforwards she was thwarted; and the worst error that she committed was, to lend the sanction of her presence to counsels which she had ceased to approve. But she had now accomplished the capital objects which her own visions had dictated. These involved all the rest. Errors were now less important; and doubtless it had now become more difficult for herself to pronounce authentically what *were* errors. The noble girl had achieved, as by a rapture of motion, the capital end of clearing out a free space around her sovereign, giving him the power to move his arms with effect; and, secondly, the inappreciable end of winning for that sovereign what seemed to all France the heavenly ratification of his rights, by crowning him with the ancient solemnities. She had made it impossible for the English now to step before her. They were caught in an irretrievable blunder, owing partly to discord amongst the uncles of Henry VI., partly to a want of funds, but partly to the very impossibility which they believed to press with tenfold force upon any French attempt to forestall theirs. They laughed at such a thought; and whilst they laughed, she *did* it. Henceforth the single redress for the English of this capital oversight, but which never *could* have redressed it effectually, was, to vitiate

and taint the coronation of Charles VII. as the work
of a witch. That policy, and not malice (as M.
Michelet is so happy to believe), was the moving
principle in the subsequent prosecution of Joanna.
Unless they unhinged the force of the first coronation
in the popular mind, by associating it with power given
from hell, they felt that the sceptre of the invader
was broken.

But she, the child that, at nineteen, had wrought
wonders so great for France, was she not elated? ` Did
she not lose, as men so often *have* lost, all sobriety of
mind when standing upon the pinnacle of success so
giddy? Let her enemies declare. During the progress of her movement, and in the centre of ferocious
struggles, she had manifested the temper of her feelings, by the pity which she had everywhere expressed
for the suffering enemy. She forwarded to the English
leaders a touching invitation to unite with the French,
as brothers, in a common crusade against infidels, thus
opening the road for a soldierly retreat. She inter-
posed to protect the captive or the wounded—she
mourned over the excesses of her countrymen—she
threw herself off her horse to kneel by the dying
English soldier, and to comfort him with such ministrations, physical or spiritual, as his situation allowed.
' Nolebat,' says the evidence, ' uti ense suo, aut quem-
quam interficere.' She sheltered the English, that
invoked her aid, in her own quarters. She wept as
she beheld, stretched on the field of battle, so many
brave enemies that had died without confession. And,
as regarded herself, her elation expressed itself thus:
—On the day when she had finished her work, she
wept; for she knew that, when her *triumphal* task was

done, her end must be approaching. Her aspirations pointed only to a place, which seemed to her more than usually full of natural piety, as one in which it would give her pleasure to die. And she uttered, between smiles and tears, as a wish that inexpressibly fascinated her heart, and yet was half-fantastic, a broken prayer, that God would return her to the solitudes from which he had drawn her, and suffer her to become a shepherdess once more. It was a natural prayer, because nature has laid a necessity upon every human heart to seek for rest, and to shrink from torment. Yet, again, it was a half-fantastic prayer, because, from childhood upwards, visions that she had no power to mistrust, and the voices which sounded in her ear for ever, had long since persuaded her mind, that for *her* no such prayer could be granted. Too well she felt that her mission must be worked out to the end, and that the end was now at hand. All went wrong from this time. She herself had created the *funds* out of which the French restoration should grow; but she was not suffered to witness their development, or their prosperous application. More than one military plan was entered upon which she did not approve. But she still continued to expose her person as before. Severe wounds had not taught her caution. And at length, in a sortie from Compeigne (whether through treacherous collusion on the part of her own friends is doubtful to this day), she was made prisoner by the Burgundians, and finally surrendered to the English.

Now came her trial. This trial, moving of course under English influence, was conducted in chief by the Bishop of Beauvais. He was a Frenchman, sold to

English interests, and hoping, by favor of the English leaders, to reach the highest preferment. *Bishop that art, Archbishop that shalt be, Cardinal that mayest be,* were the words that sounded continually in his ear; and doubtless, a whisper of visions still higher, of a triple crown, and feet upon the necks of kings, sometimes stole into his heart. M. Michelet is anxious to keep us in mind that this bishop was but an agent of the English. True. But it does not better the case for his countryman — that, being an accomplice in the crime, making himself the leader in the persecution against the helpless girl, he was willing to be all this in the spirit, and with the conscious vileness of a cat's-paw. Never from the foundations of the earth was there such a trial as this, if it were laid open in all its beauty of defence, and all its hellishness of attack. Oh, child of France! shepherdess, peasant girl! trodden under foot by all around thee, how I honor thy flashing intellect, quick as God's lightning, and true as God's lightning to its mark, that ran before France and laggard Europe by many a century, confounding the malice of the ensnarer, and making dumb the oracles of falsehood! Is it not scandalous, is it not humiliating to civilization, that, even at this day, France exhibits the horrid spectacle of judges examining the prisoner against himself; seducing him, by fraud, into treacherous conclusions against his own head; using the terrors of their power for extorting confessions from the frailty of hope; nay (which is worse), using the blandishments of condescension and snaky kindness for thawing into compliances of gratitude those whom they had failed to freeze into terror? Wicked judges! Barbarian jurisprudence! that, sitting in your own conceit on the summits of social wisdom, have yet failed to learn the first principles of criminal justice; sit ye humbly and with docility at the feet of this girl from Domrémy, that tore your webs of cruelty into shreds and dust. 'Would you examine me as a witness against myself?' was the question by which many times she defied their arts. Continually she showed that their interrogations were irrelevant to any business before the court, or that entered into the ridiculous charges against her. General questions were proposed to her on points of casuistical divinity; two-edged questions, which not one of themselves could have answered without, on the one side, landing himself in heresy (as then inter-preted), or, on the other, in some presumptuous expression of self-esteem. Next came a wretched Dominican, that pressed her with an objection, which, if applied to the Bible would tax every one of its miracles with unsoundness. The monk had the excuse of never having read the Bible. M. Michelet has no such excuse; and it makes one blush for him, as a philosopher, to find him describing such an argument as 'weighty,' whereas it is but a varied expression of rude Mahometan metaphysics. Her answer to this, if there were room to place the whole in a clear light, was as shattering as it was rapid. Another thought to entrap her by asking what language the angelic visitors of her solitude had talked; as though heavenly counsels could want polyglot interpreters for every word, or that God needed language at all in whisper-ing thoughts to a human heart. Then came a worse devil, who asked her whether the archangel Michael had appeared naked. Not comprehending the vile insinua-

tion, Joanna, whose poverty suggested to her simplicity
that it might be the *costliness* of suitable robes which
caused the demur, asked them if they fancied God,
who clothed the flowers of the valleys, unable to find
raiment for his servants. The answer of Joanna
moves a smile of tenderness, but the disappointment
of her judges makes one laugh exultingly. Others
succeeded by troops, who upbraided her with leaving
her father; as if that greater Father, whom she believed
herself to have been serving, did not retain the power
of dispensing with his own rules, or had not said,
that, for a less cause than martyrdom, man and woman
should leave both father and mother.

On Easter Sunday, when the trial had been long
proceeding, the poor girl fell so ill as to cause a belief
that she had been poisoned. It was not poison. Nobody had any interest in hastening a death so certain.
M. Michelet, whose sympathies with all feelings are so
quick, that one would gladly see them always as justly
directed, reads the case most truly. Joanna had a
twofold malady. She was visited by a paroxysm of
the complaint called *home-sickness;* the cruel nature
of her imprisonment, and its length, could not but
point her solitary thoughts, in darkness and in chains
(for chained she was), to Domrémy, And the season,
which was the most heavenly period of the spring,
added stings to this yearning. That was one of her
maladies — *nostalgia*, as medicine calls it; the other
was weariness and exhaustion from daily combats with
malice. She saw that everybody hated her, and
thirsted for her blood; nay, many kind-hearted creatures that would have pitied her profoundly, as regarded all political charges, had their natural feelings

warped by the belief that she had dealings with fiendish powers. She knew she was to die; that was *not*
the misery: the misery was, that this consummation
could not be reached without so much intermediate
strife, as if she were contending for some chance
(where chance was none) of happiness, or were dream-
ing for a moment of escaping the inevitable. Why,
then, *did* she contend? Knowing that she would reap
nothing from answering her persecutors, why did she
not retire by silence from the superfluous contest? It
was because her quick and eager loyalty to truth would
not suffer her to see it darkened by frauds, which *she*
could expose, but others, even of candid listeners,
perhaps could not; it was through that imperishable
grandeur of soul, which taught her to submit meekly
and without a struggle to her punishment, but taught
her *not* to submit — no, not for a moment — to calumny as to facts, or to misconstruction as to motives.
Besides, there were secretaries all around the court
taking down her words. That was meant for no good
to *her*. But the end does not always correspond to
the meaning. And Joanna might say to herself — these
words that will be used against me to-morrow and the
next day, perhaps in some nobler generation may rise
again for my justification. Yes, Joanna, they *are* rising
even now in Paris, and for more than justification.

Woman, sister — there are some things which you
do not execute as well as your brother, man; no, nor
ever will. Pardon me, if I doubt whether you will
ever produce a great poet from your choirs, or a Mozart, or a Phidias, or a Michael Angelo, or a great
philosopher, or a great scholar. By which last is
meant — not one who depends simply on an infinite

memory, but also on an infinite and electrical power of combination; bringing together from the four winds, like the angel of the resurrection, what else were dust from dead men's bones, into the unity of breathing life. If you *can* create yourselves into any of these great creators, why have you not?

Yet, sister woman, though I cannot consent to find a Mozart or a Michael Angelo in your sex, cheerfully, and with the love that burns in depths of admiration, I acknowledge that you can do one thing as well as the best of us men — a greater thing than even Milton is known to have done, or Michael Angelo — you can die grandly, and as goddesses would die, were goddesses mortal. If any distant worlds (which *may* be the case) are so far ahead of us Tellurians in optical resources, as to see distinctly through their telescopes all that we do on earth, what is the grandest sight to which we ever treat them? St. Peter's at Rome, do you fancy, on Easter Sunday, or Luxor, or perhaps the Himalayas? Oh, no! my friend: suggest something better; these are baubles to *them;* they see in other worlds, in their own, far better toys of the same kind. These, take my word for it, are nothing. Do you give it up? The finest thing, then, we have to show them, is a scaffold on the morning of execution. I assure you there is a strong muster in those far telescopic worlds, on any such morning, of those who happen to find themselves occupying the right hemisphere for a peep at *us.* How, then, if it be announced in some such telescopic world by those who make a livelihood of catching glimpses at our newspapers, whose language they have long since deciphered, that the poor victim in the morning's sacrifice is a woman? How,

if it be published in that distant world, that the suf-
ferer wears upon her head, in the eyes of many, the
garlands of martyrdom? How, if it should be some
Marie Antoinette, the widowed queen, coming forward
on the scaffold, and presenting to the morning air her
head turned gray by sorrow, daughter of Cæsars kneeling down humbly to kiss the guillotine, as one that
worships death? How, if it were the noble Charlotte
Corday, that in the bloom of youth, that with the
loveliest of persons, that with homage waiting upon
her smiles wherever she turned her face to scatter
them — homage that followed those smiles as surely as
the carols of birds, after showers in spring, follow the
re-appearing sun and the racing of sunbeams over the
-hills — yet thought all these things cheaper than the
dust upon her sandals, in comparison of deliverance
from hell for her dear suffering France! Ah! these
were spectacles indeed for those sympathizing people
in distant worlds ; and some, perhaps would suffer a
sort of martyrdom themselves, because they could not
testify their wrath, could not bear witness to the
strength of love and to the fury of hatred that burned
within them at such scenes; could not gather into
golden urns some of that glorious dust which rested
in the catacombs of earth.

. On the Wednesday after Trinity Sunday in 1431,
being then about nineteen years of age, the Maid of
Arc underwent her martyrdom. She was conducted
before mid-day, guarded by eight hundred spearmen,
to a platform of prodigious height, constructed of
wooden billets supported by occasional walls of lath
and plaster, and traversed by hollow spaces in every
direction for the creation of air-currents. The pile

'struck terror,' says M. Michelet, 'by its height;' and, as usual, the English purpose in this is viewed as one of pure malignity. But there are two ways of explaining all that. It is probable that the purpose was merciful. On the circumstances of the execution I shall not linger. Yet, to mark the almost fatal felicity of M. Michelet in finding out whatever may injure the English name, at a moment when every reader will be interested in Joanna's personal appearance, it is really edifying to notice the ingenuity by which he draws into light from a dark corner a very unjust account of it, and neglects, though lying upon the high road, a very pleasing one. Both are from English pens. Grafton, a chronicler but little read, being a stiff-necked John Bull, thought fit to say, that no wonder Joanna should be a virgin, since her 'foule face' was a satisfactory solution of that particular merit. Holinshead, on the other hand, a chronicler somewhat later, every way more important, and at one time universally read, has given a very pleasing testimony to the interesting character of Joanna's person and engaging manners. Neither of these men lived till the following century, so that personally this evidence is none at all. Grafton sullenly and carelessly believed as he wished to believe; Holinshead took pains to inquire, and reports undoubtedly the general impression of France. But I cite the case as illustrating M. Michelet's candor.[6]

The circumstantial incidents of the execution, unless with more space than I can now command, I should be unwilling to relate. I should fear to injure, by imperfect report, a martyrdom which to myself appears so unspeakably grand. Yet for a purpose, pointing not

at Joanna, but at M. Michelet — viz., to convince him
that an Englishman is capable of thinking more highly
of *La Pucelle* than even her admiring countryman, I
shall, in parting, allude to one or two traits in Joanna's
demeanor on the scaffold, and to one or two in that of
the bystanders, which authorize me in questioning an
opinion of his upon this martyr's firmness. The reader
ought to be reminded that Joanna D'Arc was subjected
to an unusually unfair trial of opinion. Any of the
elder Christian martyrs had not much to fear of *personal* rancor. The martyr was chiefly regarded as the
enemy of Cæsar; at times, also, where any knowledge
of the Christian faith and morals existed, with the
enmity that arises spontaneously in the worldly against
the spiritual. But the martyr, though disloyal, was
not supposed to be, therefore, anti-national; and still
less was *individually* hateful. What was hated (if
anything) belonged to his class, not to himself separately. Now, Joanna, if hated at all, was hated personally, and in Rouen on national grounds. Hence
there would be a certainty of calumny arising against
her, such as would not affect martyrs in general. That
being the case, it would follow of necessity that some
people would impute to her a willingness to recant.
No innocence could escape *that*. Now, had she really
testified this willingness on the scaffold, it would have
argued nothing at all but the weakness of a genial
nature shrinking from the instant approach of torment.
And those will often pity that weakness most, who, in
their own persons, would yield to it least. Meantime,
there never was a calumny uttered that drew less support from the recorded circumstances. It rests upon
no *positive* testimony, and it has a weight of contra-

10

dicting testimony to stem. And yet, strange to say, M. Michelet, who at times seems to admire the Maid of Arc as much as I do, is the one sole writer amongst her *friends* who lends some countenance to this odious slander. His words are, that, if she did not utter this word *recant* with her lips, she uttered it in her heart. ' Whether she *said* the word is uncertain; but I affirm that she *thought* it.'

Now, I affirm that she did not ; not in any sense of the word ' *thought* ' applicable to the case. Here is France calumniating *La Pucelle :* here is England defending her. M. Michelet can only mean that, on *à priori* principles, every woman must be. liable to such a weakness : that Joanna was a woman ; *ergo*, that she was liable to such a weakness. That is, he only supposes her to have uttered the word by an argument which presumes it impossible for anybody to have done otherwise. I, on the contrary, throw the *onus* of the argument not on presumable tendencies of nature, but on the known facts of that morning's execution, as recorded by multitudes. What else, I demand, than mere weight of metal, absolute nobility of deportment, broke the vast line of battle then arrayed against her? What else but her meek, saintly demeanor won from the enemies, that till now had believed her a witch, tears of rapturous admiration? ' Ten thousand men,' says M. Michelet himself, ' ten thousand men wept ; '. and of these ten thousand the majority were political enemies knitted together by cords of superstition. What else was it but her constancy, united with her angelic gentleness, that drove the fanatic English soldier — who had sworn to throw a faggot on her scaffold, as *his* tribute of abhorrence, that *did* so, that ful-

filled his vow — suddenly to turn away a penitent for
life, saying everywhere that he had seen a dove rising
upon wings to heaven from the ashes where she had
stood? What else drove the executioner to kneel at
every shrine for pardon to *his* share in the tragedy!
And if all this were insufficient, then I cite the closing
act of her life, as valid on her behalf, were all other
testimonies against her. The executioner had been
directed to apply his torch from below. He did so.
The fiery smoke rose upwards in billowing volumes. A
Dominican monk was then standing almost at her side.
Wrapped up in his sublime office, he saw not the danger, but still persisted in his prayers. Even then, when
the last enemy was racing up the fiery stairs to seize
her, even at that moment did this noblest of girls think
only for *him*, the one friend that would not forsake her,
and not for herself; bidding him with her last breath
to care for his own preservation, but to leave *her* to God.
That girl, whose latest breath ascended in this sublime
expression of self-oblivion, did not utter the word *recant* either with her lips or in her heart. No; she did
not, though one should rise from the dead to swear it.

   ·   ·   ·   ·   ·   ·   ·   ·   ·   ·

Bishop of Beauvais! thy victim died in fire upon a
scaffold — thou upon a down bed. But for the departing minutes of life, both are oftentimes alike. At
the farewell crisis, when the gates of death are opening, and flesh is resting from its struggles, oftentimes
the tortured and torturer have the same truce from
carnal torment; both sink together into sleep; together both, sometimes, kindle into dreams. When
the mortal mists were gathering fast upon you two,
bishop and shepherd girl — when the pavilions of life

were closing up·their shadowy curtains about you —
let us try, through the gigantic glooms, to decipher the
flying features of your separate visions.

The shepherd girl that had delivered France — she,
from her dungeon, she, from her baiting at the stake,
she, from her duel with fire, as she entered her last
dream — saw Domrémy, saw the fountain of Domrémy,
saw the pomp of forests in which her childhood had
wandered. That Easter festival, which man had de-
nied to her languishing heart — that resurrection of
spring-time, which the darkness of dungeons had intercepted from *her*, hungering after the glorious liberty
of forests — were by God given back into her hands,
as jewels that had been stolen from her by robbers.
With those, perhaps (for the minutes of dreams can
stretch into ages), was given back to her by God the
bliss of childhood. By special privilege, for *her* might
be created, in this farewell dream, a second childhood,
innocent as the first; but not, like *that*, sad with the
gloom of a fearful mission in the rear. The mission
had now been fulfilled. The storm was weathered, the
skirts even of that mighty storm were drawing off.
The blood that she was to reckon for had been exacted; the tears that she was to shed in secret had
been paid to the last. The hatred to herself in all
eyes had been faced steadily, had been suffered, had
been survived. And in her last fight upon the scaffold
she had triumphed gloriously; victoriously she had
tasted the stings of death. For all, except this comfort from her farewell dream, she had died — died,
amidst the tears of ten thousand enemies — died,
amidst the drums and trumpets of armies — died,
amidst peals redoubling upon peals, volleys upon volleys, from the saluting clarions of martyrs.

Bishop of Beauvais! because the guilt-burdened man is in dreams haunted and waylaid by the most frightful of his crimes, and because upon thàt fluctuating mirror — rising (like the mocking mirrors of *mirage* in Arabian deserts) from the fens of death — most of all are reflected the sweet countenances which the man has laid in ruins; therefore I know, bishop, that you also, entering your final dream, saw Domrémy. That fountain, of which the witnesses spoke so much, showed itself to your eyes in pure morning dews: but neither dews, nor the holy dawn, could cleanse away the bright spots of innocent blood upon its surface. By the fountain, bishop, you saw a woman seated, that hid her face. But as *you* draw near, the woman raises her wasted features. Would Domrémy know them again for the features of her child? Ah, but *you* know them, bishop, well! Oh, mercy! what a groan was *that* which the servants, waiting outside the bishop's dream at his bedside, heard from his laboring heart, as at this moment he turned away from the fountain and the woman, seeking rest in the forests afar off. Yet not *so* to escape the woman, whom once again he must behold before he dies. In the forests to which he prays for pity, will he find a respite? What a tumult, what a gathering of feet is there! In glades, where only wild deer should run, armies and nations are assembling; towering in the fluctuating crowd are phantoms that belong to departed hours. There is the great English Prince, Regent of France. There is my Lord of Winchester, the princely cardinal, that died and made no sign. There is the Bishop of Beauvais, clinging to the shelter of thickets. What building is that which hands so rapid are raising? Is it a martyr's scaffold? Will they burn the child of Domrémy a second time? No: it is a tribunal that rises to the clouds; and two nations stand around it, waiting for a trial. Shall my Lord of Beauvais sit again upon the judgment-seat, and again number the hours for the innocent? Ah! no: he is the prisoner at the bar. Already all is waiting: the mighty audience is gathered, the Court is hurrying to their seats, the witnesses are arrayed, the trumpets are sounding, the judge is taking his place. Oh! but this is sudden. My lord, have you no counsel? 'Counsel I have none: in heaven above, or on earth beneath, counsellor there is none now that would take a brief from *me*: all are silent.' Is it, indeed, come to this? Alas the time is short, the tumult is wondrous, the crowd stretches away into infinity, but yet I will search in it for somebody to take your brief: I know of somebody that will be your counsel. Who is this that cometh from Domrémy? Who is she in bloody coronation robes from Rheims? Who is she that cometh with blackened flesh from walking the furnaces of Rouen? This is she, the shepherd girl, counsellor that had none for herself, whom I choose, bishop, for yours. She it is, I engage, that shall take my lord's brief. She it is, bishop, that would plead for you: yes, bishop, SHE — when heaven and earth are silent.

NOTES.

Note 1. Page 81.

' *Arc* : '— Modern France, that should know a great deal better than myself, insists that the name is not D'Arc — *i. e.*, of Arc — but *Darc*. Now it happens sometimes, that if a person, whose position guarantees his access to the best information, will content himself with gloomy dogmatism, striking the table with his fist, and saying in a terrific voice, ' It *is* so; and there's an end of it,' one bows deferentially, and submits. But if, unhappily for himself, won by this docility, he relents too amiably into reasons and arguments, probably one raises an insurrection against him that may never be crushed; for in the fields of logic one can skirmish, perhaps, as well as he. Had he confined himself to dogmatism, he would have entrenched his position in darkness, and have hidden his own vulnerable points. But, coming down to base reasons, he lets in light, and one sees where to plant the blows. Now, the worshipful reason of modern France for disturbing the old received spelling, is — that Jean Hordal, a descendant of *La Pucelle's* brother, spelled the name *Darc*, in 1612. But what of that? It is notorious that what small matter of spelling Providence had thought fit to disburse amongst man in the seventeenth century, was all monopolized by printers; now, M. Hordal was *not* a printer.

Note 2. Page 82.

'*Those that share thy blood :* ' — a collateral relative of Joanna's was subsequently ennobled by the title of *Du Lys*.

Note 3. Page 85.

' Only *now* forthcoming : ' — In 1847 *began* the publication (from official records) of Joanna's trial. It was interrupted, I fear, by the convulsions of 1848; and whether even yet finished, I do not know.

Note 4. Page 87.

'*Jean:*'—M. Michelet asserts, that there was a mystical meaning at that era in calling a child *Jean;* it implied a secret commendation of a child, if not a dedication, to St. John the evangelist, the beloved disciple, the apostle of love and mysterious visions. But, really, as the name was so exceedingly common, few people will detect a mystery in calling a *boy* by the name of Jack, though it *does* seem mysterious to call a girl Jack. It may be less so in France, where a beautiful practice has always prevailed of giving to a boy his mother's name — preceded and strengthened by a male name, as *Charles Anne, Victor Victoire.* In cases where a mother's memory has been unusually dear to a son, this vocal memento of her, locked into the circle of his own name, gives to it the tenderness of a testamentary relique, or a funeral ring. I presume, therefore, that *La Pucelle* must have borne the baptismal names of Jeanne Jean; the latter with no reference, perhaps, to so sublime a person as St. John, but simply to some relative.

Note 5. Page 88.

And reminding one of that inscription, so justly admired by Paul Richter, which a Russian Czarina placed on a guide-post near Moscow — *This is the road that leads to Constantinople.*

Note 6. Page 112.

Amongst the many ebullitions of M. Michelet's fury against us poor English, are four which will be likely to amuse the reader ; and they are the more conspicuous in collision with the justice which he sometimes does us, and the very indignant admiration which, under some aspects, he grants to us.

1. Our English literature he admires with some gnashing of teeth. He pronounces it 'fine and sombre,' but, I lament to add, 'sceptical, Judaic, Satanic — in a word, Anti-Christian.' That Lord Byron should figure as a member of this diabolical corporation, will not surprise men. It *will* surprise them to hear that Milton is one of its Satanic leaders. Many are the generous and eloquent Frenchmen, besides Chateaubriand, who have, in the course of the last thirty years, nobly suspended their own burn-

ing nationality, in order to render a more rapturous homage at the feet of Milton; and some of them have raised Milton almost to a level with angelic natures. Not one of them has thought of looking for him *below* the earth. As to Shakspeare, M. Michelet detects in him a most extraordinary mare's nest. It is this: he does 'not recollect to have seen the name of God' in any part of his works. On reading such words, it is natural to rub one's eyes, and suspect that all one has ever seen in this world may have been a pure ocular delusion. In particular, I begin myself to suspect, that the word '*la gloire*' never occurs in any Parisian journal. 'The great English nation,' says M. Michelet, 'has one immense profound vice,' to wit, 'pride.' Why, really that may be true; but we have a neighbor not absolutely clear of an 'immense profound vice,' as like ours in color and shape as cherry to cherry. In short, M. Michelet thinks us, by fits and starts, admirable, only that we are detestable; and he would adore some of our authors, were it not that so intensely he could have wished to kick them.

2. M. Michelet thinks to lodge an arrow in our sides by a very odd remark upon Thomas a Kempis: which is, that a man of any conceivable European blood — a Finlander, suppose, or a Zantiote — might have written Tom ; only not an Englishman. Whether an Englishman could have forged Tom, must remain a matter of doubt, unless the thing had been tried long ago. That problem was intercepted for ever by Tom's perverseness in choosing to manufacture himself. Yet, since nobody is better aware than M. Michelet that this very point of Kempis *having* manufactured Kempis is furiously and hopelessly litigated, three or four nations claiming to have forged his work for him, the shocking old doubt will raise its snaky head once more — whether this forger, who rests in so much darkness, might not, after all, be of English blood. Tom, it may be feared, is known to modern English literature chiefly by an irreverent mention of his name in a line of Peter Pindar's (Dr. Wolcot) fifty years back, where he is described as

' Kempis Tom,
Who clearly shows the way to Kingdom Come.'

Few in these days can have read him, unless in the Methodist version of John Wesley. Amongst those few, however, happens

11

to be myself; which arose from the accident of having, when a boy of eleven, received a copy of the 'De Imitatione Christi,' as a bequest from a relation, who died very young; from which cause, and from the external prettiness of the book, being a Glasgow reprint, by the celebrated Foulis, and gayly bound, I was induced to look into it; and finally read it many times over, partly out of some sympathy which, even in those days, I had with its simplicity and devotional fervor; but much more from the savage delight I found in laughing at Tom's Latinity. *That*, I freely grant to M. Michelet, is inimitable. Yet, after all, it is not certain whether the original *was* Latin. But, however *that* may have been, if it is possible that M. Michelet* can be accurate in saying that there are no less than *sixty* French versions (not editions, observe, but separate versions) existing of the 'De Imitatione,' how prodigious must have been the adaptation of the book to the religious heart of the fifteenth century! Excepting the Bible, but excepting *that* only, in Protestant lands, no book known to man has had the same distinction. It is the most marvellous bibliographical fact on record.

3. Our English girls, it seems, are as faulty in one way as we English males in another. None of us men could have written the *Opera Omnia* of Mr. à Kempis; neither could any of our girls have assumed male attire like *La Pucelle*. But why? Because, says Michelet, English girls and German think so much

---

* ' *If M. Michelet can be accurate :* '— However, on consideration, this statement does not depend on Michelet. The bibliographer Barbier has absolutely *specified* sixty in a separate dissertation, *soixante traductions*, amongst those even that have not escaped the search. The Italian translations are said to be thirty. As to mere *editions*, not counting the early MSS. for half a century before printing was introduced, those in Latin amount to two thousand, and those in French to one thousand. Meantime, it is very clear to me that this astonishing popularity, so entirely unparalleled in literature, could not have existed except in Roman Catholic times, nor subsequently have lingered in any Protestant land. It was the denial of Scripture fountains to thirsty lands which made this slender rill of Scripture truth so passionately welcome.

of an indecorum. Well, that is a good fault, generally speaking. But M. Michelet ought to have remembered a fact in the martyrologies which justifies both parties — the French heroine for doing, and the general choir of English girls for *not* doing. A female saint, specially renowned in France, had, for a reason as weighty as Joanna's — viz., expressly to shield her modesty amongst men — worn a male military harness. That reason and that example authorized *La Pucelle;* but our English girls, as a body, have seldom any such reason, and certainly no such saintly example, to plead. This excuses *them.* Yet, still, if it is indispensable to the national character that our young women should now and then trespass over the frontier of decorum, it then becomes a patriotic duty in me to assure M. Michelet that we have such ardent females amongst us, and in a long series ; some detected in naval hospitals, when too sick to remember their disguise; some on fields of battle; multitudes never detected at all; some only suspected; and others discharged without noise by war offices and other absurd people. In our navy, both royal and commercial, and generally from deep remembrances of slighted love, women have sometimes served in disguise for many years, taking contentedly their daily allowance of burgoo, biscuit, or cannon-balls — anything, in short, digestible or indigestible, that it might please Providence to send. One thing, at least, is to their credit : never any of these poor masks, with their deep silent remembrances, have been detected through murmuring, or what is nautically understood by 'skulking.' So, for once, M. Michelet has an *erratum* to enter upon the fly-leaf of his book in presentation copies.

4. But the last of these ebullitions is the most lively. We English, at Orleans, and after Orleans (which is not quite so extraordinary, if all were told), fled before the Maid of Arc. Yes, says M. Michelet, you *did:* deny it, if you can. Deny it, *mon cher?* I don't mean to deny it. Running away, in many cases, is a thing so excellent, that no philosopher would, at times, condescend to adopt any other step. All of us nations in Europe, without one exception, have shown our philosophy in that way at times. Even people, ' *qui ne se rendent pas,*' have deigned both to run and to shout, ' *Sauve qui peut!* ' at odd times of sunset ; though, for my part, I have no pleasure in recalling unpleasant

remembrances to brave men ; and yet, really, being so philosophic, they ought *not* to be unpleasant.　But the amusing feature in M. Michelet's reproach is the way in which he *improves*
and varies against us the charge of running, as if he were singing
a catch.　Listen to him.　They *'showed their backs,'* did these
English.　(Hip, hip, hurrah! three times three!)　*'Behind*
good walls, they let themselves be taken.'　(Hip, hip ! nine times
nine !)　They *'ran as fast as their legs could carry them.'*
(Hurrah ! twenty-seven times twenty-seven !)　They *'ran before*
a girl;' they did.　(Hurrah ! eighty-one times eighty-one!)
This reminds one of criminal indictments on the old model in
English courts, where (for fear the prisoner should escape) the
crown lawyer varied the charge perhaps through forty counts.
The law laid its guns so as to rake the accused at every possible
angle.　Whilst the indictment was reading, he seemed a monster
of crime in his own eyes; and yet, after all, the poor fellow had
but committed one offence, and not always *that.*　N. B. — Not
having the French original at hand, I make my quotations from
a friend's copy of Mr. Walter Kelly's translation, which seems
to me faithful, spirited, and idiomatically English — liable, in
fact, only to the single reproach of occasional provincialisms.

THE ENGLISH MAIL-COACH.

SECTION THE FIRST.—THE GLORY OF MOTION.

Some twenty or more years before I matriculated at Oxford, Mr. Palmer, at that time M. P. for Bath, had accomplished two things, very hard to do on our little planet, the Earth, however cheap they may be held by eccentric people in comets—he had invented mail-coaches, and he had married the daughter [1] of a duke. He was, therefore, just twice as great a man as Galileo, who did certainly invent (or which is the same thing,[2] discover) the satellites of Jupiter, those very next things extant to mail-coaches in the two capital pretensions of speed and keeping time, but, on the other hand, who did not marry the daughter of a duke.

These mail-coaches, as organzied by Mr. Palmer, are entitled to a circumstantial notice from myself, having had so large a share in developing the anarchies of my subsequent dreams; an agency which they accomplished, 1st, through velocity, at that time unprecedented—for they first revealed the glory of motion; 2dly, through grand effects for the eye between lamp-light and the darkness upon solitary roads; 3dly, through animal beauty and power so often displayed in the class of horses selected for this mail service; 4thly, through the conscious presence of a central intellect, that, in the midst of vast distances [3] —of storms, of darkness, of danger—overruled all

[125]

obstacles into one steady co-operation to a national result. For my own feeling, this post-office service spoke as by some mighty orchestra, where a thousand instruments, all disregarding each other, and so far in danger of discord, yet all obedient as slaves to the supreme *baton* of some great leader, terminate in a perfection of harmony like that of heart, brain, and lungs, in a healthy animal organization. But, finally, that particular element in this whole combination which most impressed myself, and through which it is that to this hour Mr. Palmer's mail-coach system tyrannizes over my dreams by terror and terrific beauty, lay in the awful *political* mission which at that time it fulfilled. The mail-coach it was that distributed over the face of the land, like the opening of apocalyptic vials, the heart-shaking news of Trafalgar, of Salamanca, of Vittoria, of Waterloo. These were the harvests that, in the grandeur of their reaping, redeemed the tears and blood in which they had been sown. Neither was the meanest peasant so much below the grandeur and the sorrow of the times as to confound battles such as these, which were gradually moulding the destinies of Christendom, with the vulgar conflicts of ordinary warfare, so often no more than gladiatorial trials of national prowess. The victories of England in this stupendous contest rose of themselves as natural *Te Deums* to heaven; and it was felt by the thoughtful that such victories, at such a crisis of general prostration, were not more beneficial to ourselves than finally to France, our enemy, and to the nations of all western or central Europe, through whose pusillanimity it was that the French domination had prospered.

The mail-coach, as the national organ for publishing these mighty events thus diffusively influential, became itself a spiritualized and glorified object to an impassioned heart; and naturally, in the Oxford of that day, *all* hearts were impassioned, as being all (or nearly all) in *early* manhood. In most universities there is one single college; in Oxford there were five-and-twenty, all of which were peopled by young men, the *élite* of their own generation; not boys, but men; none under eighteen. In some of these many colleges, the custom permitted the student to keep what are called ' short terms ; ' that is, the four terms of Michaelmas, Lent, Easter, and Act, were kept by a residence, in the aggregate of ninety-one days, or thirteen weeks. Under this interrupted residence, it was possible that a student might have a reason for going down to his home four times in the year. This made eight journeys to and fro. But, as the homes lay dispersed through all the shires of the island, and most of us disdained all coaches except his majesty's mail, no city out of London could pretend to so extensive a connection with Mr. Palmer's establishment as Oxford. Three mails, at the least, I remember as passing every day through Oxford, and benefiting by my personal patronage — viz., the Worcester, the Gloucester, and the Holyhead mail. Naturally, therefore, it became a point of some interest with us, whose journeys revolved every six weeks on an average, to look a little into the executive details of the system. With some of these Mr. Palmer had no concern ; they rested upon bye-laws enacted by posting-houses for their own benefit, and upon other bye-laws, equally stern, enacted by the inside passengers for the illustration of their own

haughty exclusiveness. These last were of a nature to
rouse our scorn, from which the transition was not
very long to systematic mutiny. Up to this time, say
1804, or 1805 (the year of Trafalgar), it had been the
fixed assumption of the four inside people (as an old
tradition of all public carriages derived from the reign
of Charles II.), that they, the illustrious quaternion,
constituted a porcelain variety of the human race,
whose dignity would have been compromised by ex-
changing one word of civility with the three miserable
delf-ware outsides. Even to have kicked an outsider,
might have been held to attaint the foot concerned in
that operation ; so that, perhaps, it would have required an act of parliament to restore its purity of
blood. What words, then, could express the horror,
and the sense of treason, in that case, which *had* happened, where all three outsides (the trinity of Pariahs)
made a vain attempt to sit down at the same breakfast-
table or dinner-table with the consecrated four ? I
myself witnessed such an attempt; and on that occasion a benevolent old gentleman endeavored to soothe
his three holy associates, by suggesting that, if the
outsides were indicted for this criminal attempt at the
next assizes, the court would regard it as a case of
lunacy, or *delirium tremens*, rather than of treason.
England owes much of her grandeur to the depth of
the aristocratic element in her social composition, when
pulling against her strong democracy. I am not the
man to laugh at it. But sometimes, undoubtedly, it
expressed itself in comic shapes. The course taken
with the infatuated outsiders, in the particular attempt
which I have noticed, was, that the waiter, beckoning
them away from the privileged *salle-à-manger*, sang

out, 'This way, my good men,' and then enticed these good men away to the kitchen. But that plan had not always answered. Sometimes, though rarely, cases occurred where the intruders, being stronger than usual, or more vicious than usual, resolutely refused to budge, and so far carried their point, as to have a separate table arranged for themselves in a corner of the general room. Yet, if an Indian screen could be found ample enough to plant them out from the very eyes of the high table, or *dais*, it then became possible to assume as a fiction of law — that the three delf fellows, after all, were not present. They could be ignored by the porcelain men, under the maxim, that objects not appearing, and not existing, are governed by the same logical construction.[4]

Such being, at that time, the usages of mail-coaches, what was to be done by us of young Oxford? We, the most aristocratic of people, who were addicted to the practice of looking down superciliously even upon the insides themselves as often very questionable characters — were we, by voluntarily going outside, to court indignities? If our dress and bearing sheltered us, generally, from the suspicion of being 'raff' (the name at that period for 'snobs '[5]), we really *were* such constructively, by the place we assumed. If we did not submit to the deep shadow of eclipse, we entered at least the skirts of its penumbra. And the analogy of theatres was valid against us, where no man can complain of the annoyances incident to the pit or gallery, having his instant remedy in paying the higher price of the boxes. But the soundness of this analogy we disputed. In the case of the theatre, it cannot be pretended that the inferior situations have any separate attractions, unless the pit may be supposed to have an advantage for the purposes of the critic or the dramatic reporter. But the critic or reporter is a rarity. For most people, the sole benefit is in the price. Now, on the contrary, the outside of the mail had its own incommunicable advantages. These we could not forego. The higher price we would willingly have paid, but not the price connected with the condition of riding inside ; which condition we pronounced insufferable. The air, the freedom of prospect, the proximity to the horses, the elevation of seat — these were what we required ; but, above all, the certain anticipation of purchasing occasional opportunities of driving.

Such was the difficulty which pressed us ; and under the coercion of this difficulty, we instituted a searching inquiry into the true quality and valuation of the different apartments about the mail. We conducted this inquiry on metaphysical principles ; and it was ascertained satisfactorily, that the roof of the coach, which by some weak men had been called the attics, and by some the garrets, was in reality the drawing-room ; in which drawing-room the box was the chief ottoman or sofa ; whilst it appeared that the *inside*, which had been traditionally regarded as the only room tenantable by gentlemen, was, in fact, the coal-cellar in disguise.

Great wits jump. The very same idea had not long before struck the celestial intellect of China. Amongst the presents carried out by our first embassy to that country was a state-coach. It had been specially selected as a personal gift by George III. ; but the exact mode of using it was an immense mystery to Pekin. The ambassador, indeed (Lord Macartney), had made some imperfect explanations upon this point ; but, as his excellency communicated these in a diplomatic whisper, at the very moment of his departure, the celestial intellect was very feebly illuminated, and it became necessary to call a cabinet council on the grand state question, ' Where was the emperor to sit ? ' The hammer-cloth happened to be unusually gorgeous ; and partly on that consideration, but partly also because the box offered the most elevated seat, was nearest to the moon, and undeniably went foremost,.it was resolved by acclamation that the box was the imperial throne, and for the scoundrel who drove, he might sit where he could find a perch. The horses, therefore, being harnessed, solemnly his imperial majesty ascended his new English throne under a flourish of trumpets, having the first lord of the treasury on his right hand, and the chief jester on his left. Pekin gloried in the spectacle ; and in the whole flowery people, constructively present by representation, there was but one discontented person, and *that* was the coachman. This mutinous individual audaciously shouted, ' Where am *I* to sit ? ' But the privy council, incensed by his disloyalty, unanimously opened the door, and kicked him into the inside. He had all the inside places to himself ; but such is the rapacity of ambition, that he was still dissatisfied. ' I say,' he cried out in an extempore petition, addressed to the emperor through the window — ' I say, how am I to catch hold of the reins ? ' — ' Anyhow,' was the imperial answer ; ' don't trouble *me*, man, in my glory. How catch the reins ? Why, through the windows, through the keyholes — *any*how.' Finally this contumacious coachman lengthened the check-strings into

a sort of jury-reins, communicating with the horses;
with these he drove as steadily as Pekin had any right
to expect. The emperor returned after the briefest of
circuits; he descended in great pomp from his throne,
with the severest resolution never to remount it. A
public thanksgiving was ordered for his majesty's
happy escape from the disease of broken neck; and
the state-coach was dedicated thenceforward as a
votive offering to the god Fo, Fo — whom the learned
more accurately called Fi, Fi.

A revolution of this same Chinese character did
young Oxford of that era effect in the constitution of
mail-coach society. It was a perfect French revolution; and we had good reason to say, *ça ira*. In fact,
it soon became *too* popular. The ' public,' a well-
known character, particularly disagreeable, though
slightly respectable, and notorious for affecting the
chief seats in synagogues — had at first loudly opposed this revolution; but when the opposition showed
itself to be ineffectual, our disagreeable friend went
into it with headlong zeal. At first it was a sort of
race between us; and, as the public is usually from
thirty to fifty years old, naturally we of young Oxford,
that averaged about twenty, had the advantage. Then
the public took to bribing, giving fees to horse-keep-
ers, &c., who hired out their persons as warming-pans
on the box-seat. *That*, you know, was shocking to
all moral sensibilities. Come to bribery, said we, and
there is an end to all morality, Aristotle's, Zeno's,
Cicero's, or anybody's. And, besides, of what use
was it? For *we* bribed also. And as our bribes to
those of the public were as five shillings to sixpence,
here again young Oxford had the advantage. But the

contest was ruinous to the principles of the stables connected with the mails. This whole corporation was constantly bribed, rebribed, and often sur-rebribed; a mail-coach yard was like the hustings in a contested election; and a horse-keeper, hostler, or helper, was held by the philosophical at that time to be the most corrupt character in the nation.

There was an impression upon the public mind, natural enough from the continually augmenting velocity of the mail, but quite erroneous, that an outside seat on this class of carriages was a post of danger. On the contrary, I maintained that, if a man had become nervous from some gipsy prediction in his childhood, allocating to a particular moon now approaching some unknown danger, and he should inquire earnestly, ' Whither can I fly for shelter? Is a prison the safest retreat? or a lunatic hospital? or the British Museum?' I should have replied, ' Oh, no; I'll tell you what to do. Take lodgings for the next forty days on the box of his majesty's mail. Nobody can touch you there. If it is by bills at ninety days after date that you are made unhappy — if noters and protesters are the sort of wretches whose astrological shadows darken the house of life — then note you what I vehemently protest — viz., that no matter though the sheriff and under-sheriff in every county should be running after you with his *posse*, touch a hair of your head he cannot whilst you keep house, and have your legal domicile on the box of the mail. It is felony to stop the mail; even the sheriff cannot do that. And an *extra* touch of the whip to the leaders (no great matter if it grazes the sheriff) at any time guarantees your safety.' In fact, a bedroom in a quiet house

seems a safe enough retreat, yet it is liable to its own
notorious nuisances — to robbers by night, to rats, to
fire. But the mail laughs at these terrors. To robbers,
the answer is packed up and ready for delivery in the
barrel of the guard's blunderbuss. Rats again! — there
are none about mail-coaches, any more than snakes in
Von Troil's Iceland ; [6] except, indeed, now and then a
parliamentary rat, who always hides his shame in what
I have shown to be the ' coal-cellar.' And as to fire,
I never knew but one in a mail-coach, which was in
the Exeter mail, and caused by an obstinate sailor
bound to Devonport. Jack, making light of the law
and the lawgiver that had set their faces against his
offence, insisted on taking up a forbidden seat [7] in the
rear of the roof, from which he could exchange his
own yarns with those of the guard. No greater offence was then known to mail-coaches ; it was treason,
it was *læsa majestas*, it was by tendency arson ; and
the ashes of Jack's pipe, falling amongst the straw of
the hinder boot containing the mail-bags, raised a
flame which (aided by the wind of our motion) threatened a revolution in the republic of letters. Yet even
this left the sanctity of the box unviolated. In dignified repose, the coachman and myself sat on, resting
with benign composure upon our knowledge that the
fire would have to burn its way through four inside
passengers before it could reach ourselves. I remarked to the coachman, with a quotation from Virgil's
' Æneid ' really too hackneyed —

> ' Jam proximus ardet
> Ucalegon.'

But, recollecting that the Virgilian part of the coachman's education might have been neglected, I inter-

preted so far as to say, that perhaps at that moment the flames were catching hold of our worthy brother and inside passenger, Ucalegon. The coachman made no answer, which is my own way when a stranger addresses me either in Syriac or in Coptic, but by his faint sceptical smile he seemed to insinuate that he knew better; for that Ucalegon, as it happened, was not in the way-bill, and therefore could not have been booked.

No dignity is perfect which does not at some point ally itself with the mysterious. The connection of the mail with the state and the executive government —a connection obvious, but yet not strictly defined — gave to the whole mail establishment an official grandeur which did us service on the roads, and invested us with seasonable terrors. Not the less impressive were those terrors, because their legal limits were imperfectly ascertained. Look at those turnpike gates; with what deferential hurry, with what an obedient start, they fly open at our approach! Look at that long line of carts and carters ahead, audaciously usurping the very crest of the road. Ah! traitors, they do not hear us as yet; but, as soon as the dreadful blast of our horn reaches them with proclamation of our approach, see with what frenzy of trepidation they fly to their horses' heads, and deprecate our wrath by the precipitation of their crane-neck quarterings. Treason they feel to be their crime; each individual carter feels himself under the ban of confiscation and attainder; his blood is attainted through six generations; and nothing is wanting but the headsman and his axe, the block and the saw-dust, to close up the vista of his horrors. What! shall it be within benefit of clergy to delay the king's message on the high road? — to interrupt the great respirations, ebb and flood, *systole* and *diastole*, of the national intercourse? — to endanger the safety of tidings, running day and night between all nations and languages? Or can it be fancied, amongst the weakest of men, that the bodies of the criminals will be given up to their widows for Christian burial? Now the doubts which were raised as to our powers did more to wrap them in terror, by wrapping them in uncertainty, than could have been effected by the sharpest definitions of the law from the Quarter Sessions. We, on our parts (we, the collective mail, I mean), did our utmost to exalt the idea of our privileges by the insolence with which we wielded them. Whether this insolence rested upon law that gave it a sanction, or upon conscious power that haughtily dispensed with that sanction, equally it spoke from a potential station; and the agent, in each particular insolence of the moment, was viewed reverentially, as one having authority.

Sometimes after breakfast his majesty's mail would become frisky; and in its difficult wheelings amongst the intricacies of early markets, it would upset an apple-cart, a cart loaded with eggs, &c. Huge was the affliction and dismay, awful was the smash. I, as far as possible, endeavored in such a case to represent the conscience and moral sensibilities of the mail; and, when wildernesses of eggs were lying poached under our horses' hoofs, then would I stretch forth my hands in sorrow saying (in words too celebrated at that time, from the false echoes[8] of Marengo), 'Ah! wherefore have we not time to weep over you?' which was evidently impossible, since, in fact, we had not time to laugh over them. Tied to post-office allowance, in some cases of fifty minutes for eleven miles, could the royal mail pretend to undertake the offices of sympathy and condolence? Could it be expected to provide tears for the accidents of the road? If even it seemed to trample on humanity, it did so, I felt, in discharge of its own more peremptory duties.

Upholding the morality of the mail, *à fortiori* I upheld its rights; as a matter of duty, I stretched to the uttermost its privilege of imperial precedency, and astonished weak minds by the feudal powers which I hinted to be lurking constructively in the charters of this proud establishment. Once I remember being on the box of the Holyhead mail, between Shrewsbury and Oswestry, when a tawdry thing from Birmingham, some 'Tallyho' or 'Highflyer,' all flaunting with green and gold, came up alongside of us. What a contrast to our royal simplicity of form and color in this plebeian wretch! The single ornament on our dark ground of chocolate color was the mighty shield of the imperial arms, but emblazoned in proportions as modest as a signet-ring bears to a seal of office. Even this was displayed only on a single panel, whispering, rather than proclaiming, our relations to the mighty state; whilst the beast from Birmingham, our green-and-gold friend from false, fleeting, perjured Brummagem, had as much writing and painting on its sprawling flanks as would have puzzled a decipherer from the tombs of Luxor. For some time this Birmingham machine ran along by our side — a piece of familiarity that already of itself seemed to me sufficiently jacobinical. But all at once a movement of the horses announced a desperate intention of

12

leaving us behind. 'Do you see *that* ?' I said to the
coachman. — 'I see,' was his short answer. He was
wide awake, yet he waited longer than seemed prudent; for the horses of our audacious opponent had a
disagreeable air of freshness and power. But his
motive was loyal; his wish was, that the Birmingham
conceit should be full-blown before he froze it. When
that seemed right, he unloosed, or, to speak by a
stronger word, he *sprang*, his known resources: he
slipped our royal horses like cheetahs, or hunting-
leopards, after the affrighted game. How they could
retain such a reserve of fiery power after the work
they had accomplished, seemed hard to explain. But
on our side, besides the physical superiority, was a
tower of moral strength, namely, the king's name,
'which they upon the adverse faction wanted.' Passing them without an effort, as it seemed, we threw
them into the rear with so lengthening an interval
between us, as proved in itself the bitterest mockery
of their presumption; whilst our guard blew back a
shattering blast of triumph, that was really too painfully full of derision.

I mention this little incident for its connection with
what followed. A Welsh rustic, sitting behind me,
asked if I had not felt my heart burn within me
during the progress of the race? I said, with philosophic calmness, *No;* because we were not racing
with a mail, so that no glory could be gained. In
fact, it was sufficiently mortifying that such a Birmingham thing should dare to challenge us. The Welshman replied, that he didn't see *that;* for that a cat
might look at a king, and a Brummagem coach might
lawfully race the Holyhead mail. '*Race* us, if you

like,' I replied, 'though even *that* has an air of sedi-
tion, but not *beat* us. This would have been treason;
and for its own sake I am glad that the "Tallyho" was
disappointed.' So dissatisfied did the Welshman seem
with this opinion, that at last I was obliged to tell him a
very fine story from one of our elder dramatists — viz.,
that once, in some far oriental kingdom, when the
sultan of all the land, with his princes, ladies, and
chief omrahs, were flying their falcons, a hawk suddenly flew at a majestic eagle; and in defiance of the
eagle's natural advantages, in contempt also of the
eagle's traditional royalty, and before the whole assembled field of astonished spectators from Agra, and
Lahore, killed the eagle on the spot. Amazement
seized the sultan at the unequal contest, and burning
admiration for its unparalleled result. He commanded
that the hawk should be brought before him; he
caressed the bird with enthusiasm; and he ordered
that, for the commemoration of his matchless courage,
a diadem of gold and rubies should be solemnly placed
on the hawk's head; but then that, immediately after
this solemn coronation, the bird should be led off to
execution, as the most valiant indeed of traitors, but
not the less a traitor, as having dared to rise rebel-
liously against his liege lord and anointed sovereign,
the eagle. 'Now,' said I to the Welshman, 'to you
and me, as men of refined sensibilities, how painful it
would have been that this poor Brummagem brute,
the "Tallyho," in the impossible case of a victory over
us, should have been crowned with Birmingham tinsel,
with paste diamonds, and Roman pearls, and then led
off to instant execution.' The Welshman doubted if
that could be warranted by law. And when I hinted

at the 6th of Edward Longshanks, chap. 18, for regulating the precedency of coaches, as being probably the statute relied on for the capital punishment of such offences, he replied drily, that if the attempt to pass a mail really were treasonable, it was a pity that the 'Tallyho' appeared to have so imperfect an acquaintance with law.

The modern modes of travelling cannot compare with the old mail-coach system in grandeur and power. They boast of more velocity, not, however, as a consciousness, but as a fact of our lifeless knowledge, resting upon *alien* evidence; as, for instance, because somebody *says* that we have gone fifty miles in the hour, though we are far from feeling it as a personal experience, or upon the evidence of a result, as that actually we find ourselves in York four hours after leaving London. Apart from such an assertion, or such a result, I myself am little aware of the pace. But, seated on the old mail-coach, we needed no evidence out of ourselves to indicate the velocity. On this system the word was, *Non magna loquimur*, as upon railways, but *vivimus*. Yes, 'magna *vivimus;*' we do not make verbal ostentation of our grandeurs, we realize our grandeurs in act, and in the very experience of life. The vital experience of the glad animal sensibilities made doubts impossible on the question of our speed; we heard our speed, we saw it, we felt it as a thrilling; and this speed was not the product of blind insensate agencies, that had no sympathy to give, but was incarnated in the fiery eyeballs of the noblest amongst brutes, in his dilated nostril, spasmodic muscles, and thunder-beating hoofs. The sensibility of the horse, uttering itself in the maniac light of his eye, might be the last vibration of such a movement; the glory of Salamanca might be the first. But the intervening links that connected them, that spread the earthquake of battle into the eyeball of the horse, were the heart of man and its electric thrillings — kindling in the rapture of the fiery strife, and then propagating its own tumults by contagious shouts and gestures to the heart of his servant the horse.

But now, on the new system of travelling, iron tubes and boilers have disconnected man's heart from the ministers of his locomotion. Nile nor Trafalgar has power to raise an extra bubble in a steam-kettle. The galvanic cycle is broken up for ever; man's imperial nature no longer sends itself forward through the electric sensibility of the horse; the inter-agencies are gone in the mode of communication between the horse and his master, out of which grew so many aspects of sublimity under accidents of mists that hid, or sudden blazes that revealed, of mobs that agitated, or midnight solitudes that awed. Tidings, fitted to convulse all nations, must henceforwards travel by culinary process; and the trumpet that once announced from afar the laurelled mail, heart-shaking, when heard screaming on the wind, and proclaiming itself through the darkness to every village or solitary house on its route, has now given way for ever to the pot-wallopings of the boiler.

Thus have perished multiform openings for public expressions of interest, scenical yet natural, in great national tidings; for revelations of faces and groups that could not offer themselves amongst the fluctuating mobs of a railway station. The gatherings of gazers about a laurelled mail had one centre, and acknowl-

edged one sole interest. But the crowds attending at
a railway station have as little unity as running water,
and own as many centres as there are separate carriages in the train.

How else, for example, than as a constant watcher
for the dawn, and for the London mail that in summer
months entered about daybreak amongst the lawny
thickets of Marlborough forest, couldst thou, sweet
Fanny of the Bath road, have become the glorified
inmate of my dreams? Yet Fanny, as the loveliest
young woman for face and person that perhaps in my
whole life I have beheld, merited the station which
even now, from a distance of forty years, she holds in
my dreams; yes, though by links of natural association
she brings along with her a troop of dreadful creatures,
fabulous and not fabulous, that are more abominable
to the heart, than Fanny and the dawn are delightful.

Miss Fanny of the Bath road, strictly speaking,
lived at a mile's distance from the road; but came so
continually to meet the mail, that I on my frequent
transits rarely missed her, and naturally connected her
image with the great thoroughfare where only I had
ever seen her. Why she came so punctually, I do not
exactly know; but I believe with some burden of
commissions to be executed in Bath, which had gathered to her own residence as a central rendezvous for
converging them. The mail-coachman who drove the
Bath mail, and wore the royal livery,[9] happened to be
Fanny's grandfather. A good man he was, that loved
his beautiful granddaughter; and, loving her wisely,
was vigilant over her deportment in any case where
young Oxford might happen to be concerned. Did my
vanity then suggest that I myself, individually, could fall

within the line of his terrors? Certainly not, as
regarded any physical pretensions that I could plead;
for Fanny (as a chance passenger from her own neighborhood once told me) counted in her train a hundred
and ninety-nine professed admirers, if not open aspi-
rants to her favor; and probably not one of the whole
brigade but excelled myself in personal advantages.
Ulysses even, with the unfair advantage of his accursed
bow, could hardly have undertaken that amount of
suitors. So the danger might have seemed slight —
only that woman is universally aristocratic; it 'is
amongst her nobilities of heart that she *is* so. Now,
the aristocratic distinctions in my favor might easily
with Miss Fanny have compensated my physical defi-
ciencies. Did I then make love to Fanny? Why,
yes; about as much love as one *could* make whilst the
mail was changing horses — a process which, ten years
later, did not occupy above eighty seconds; but *then*
— viz., about Waterloo — it occupied five times eighty.
Now, four hundred seconds offer a field quite ample
enough for whispering into a young woman's ear a
great deal of truth, and (by way of parenthesis) some
trifle of falsehood. Grandpapa did right, therefore, to
watch me. And yet, as happens too often to the
grandpapas of earth, in a contest with the admirers of
granddaughters, how vainly would he have watched
me had I meditated any evil whispers to Fanny! She,
it is my belief, would have protected herself against
any man's evil suggestions. But he, as the result
showed, could not have intercepted the opportunities
for such suggestions. Yet, why not? Was he not
active? Was he not blooming? Blooming he was as
Fanny herself.

‘ Say, all our praises why should lords ———’
Stop, that’s not the line.
    ‘ Say, all our roses why should girls engross ? ’

The coachman showed rosy blossoms on his face
deeper even than his granddaughter’s — *his* being
drawn from the ale cask, Fanny’s from the fountains
of the dawn. But, in spite of his blooming face, some
infirmities he had; and one particularly in which he
too much resembled a crocodile. This lay in a monstrous inaptitude for turning round. The crocodile, I
presume, owes that inaptitude to the absurd *length* of
his back; but in our grandpapa it arose rather from
the absurd *breadth* of his back, combined, possibly,
with some growing stiffness in his legs. Now, upon
this crocodile infirmity of his I planted a human advantage for tendering my homage to Miss Fanny. In
defiance of all his honorable vigilance, no sooner had
he presented to us his mighty Jovian back (what a
field for displaying to mankind his royal scarlet !’),
whilst inspecting professionally the buckles, the straps,
and the silvery turrets [10] of his harness, than I raised
Miss Fanny’s hand to my lips, and, by the mixed tenderness and respectfulness of my manner, caused her
easily to understand how happy it would make me to
rank upon her list as No. 10 or 12, in which case a
few casualties amongst her lovers (and observe, they
hanged liberally in those days might have promoted
me speedily to the top of the tree ; as, on the other
hand, with how much loyalty of submission I acqui-
esced by anticipation in her award, supposing that she
should plant me in the very rearward of her favor, as
No. 199 + 1. Most truly I loved this beautiful and
ingenuous girl ; and had it not been for the Bath

mail, timing all courtships by post-office allowance,
heaven only knows what might have come of it. People talk of being over head and ears in love ; now, the
mail was the cause that I sank only over ears in love,
which, you know, still left a trifle of brain to overlook
the whole conduct of the affair.

Ah, reader ! when I look back upon those days, it
seems to me that all things change — all things perish
' Perish the roses and the palms of kings : ' perish even
the crowns and trophies of Waterloo : thunder and
lightning are not the thunder and lightning which I
remember. Roses are degenerating. The Fannies of
our island — though this I say with reluctance — are
not visibly improving ; and the Bath road is notoriously
superannuated. Crocodiles, you will say, are stationary. Mr. Waterton tells me that the crocodile does
not change ; that a cayman, in fact, or an alligator, is
just as good for riding upon as he was in the time of
the Pharaohs. *That* may be ; but the reason is, that
the crocodile does not live fast — he is a slow coach.
I believe it is generally understood among naturalists,
that the crocodile is a blockhead. It is my own impression that the Pharaohs were also blockheads.
Now, as the Pharaohs and the crocodile domineered
over Egyptian society, this accounts for a singular
mistake that prevailed through innumerable generations on the Nile. The crocodile made the ridiculous
blunder of supposing man to be meant chiefly for his
own eating. Man, taking a different view of the subject, naturally met that mistake by another : he viewed
the crocodile as a thing sometimes to worship, but always to run away from. And this continued until Mr.
Waterton [11] changed the relations between the animals.

13

The mode of escaping from the reptile he showed to
be, not by running away, but by leaping on its back,
booted and spurred. The two animals had misunderstood each other. The use of the crocodile has now
been cleared up — viz., to be ridden; and the final
cause of man is, that he may improve the health of the
crocodile by riding him a fox-hunting before breakfast.
And it is pretty certain that any crocodile, who has
been regularly hunted through the season, and is master of the weight he carries, will take a six-barred gate
now as well as ever he would have done in the infancy
of the pyramids.

If, therefore, the crocodile does *not* change, all things
else undeniably *do* : even the shadow of the pyramids
grows less. And often the restoration in vision of
Fanny and the Bath road, makes me too pathetically
sensible of that truth. Out of the darkness, if I happen to call back the image of Fanny, up rises suddenly
from a gulf of forty years a rose in June ; or, if I think
for an instant of the rose in June, up rises the heavenly
face of Fanny. One after the other, like the antipho-
nies in the choral service, rise Fanny and the rose in
June, then back again the rose in June and Fanny.
Then come both together, as in a chorus — roses and
Fannies, Fannies and roses, without end, thick as blossoms in paradise. Then comes a venerable crocodile,
in a royal livery of scarlet and gold, with sixteen
capes; and the crocodile is driving four-in-hand from
the box of the Bath mail. And suddenly we upon the
mail are pulled up by a mighty dial, sculptured with
the hours, that mingle with the heavens and the heavenly host. Then all at once we are arrived at Marlborough forest, amongst the lovely households [12] of the

roe-deer; the deer and their fawns retire into the
dewy thickets; the thickets are rich with roses; once
again the roses call up the sweet countenance of Fanny;
and she, being the granddaughter of a crocodile, awak-
ens a dreadful host of semi-legendary animals—griffins,
dragons, basilisks, sphinxes — till at length the whole
vision of fighting images crowds into one towering
armorial shield, a vast emblazonry of human charities
and human loveliness that have perished, but quartered
heraldically with unutterable and demoniac natures,
whilst over all rises, as a surmounting crest, one fair
female hand, with the forefinger pointing, in sweet,
sorrowful admonition, upwards to heaven, where is
sculptured the eternal writing which proclaims the
frailty of earth and her children.

GOING DOWN WITH VICTORY.

But the grandest chapter of our experience, within
the whole mail-coach service, was on those occasions
when we went down from London with the news of
victory. A period of about ten years stretched from
Trafalgar to Waterloo; the second and third years of
which period (1806 and 1807) were comparatively
sterile; but the other nine (from 1805 to 1815 inclu-
sively) furnished a long succession of victories; the
least of which, in such a contest of Titans, had an
inappreciable value of position — partly for its absolute
interference with the plans of our enemy, but still more
from its keeping alive through central Europe the
sense of a deep-seated vulnerability in France. Even
to tease the coasts of our enemy, to mortify them by
continual blockades, to insult them by capturing if it
were but a baubling schooner under the eyes of their

arrogant armies, repeated from time to time a sullen proclamation of power lodged in one quarter to which the hopes of Christendom turned in secret. How much more loudly must this proclamation have spoken in the audacity [13] of having bearded the *élite* of their troops, and having beaten them in pitched battles! Five years of life it was worth paying down for the privilege of an outside place on a mail-coach, when carrying down the first tidings of any such event. And it is to be noted that, from our insular situation, and the multitude of our frigates disposable for the rapid transmission of intelligence, rarely did any unauthorized rumor steal away a prelibation from the first aroma of the regular despatches. The government news was generally the earliest news.

From eight P. M., to fifteen or twenty minutes later, imagine the mails assembled on parade in Lombard Street, where, at that time, [14] and not in St. Martin's-le-Grand, was seated the General Post-office. In what exact strength we mustered I do not remember; but, from the length of each separate *attelage*, we filled the street, though a long one, and though we were drawn up in double file. On *any* night the spectacle was beautiful. The absolute perfection of all the appointments about the carriages and the harness, their strength, their brilliant cleanliness, their beautiful simplicity — but, more than all, the royal magnificence of the horses — were what might first have fixed the attention. Every carriage, on every morning in the year, was taken down to an official inspector for examination — wheels, axles, linchpins, poles, glasses, lamps, were all critically probed and tested. Every part of every carriage had been cleaned, every horse had been

groomed, with as much rigor as if they belonged to a
private gentleman; and that part of the spectacle
offered itself always. But the night before us is a
night of victory; and, behold! to the ordinary display,
what a heart-shaking addition! — horses, men, carriages, all are dressed in laurels and flowers, oak-leaves
and ribbons. The guards, as being officially his Majesty's servants, and of the coachmen such as are within
the privilege of the post-office, wear the royal liveries
of course; and as it is summer (for all the *land* victories were naturally won in summer), they wear, on this
fine evening, these liveries exposed to view, without
any covering of upper coats. Such a costume, and the
elaborate arrangement of the laurels in their hats, dilate
their hearts, by giving to them openly a personal connection with the great news, in which already they
have the general interest of patriotism. That great
national sentiment surmounts and quells all sense of
ordinary distinctions. Those passengers who happen
to be gentlemen are now hardly to be distinguished as
such except by dress; for the usual reserve of their
manner in speaking to the attendants has on this night
melted away. One heart, one pride, one glory, con-
nects every man by the transcendent bond of his
national blood. The spectators, who are numerous
beyond precedent, express their sympathy with these
fervent feelings by continual hurrahs. Every moment
are shouted aloud by the post-office servants, and summoned to draw up, the great ancestral names of cities
known to history through a thousand years — Lincoln,
Winchester, Portsmouth, Gloucester, Oxford, Bristol,
Manchester, York, Newcastle, Edinburgh, Glasgow,
Perth, Stirling, Aberdeen — expressing the grandeur

of the empire by the antiquity of its towns, and the
grandeur of the mail establishment by the diffusive
radiation of its separate missions.   Every moment you
hear thunder of lids locked down upon the mail-bags.
That sound to each individual mail is the signal for
drawing off, which process is the finest part of the
entire spectacle.   Then come the horses into play.
Horses! can these be horses that bound off with the
action and gestures of leopards ?   What stir! — what
sea-like ferment! — what a thundering of wheels! —
what a trampling of hoofs! — what a sounding of
trumpets! — what farewell cheers — what redoubling
peals of brotherly congratulation, connecting the name
of the particular mail — 'Liverpool for ever!' — with
the name of the particular victory — 'Badajoz for
ever!' or 'Salamanca for ever!'   The half-slumbering
consciousness that, all night long and all the next
day — perhaps for even a longer period — many of
these mails, like fire racing along a train of gunpow-
der, will be kindling at every instant new successions
of burning joy, has an obscure effect of multiplying
the victory itself, by multiplying to the imagination
into infinity the stages of its progressive diffusion.   A
fiery arrow seems to be let loose, which from that moment is destined to travel, without intermission, west-
wards for three hundred [15] miles — northwards for
six hundred; and the sympathy of our Lombard
Street friends at parting is exalted a hundredfold by
a sort of visionary sympathy with the yet slumbering
sympathies which in so vast a succession we are going
to awake.

Liberated from the embarrassments of the city, and
issuing into the broad uncrowded avenues of the north-

ern suburbs, we soon begin to enter upon our natural
pace of ten miles an hour. In the broad light of the
summer evening, the sun, perhaps, only just at the
point of setting, we are seen from every story of every
house. Heads of every age crowd to the windows —
young and old understand the language of our victorious symbols — and rolling volleys of sympathizing
cheers ran along us, behind us, and before us. The
beggar, rearing himself against the wall, forgets his
lameness — real or assumed — thinks not of his whin-
ing trade, but stands erect, with bold exulting smiles,
as we pass him. The victory has healed him, and
says, Be thou whole! Women and children, from
garrets alike and cellars, through infinite London, look
down or look up with loving eyes upon our gay ribbons and our martial laurels; sometimes kiss their
hands; sometimes hang out, as signals of affection,
pocket-handkerchiefs, aprons, dusters, anything that,
by catching the summer breezes, will express an aerial
jubilation. On the London side of Barnet, to which
we draw near within a few minutes after nine, observe
that private carriage which is approaching us. The
weather being so warm, the glasses are all down; and
one may read, as on the stage of a theatre, everything
that goes on within. It contains three ladies — one
likely to be ' mamma,' and two of seventeen or eighteen, who are probably her daughters. What lovely
animation, what beautiful unpremeditated pantomime,
explaining to us every syllable that passes, in these ingenuous girls! By the sudden start and raising of the
hands, on first discovering our laurelled equipage! —
by the sudden movement and appeal to the elder lady
from both of them — and by the heightened color on

their animated countenances, we can almost hear them saying, 'See, see! Look at their laurels! Oh, mamma! there has been a great battle in Spain; and it has been a great victory.' In a moment we are on the point of passing them. We passengers — I on the box, and the two on the roof behind me — raise our hats to the ladies; the coachman makes his professional salute with the whip; the guard even, though punctilious on the matter of his dignity as an officer under the crown, touches his hat. The ladies move to us, in return, with a winning graciousness of gesture; all smile on each side in a way that nobody could misunderstand, and that nothing short of a grand national sympathy could so instantaneously prompt. Will these ladies say that we are nothing to *them*? Oh, no; they will not say *that*. They cannot deny — they do not deny — that for this night they are our sisters; gentle or simple, scholar or illiterate servant, for twelve hours to come, we on the outside have the honor to be their brothers. Those poor women, again, who stop to gaze upon us with delight at the entrance of Barnet, and seem, by their air of weariness, to be returning from labor — do you mean to say that they are washerwomen and charwomen? Oh, my poor friend, you are quite mistaken. I assure you they stand in a far higher rank; for this one night they feel themselves by birthright to be daughters of England, and answer to no humbler title.

Every joy, however, even rapturous joy — such is the sad law of earth — may carry with it grief, or fear of grief, to some. Three miles beyond Barnet, we see approaching us another private carriage, nearly repeating the circumstances of the former case. Here, also, the glasses are all down — here, also, is an elderly lady seated; but the two daughters are missing; for the single young person sitting by the lady's side, seems to be an attendant — so I judge from her dress, and her air of respectful reserve. The lady is in mourning; and her countenance expresses sorrow. At first she does not look up; so that I believe she is not aware of our approach, until she hears the measured beating of our horses' hoofs. Then she raises her eyes to settle them painfully on our triumphal equipage. Our decorations explain the case to her at once; but she beholds them with apparent anxiety, or even with terror. Some time before this, I, finding it difficult to hit a flying mark, when embarrassed by the coachman's person and reins intervening, had given to the guard a 'Courier' evening paper, containing the gazette, for the next carriage that might pass. Accordingly he tossed it in, so folded that the huge capitals expressing some such legend as — GLORIOUS VICTORY, might catch the eye at once. To see the paper, however, at all, interpreted as it was by our ensigns of triumph, explained everything; and, if the guard were right in thinking the lady to have received it with a gesture of horror, it could not be doubtful that she had suffered some deep personal affliction in connection with this Spanish war.

Here, now, was the case of one who, having formerly suffered, might, erroneously perhaps, be distressing herself with anticipations of another similar suffering. That same night, and hardly three hours later, occurred the reverse case. A poor woman, who too probably would find herself, in a day or two, to

have suffered the heaviest afflictions by the battle,
blindly allowed herself to express an exultation so
unmeasured in the news and its details, as gave to her
the appearance which amongst Celtic Highlanders is
called *fey*. This was at some little town where we
changed horses an hour or two after midnight. Some
fair or wake had kept the people up out of their beds,
and had occasioned a partial illumination of the stalls
and booths, presenting an unusual but very impressive
effect. We saw many lights moving about as we drew
near; and perhaps the most striking scene on the
whole route was our reception at this place. The
flashing of torches and the beautiful radiance of blue
lights (technically, Bengal lights) upon the heads of
our horses; the fine effect of such a showery and
ghostly illumination falling upon our flowers and
glittering laurels; [16] whilst all around ourselves, that
formed a centre of light, the darkness gathered on the
rear and flanks in massy blackness; these optical
splendors, together with the prodigious enthusiasm
of the people, composed a picture at once scenical
and affecting, theatrical and holy. As we staid for
three or four minutes, I alighted; and immediately
from a dismantled stall in the street, where no doubt
she had been presiding through the earlier part of the
night, advanced eagerly a middle-aged woman. The
sight of my newspaper it was that had drawn her attention upon myself. The victory which we were
carrying down tô the provinces on *this* occasion, was
the imperfect one of Talavera — imperfect for its results, such was the virtual treachery of the Spanish
general, Cuesta, but not imperfect in its ever-memora-
ble heroism. I told her the main outline of the battle.

The agitation of her enthusiasm had been so conspicuous when listening, and when first applying for
information, that I could not but ask her if she had
not some relative in the Peninsular army. Oh, yes ;
her only son was there.   In what regiment? He was
a trooper in the 23d Dragoons.   My heart sank within
me as she made that answer.   This sublime regiment,
which an Englishman should never mention without
raising his hat to their memory, had made the most
memorable and effective charge recorded in military
annals.   They leaped their horses — *over* a trench
where they could, *into* it, and with the result of death
or mutilation when they could *not*.   What proportior
cleared the trench is nowhere stated.   Those who *did*,
closed up and went down upon the enemy with such
divinity of fervor (I use the word *divinity* by design :
the inspiration of God must have prompted this movement to those whom even then he was calling to his
presence), that two results followed.   As regarded the
enemy, this 23d Dragoons, not, I believe, originally
three hundred and fifty strong, paralyzed a French
column, six thousand strong, then ascended the hill,
and fixed the gaze of the whole French army.   As
regarded themselves, the 23d were supposed at first
to have been barely not annihilated ; but eventually,
I believe, about one in four survived.   And this, then,
was the regiment — a regiment already for some hours
glorified and hallowed to the ear of all London. as
lying stretched, by a large majority, upon one bloody
aceldama — in which the young trooper served whose
mother was now talking in a spirit of such joyous
enthusiasm.   Did I tell her the truth? Had I the
heart to break up her dreams ? No. To-morrow, said
I to myself — to-morrow, or the next day, will publish

the worst. For one night more, wherefore should she not sleep in peace? After to-morrow, the chances are too many that peace will forsake her pillow. This brief respite, then, let her owe to *my* gift and *my* forbearance. But, if I told her not of the bloody price that had been paid, not, therefore, was I silent on the contributions from her son's regiment to that day's service and glory. I showed her not the funeral banners under which the noble regiment was sleeping. I lifted not the overshadowing laurels from the bloody trench in which horse and rider lay mangled together. But I told her how these dear children of England, officers and privates, had leaped their horses over all obstacles as gayly as hunters to the morning's chase. I told her how they rode their horses into the mists of death (saying to myself, but not saying to *her*), and laid down their young lives for thee, O mother England! as willingly — poured out their noble blood as cheerfully — as ever, after a long day's sport, when infants, they had rested their wearied heads upon their mother's knees, or had sunk to sleep in her arms. Strange it is, yet true, that she seemed to have no fears for her son's safety, even after this knowledge that the 23d Dragoons had been memorably engaged ; but so much was she enraptured by the knowledge that *his* regiment, and therefore that *he*, had rendered conspicuous service in the dreadful conflict — a service which had actually made them, within the last twelve hours, the foremost topic of conversation in London — so absolutely was fear swallowed up in joy — that, in the mere simplicity of her fervent nature, the poor woman threw her arms round my neck, as she thought of her son, and gave to *me* the kiss which secretly was meant for *him*.

THE ENGLISH MAIL-COACH.

SECTION THE SECOND. — THE VISION OF SUDDEN DEATH.

WHAT is to be taken as the predominant opinion of man, reflective and philosophic, upon SUDDEN DEATH? It is remarkable that, in different conditions of society, sudden death has been variously regarded as the consummation of an earthly career most fervently to be desired, or, again, as that consummation which is with most horror to be deprecated. Cæsar the Dictator, at his last dinner party (*cœna*), on the very evening before his assassination, when the minutes of his earthly career were numbered, being asked what death, in *his* judgment, might be pronounced the most eligible, replied, 'That which should be most sudden.' On the other hand, the divine Litany of our English Church, when breathing forth supplications, as if in some representative character for the whole human race prostrate before God, places such a death in the very van of horrors : — 'From lightning and tempest; from plague, pestilence, and famine; from battle and murder, and from SUDDEN DEATH — *Good Lord, deliver us.*' Sudden death is here made to crown the climax in a grand ascent of calamities; it is ranked among the last of curses; and yet, by the noblest of

[157]

Romans, it was ranked as the first of blessings. In
that difference, most readers will see little more than
the essential difference between Christianity and Pa-
ganism. But this, on consideration, I doubt. The
Christian Church may be right in its estimate of sudden death; and it is a natural feeling, though after all
it may also be an infirm one, to wish for a quiet dis-
missal from life — as that which *seems* most reconcil-
able with meditation, with penitential retrospects, and
with the humilities of farewell prayer. There does
not, however, occur to me any direct scriptural warrant for this earnest petition of the English Litany,
unless under a special construction of the word ' sudden.' It seems a petition — indulged rather and conceded to human infirmity, than exacted from human
piety. It is not so much a doctrine built upon the
eternities of the Christian system, as a plausible opinion built upon special varieties of physical temperament. Let that, however, be as it may, two remarks
suggest themselves as prudent restraints upon a doctrine, which else *may* wander, and *has* wandered, into
an uncharitable superstition. The first is this : that
many people are likely to exaggerate the horror of a
sudden death, from the disposition to lay a false stress
upon words or acts, simply because by an accident
they have become *final* words or acts. If a man dies,
for instance, by some sudden death when he happens
to be intoxicated, such a death is falsely regarded with
peculiar horror ; as though the intoxication were suddenly exalted into a blasphemy. But *that* is unphilo-
sophic. The man was, or he was not, *habitually* a
drunkard. If not, if his intoxication were a solitary
accident, there can be no reason for allowing special

emphasis to this act, simply because through misfortune it became his final act. Nor, on the other hand,
if it were no accident, but one of his *habitual* trans-
gressions, will it be the more habitual or the more a
transgression, because some sudden calamity surprising
him, has caused this habitual transgression to be also
a final one. Could the man have had any reason even
dimly to foresee his own sudden death, there would
have been a new feature in his act of intemperance.—
feature of presumption and irreverence, as in one that,
having known himself drawing near to the presence of
God, should have suited his demeanor to an expectation so awful. But this is no part of the case supposed. And the only new element in the man's act is
not any element of special immorality, but simply of
special misfortune.

The other remark has reference to the meaning of
the word *sudden.* Very possibly Cæsar and the Christian Church do not differ in the way supposed ; that
is, do not differ by any difference of doctrine as between Pagan and Christian views of the moral temper
appropriate to death, but perhaps they are contemplating different cases. Both contemplate a violent
death, a βιαθανατος — death that is βιαιος, or, in other
words, death that is brought about, not by internal
and spontaneous change, but by active force, having
its origin from without. In this meaning the two
authorities agree. Thus far they are in harmony.
But the difference is, that the Roman by the word
'sudden' means *unlingering;* whereas the Christian
Litany by 'sudden death' means a death *without
warning,* consequently without any available summons
to religious preparation. The poor mutineer, who

kneels down to gather into his heart the bullets from twelve firelocks of his pitying comrades, dies by a most sudden death in Cæsar's sense; one shock, one mighty spasm, one (possibly *not* one) groan, and all is over. But in the sense of the Litany, the mutineer's death is far from sudden; his offence originally, his imprisonment, his trial, the interval between his sentence and its execution, having all furnished him with separate warnings of his fate — having all summoned him to meet it with solemn preparation.

Here at once, in this sharp verbal distinction, we comprehend the faithful earnestness with which a holy Christian Church pleads on behalf of her poor departing children, that God would vouchsafe to them the last great privilege and distinction possible on a death-bed — viz., the opportunity of untroubled preparation for facing this mighty trial. Sudden death, as a mere variety in the modes of dying, where death in some shape is inevitable, proposes a question of choice which, equally in the Roman and the Christian sense, will be variously answered according to each man's variety of temperament. Meantime, one aspect of sudden death there is, one modification, upon which no doubt can arise, that of all martyrdoms it is the most agitating — viz., where it surprises a man under circumstances which offer (or which seem to offer) some hurrying, flying, inappreciably minute chance of evading it. Sudden as the danger which it affronts, must be any effort by which such an evasion can be accomplished. Even *that*, even the sickening necessity for hurrying in extremity where all hurry seems destined to be vain, even that anguish is liable to a hideous exasperation in one particular case — viz., where the appeal is made not exclusively to the instinct of self-preservation, but to the conscience, on behalf of some other life besides your own, accidentally thrown upon *your* protection. To fail, to collapse in a service merely your own, might seem comparatively venial; though, in fact, it is far from venial. But to fail in a case where Providence has suddenly thrown into your hands the final interests of another — a fellow-creature shuddering between the gates of life and death; this, to a man of apprehensive conscience, would mingle the misery of an atrocious criminality with the misery of a bloody calamity. You are called upon, by the case supposed, possibly to die; but to die at the very moment when, by any even partial failure, or effeminate collapse of your energies, you will be self-denounced as a murderer. You had but the twinkling of an eye for your effort, and that effort might have been unavailing; but to have risen to the level of such an effort, would have rescued you, though not from dying, yet from dying as a traitor to your final and farewell duty.

The situation here contemplated exposes a dreadful ulcer, lurking far down in the depths of human nature. It is not that men generally are summoned to face such awful trials. But potentially, and in shadowy outline, such a trial is moving subterraneously in perhaps all men's natures. Upon the secret mirror of our dreams such a trial is darkly projected, perhaps, to every one of us. That dream, so familiar to childhood, of meeting a lion, and, through languishing prostration in hope and the energies of hope, that constant sequel of lying down before the lion, publishes the secret frailty of human nature — reveals its

14

deep-seated falsehood to itself—records its abysmal
treachery. Perhaps not one of us escapes that dream;
perhaps, as by some sorrowful doom of man, that
dream repeats for every one of us, through every
generation, the original temptation in Eden. Every
one of us, in this dream, has a bait offered to the
infirm places of his own individual will; once again
a snare is presented for tempting him into captivity to
a luxury of ruin; once again, as in aboriginal Paradise, the man falls by his own choice; again, by
infinite iteration, the ancient Earth groans to Heaven,
through her secret caves, over the weakness of her
child: 'Nature, from her seat, sighing through all her
works,' again 'gives signs of wo that all is lost;' and
again the counter sigh is repeated to the sorrowing
heavens for the endless rebellion against God. It is
not without probability that in the world of dreams
every one of us ratifies for himself the original transgression. In dreams, perhaps under some secret
conflict of the midnight sleeper, lighted up to the
consciousness at the time, but darkened to the memory as soon as all is finished, each several child of our
mysterious race completes for himself the treason of
the aboriginal fall.

. . . .

The incident, so memorable in itself by its features
of horror, and so scenical by its grouping for the eye,
which furnished the text for this reverie upon *Sudden
Death*, occurred to myself in the dead of night, as a
solitary spectator, when seated on the box of the
Manchester and Glasgow mail, in the second or third
summer after Waterloo. I find it necessary to relate
the circumstances, because they are such as could not

have occurred unless under a singular combination of
accidents. In those days, the oblique and lateral
communications with many rural post-offices were so
arranged, either through necessity or through defect
of system, as to make it requisite for the main north-
western mail (*i. e.,* the *down* mail), on reaching Manchester, to halt for a number of hours ; how many, I
do not remember ; six or seven, I think ; but the
result was, that, in the ordinary course, the mail
recommenced its journey northwards about midnight.
Wearied with the long detention at a gloomy hotel,
I walked out about eleven o'clock at night for the
sake of fresh air; meaning to fall in with the mail
and resume my seat at the post-office. The night,
however, being yet dark, as the moon had scarcely
risen, and the streets being at that hour empty, so as to
offer no opportunities for asking the road, I lost my
way ; and did not reach the post-office until it was considerably past midnight ; but, to my great relief (as it
was important for me to be in Westmoreland by the
morning), I saw in the huge saucer eyes of the mail,
blazing through the gloom, an evidence that my
chance was not yet lost. Past the time it was, but,
by some rare accident, the mail was not even yet
ready to start. I ascended to my seat on the box,
where my cloak was still lying as it had lain at the
Bridgewater Arms. I had left it there in imitation
of a nautical discoverer, who leaves a bit of bunting
on the shore of his discovery, by way of warning off
the ground the whole human race, and notifying to
the Christian and the heathen worlds, with his best
compliments, that he has hoisted his pocket-handkerchief once and for ever upon that virgin soil; thence-

forward claiming the *jus dominii* to the top of the atmosphere above it, and also the right of driving shafts to the centre of the earth below it; so that all people found after this warning, either aloft in upper chambers of the atmosphere, or groping in subterraneous shafts, or squatting audaciously on the surface of the soil, will be treated as trespassers — kicked, that is to say, or decapitated, as circumstances may suggest, by their very faithful servant, the owner of the said pocket-handkerchief. In the present case, it is probable that my cloak might not have been respected, and the *jus gentium* might have been cruelly violated in my person — for, in the dark, people commit deeds of darkness, gas being a great ally of morality — but it so happened that, on this night, there was no other outside passenger; and thus the crime, which else was but too probable, missed fire for want of a criminal.

Having mounted the box, I took a small quantity of laudanum, having already travelled two hundred and fifty miles — viz., from a point seventy miles beyond London. In the taking of laudanum there was nothing extraordinary. But by accident it drew upon me the special attention of my assessor on the box, the coachman. And in *that* also there was nothing extraordinary. But by accident, and with great delight, it drew my own attention to the fact that this coachman was a monster in point of bulk, and that he had but one eye. In fact, he had been foretold by Virgil as

'Monstrum horrendum, informe, ingens cui lumen ademptum.'

He answered to the conditions in every one of the items: — 1, a monster he was; 2, dreadful; 3, shapeless; 4, huge; 5, who had lost an eye. But why

should *that* delight me? Had he been one of the
Calendars in the 'Arabian Nights,' and had paid
down his eye as the price of his criminal curiosity,
what right had *I* to exult in his misfortune? I did
not exult: I delighted in no man's punishment, though
it were even merited. But these personal distinctions
(Nos. 1, 2, 3, 4, 5) identified in an instant an old
friend of mine, whom I had known in the south for
some years as the most masterly of mail-coachmen.
He was the man in all Europe that could (if *any*
could) have driven six-in-hand full gallop over *Al
Sirat* — that dreadful bridge of Mahomet, with no
side battlements, and of *extra* room not enough for a
razor's edge — leading right across the bottomless
gulf. Under this eminent man, whom in Greek I
cognominated Cyclops *diphrélates* (Cyclops the cha-
rioteer), I, and others known to me, studied the
diphrelatic art. Excuse, reader, a word too elegant
to be pedantic. As a pupil, though I paid extra fees,
it is to be lamented that I did not stand high in his
esteem. It showed his dogged honesty (though, observe, not his discernment), that he could not see my
merits. Let us excuse his absurdity in this particular,
by remembering his want of an eye. Doubtless *that*
made him blind to my merits. In the art of conversation, however, he admitted that I had the whip-hand
of him. On this present occasion, great joy was at
our meeting. But what was Cyclops doing here?
Had the medical men recommended northern air, or
how? I collected, from such explanations as he vol-
unteered, that he had an interest at stake in some suit-
at-law now pending at Lancaster; so that probably he
had got himself transferred to this station, for the pur-

pose of connecting with his professional pursuits an instant readiness for the calls of his lawsuit.

Meantime, what are we stopping for? Surely we have now waited long enough. Oh, this procrastinating mail, and this procrastinating post-office! Can't they take a lesson upon that subject from *me*? Some people have called *me* procrastinating. Yet you are witness, reader, that I was kept here waiting for the post-office. Will the post-office lay its hand on its heart, in its moments of sobriety, and assert that ever it waited for me? What are they about? The guard tells me that there is a large extra accumulation of foreign mails this night, owing to irregularities caused by war, by wind, by weather, in the packet service, which as yet does not benefit at all by steam. For an *extra* hour, it seems, the post-office has been engaged in threshing out the pure wheaten correspondence of Glasgow, and winnowing it from the chaff of all baser intermediate towns. But at last all is finished. Sound your horn, guard. Manchester, good-by; we've lost an hour by your criminal conduct at the post-office: which, however, though I do not mean to part with a serviceable ground of complaint, and one which really *is* such for the horses, to me secretly is an advantage, since it compels us to look sharply for this lost hour amongst the next eight or nine, and to recover it (if we can) at the rate of one mile extra per hour. Off we are at last, and at eleven miles per hour: and for the moment I detect no changes in the energy or in the skill of Cyclops.

From Manchester to Kendal, which virtually (though not in law) is the capital of Westmoreland, there were at this time seven stages of eleven miles each. The

first five of these, counting from Manchester, terminate
in Lancaster, which is therefore fifty-five miles north
of Manchester, and the same distance exactly from
Liverpool. The first three stages terminate in Preston
(called, by way of distinction from other towns of that
name, *proud* Preston), at which place it is that the
separate roads from Liverpool and from Manchester to
the north become confluent.[17] Within these first three
stages lay the foundation, the progress, and termination of our night's adventure. During the first stage,
I found out that Cyclops was mortal : he was liable to
the shocking affection of sleep — a thing which previously I had never suspected. If a man indulges in
the vicious habit of sleeping, all the skill in aurigation
of Apollo himself, with the horses of Aurora to execute his notions, avail him nothing. ' Oh, Cyclops ! '
I exclaimed, ' thou art mortal. My friend, thou snor-
est.' Through the first eleven miles, however, this
infirmity — which I grieve to say that he shared with
the whole Pagan Pantheon — betrayed itself only by
brief snatches. On waking up, he made an apology
for himself, which, instead of mending matters, laid
open a gloomy vista of coming disasters. The summer assizes, he reminded me, were now going on at
Lancaster : in consequence of which, for three nights
and three days, he had not lain down in a bed. During the day, he was waiting for his own summons as a
witness on the trial in which he was interested : or
else, lest he should be missing at the critical moment,
was drinking with the other witnesses, under the pastoral surveillance of the attorneys. During the night,
or that part of it which at sea would form the middle
watch, he was driving. This explanation certainly

accounted for his drowsiness, but in a way which made
it much more alarming; since now, after several days'
resistance to this infirmity, at length he was steadily
giving way. Throughout the second stage he grew
more and more drowsy. In the second mile of the
third stage, he surrendered himself finally and without
a struggle to his perilous temptation. All his past
resistance had but deepened the weight of this final
oppression. Seven atmospheres of sleep rested upon
him; and to consummate the case, our worthy guard,
after singing ' Love amongst the Roses ' for perhaps
thirty times, without invitation, and without applause,
had in revenge moodily resigned himself to slumber —
not so deep, doubtless, as the coachman's, but deep
enough for mischief. And thus at last, about ten
miles from Preston, it came about that I found myself
left in charge of his Majesty's London and Glasgow
mail, then running at the least twelve miles an hour.

What made this negligence less criminal than else it
must have been thought, was the condition of the
roads at night during the assizes. At that time, all
the law business of populous Liverpool, and also of
populous Manchester, with its vast cincture of populous rural districts, was called up by ancient usage to
the tribunal of Lilliputian Lancaster. To break up
this old traditional usage required, 1, a conflict with
powerful established interests; 2, a large system of
new arrangements; and 3, a new parliamentary statute.
But as yet this change was merely in contemplation.
As things were at present, twice in the year [18] so vast
a body of business rolled northwards, from the southern quarter of the county, that for a fortnight at least
it occupied the severe exertions of two judges in its

despatch. The consequence of this was, that every horse available for such a service, along the whole line of road, was exhausted in carrying down the multitudes of people who were parties to the different suits. By sunset, therefore, it usually happened that, through utter exhaustion amongst men and horses, the roads sank into profound silence. Except the exhaustion in the vast adjacent county of York from a contested election, no such silence succeeding to no such fiery uproar was ever witnessed in England.

On this occasion, the usual silence and solitude prevailed along the road. Not a hoof nor a wheel was to be heard. And to strengthen this false luxurious confidence in the noiseless roads, it happened also that the night was one of peculiar solemnity and peace. For my own part, though slightly alive to the possibilities of peril, I had so far yielded to the influence of the mighty calm as to sink into a profound reverie. The month was August, in the middle of which lay my own birth-day — a festival to every thoughtful man suggesting solemn and often sigh-born [19] thoughts. The county was my own native county — upon which, in its southern section, more than upon any equal area known to man past or present, had descended the original curse of labor in its heaviest form, not mastering the bodies only of men as of slaves, or criminals in mines, but working through the fiery will. Upon no equal space of earth was, or ever had been, the same energy of human power put forth daily. At this particular season also of the assizes, that dreadful hurricane of flight and pursuit, as it might have seemed to a stranger, which swept to and from Lancaster all day long, hunting the county up and down, and regularly

15

subsiding back into silence about sunset, could not fail
(when united with this permanent distinction of Lancashire as the very metropolis and citidal of labor) to
point the thoughts pathetically upon that counter vision of rest, of saintly repose from strife and sorrow,
towards which, as to their secret haven, the profounder
aspirations of man's heart are in solitude continually
travelling. Obliquely upon our left we were nearing
the sea, which also must, under the present circumstances, be repeating the general state of halcyon
repose. The sea, the atmosphere, the light, bore each
an orchestral part in this universal lull. Moonlight,
and the first timid tremblings of the dawn, were by
this time blending; and the blendings were brought
into a still more exquisite state of unity by a slight
silvery mist, motionless and dreamy, that covered the
woods and fields, but with a veil of equable transpa-
rency. Except the feet of our own horses, which,
running on a sandy margin of the road, made but little
disturbance, there was no sound abroad. In the
clouds, and on the earth, prevailed the same majestic
peace; and in spite of all that the villain of a schoolmaster has done for the ruin of our sublimer thoughts,
which are the thoughts of our infancy, we still believe
in no such nonsense as a limited atmosphere. Whatever we may swear with our false feigning lips, in our
faithful hearts we still believe, and must for ever believe, in fields of air traversing the total gulf between
earth and the central heavens. Still in the confidence
of children that tread without fear *every* chamber in
their father's house, and to whom no door is closed,
we, in that Sabbatic vision which sometimes is revealed
for an hour upon nights like this, ascend with easy

steps from the sorrow-stricken fields of earth, upwards
to the sandals of God.

Suddenly, from thoughts like these, I was awakened
to a sullen sound, as of some motion on the distant
road. It stole upon the air for a moment; I listened
in awe; but then it died away. Once roused, however, I could not but observe with alarm the quickened
motion of our horses. Ten years' experience had
made my eye learned in the valuing of motion; and I
saw that we were now running thirteen miles an hour.
I pretend to no presence of mind. On the contrary,
my fear is, that I am miserably and shamefully de-
ficient in that quality as regards action. The palsy
of doubt and distraction hangs like some guilty weight
of dark unfathomed remembrances upon my energies,
when the signal is flying for *action*. But, on the
other hand, this accursed gift I have, as regards *thought*,
that in the first step towards the possibility of a misfortune, I see its total evolution; in the radix of the
series I see too certainly and too instantly its entire
expansion; in the first, syllable of the dreadful sentence, I read already the last. It was not that I feared
for ourselves. *Us*, our bulk and impetus charmed
against peril in any collision. And I had ridden
through too many hundreds of perils that were frightful to approach, that were matter of laughter to look
back upon, the first face of which was horror — the
parting face a jest, for any anxiety to rest upon *our*
interests. The mail was not built, I felt assured, nor
bespoke, that could betray *me* who trusted to its protection. But any carriage that we could meet would
be frail and light in comparison of ourselves. And
I remark this ominous accident of our situation. We

were on the wrong side of the road. But then, it may be said, the other party, if other there was, might also be on the wrong side; and two wrongs might make a right. *That* was not likely. The same motive which had drawn *us* to the right-hand side of the road — viz., the luxury of the soft beaten sand, as contrasted with the paved centre — would prove attractive to others. The two adverse carriages would therefore, to a certainty, be travelling on the same side; and from this side, as not being ours in law, the crossing over to the other would, of course, be looked for from *us*.[20] Our lamps, still lighted, would give the impression of vigilance on our part. And every creature that met us, would rely upon *us* for quartering.[21] All this, and if the separate links of the anticipation had been a thousand times more, I saw, not discursively, or by effort, or by succession, but by one flash of horrid simultaneous intuition.

Under this steady though rapid anticipation of the evil which *might* be gathering ahead, ah! what a sullen mystery of fear, what a sigh of wo, was that which stole upon the air, as again the far-off sound of a wheel was heard? A whisper it was — a whisper from, perhaps, four miles off — secretly announcing a ruin that, being foreseen, was not the less inevitable; that, being known, was not, therefore, healed. What could be done — who was it that could do it — to check the storm-flight of these maniacal horses? Could I not seize the reins from the grasp of the slumbering coachman? You, reader, think that it would have been in *your* power to do so. And I quarrel not with your estimate of yourself. But, from the way in which the coachman's hand was viced between his upper and lower thigh, this was impossible. Easy, was it? See, then, that bronze equestrian statue. The cruel rider has kept the bit in his horse's mouth for two centuries. Unbridle him, for a minute, if you please, and wash his mouth with water. Easy, was it? Unhorse me, then, that imperial rider; knock me those marble feet from those marble stirrups of Charlemagne.

The sounds ahead strengthened, and were now too clearly the sounds of wheels. Who and what could t be? Was it industry in a taxed cart? Was it youthful gayety in a gig? Was it sorrow that loitered, or joy that raced? For as yet the snatches of sound were too intermitting, from distance, to decipher the character of the motion. Whoever were the travellers, something must be done to warn them. Upon the other party rests the active responsibility, but upon us — and, wo is me! that us was reduced to my frail opium-shattered self — rests the responsibility of warning. Yet how should this be accomplished? Might I not sound the guard's horn? Already, on the first thought, I was making my way over the roof to the guard's seat. But this, from the accident which I have mentioned, of the foreign mails' being piled upon the roof, was a difficult and even dangerous attempt to one cramped by nearly three hundred miles of outside travelling. And, fortunately, before I had lost much time in the attempt, our frantic horses swept round an angle of the road, which opened upon us that final stage where the collision must be accomplished, and the catastrophe sealed. All was apparently finished. The court was sitting; the case was heard; the judge had finished; and the only verdict was yet in arrear.

Before us lay an avenue, straight as an arrow, six hundred yards, perhaps, in length; and the umbrageous trees, which rose in a regular line from either side, meeting high overhead, gave to it the character of a cathedral aisle. These trees lent a deeper solemnity to the early light; but there was still light enough to perceive, at the further end of this Gothic aisle, a frail reedy gig, in which were seated a young man, and by his side a young lady. Ah, young sir! what are you about? If it is requisite that you should whisper your communications to this young lady — though really I see nobody, at an hour and on a road so solitary, likely to overhear you — is it therefore requisite that you should carry your lips forward to hers? The little carriage is creeping on at one mile an hour; and the parties within it being thus tenderly engaged, are naturally bending down their heads. Between them and eternity, to all human calculation, there is but a minute and a-half. Oh heavens! what is it that I shall do? Speaking or acting, what help can I offer? Strange it is, and to a mere auditor of the tale might seem laughable, that I should need a suggestion from the ' Iliad ' to prompt the sole resource that remained. Yet so it was. Suddenly I remembered the shout of Achilles, and its effect. But could I pretend to shout like the son of Peleus, aided by Pallas? No : but then I needed not the shout that should alarm all Asia militant; such a shout would suffice as might carry terror into the hearts of two thoughtless young people, and one gig horse. I shouted — and the young man heard me not. A second time I shouted — and now he heard me, for now he raised his head.

Here, then, all had been done that, by me, *could* be

done: more on *my* part was not possible. Mine had
been the first step; the second was for the young
man; the third was for God. If, said I, this stranger
is a brave man, and if, indeed, he loves the young girl
at his side — or, loving her not, if he feels the obliga-
tion, pressing upon every man worthy to be called a
man, of doing his utmost for a woman confided to his
protection — he will, at least, make some effort to
save her. If *that* fails, he will not perish the more, or
by a death more cruel, for having made it; and he will
die as a brave man should, with his face to the danger, and with his arm about the woman that he sought
in vain to save. But, if he makes no effort, shrinking,
without a struggle, from his duty, he himself will not
the less certainly perish for this baseness of poltroon-
ery. He will die no less: and why not? Wherefore
should we grieve that there is one craven less in the
world? No; *let* him perish, without a pitying thought
of ours wasted upon him; and, in that case, all our
grief will be reserved for the fate of the helpless girl
who now, upon the least shadow of failure in *him*,
must, by the fiercest of translations — must, without
time for a prayer — must, within seventy seconds,
stand before the judgment-seat of God.

But craven he was not: sudden had been the call
upon him, and sudden was his answer to the call.
He saw, he heard, he comprehended, the ruin that
was coming down: already its gloomy shadow darkened above him; and already he was measuring his
strength to deal with it. Ah! what a vulgar thing
does courage seem, when we see nations buying it and
selling it for a shilling a-day: ah! what a sublime
thing does courage seem, when some fearful summons

on the great deeps of life carries a man, as if running
before a hurricane, up to the giddy crest of some
tumultuous crisis, from which lie two courses, and a
voice says to him audibly, ' One way lies hope ; take
the other, and mourn for ever!' How grand a
triumph, if, even then, amidst the raving of all around
him, and the frenzy of the danger, the man is able
to confront his - situation — is able to retire for a
moment into solitude with God, and to seek his
counsel from *him !*

For seven seconds, it might be, of his seventy, the
stranger settled his countenance steadfastly upon us,
as if to search and value every element in the conflict
before him. For five seconds more of his seventy he
sat immovably, like one that mused on some great
purpose. For five more, perhaps, he sat with eyes
upraised, like one that prayed in sorrow, under some
extremity of doubt, for light that should guide him to
the better choice. Then suddenly he rose ; stood
upright ; and by a powerful strain upon the reins,
raising his horse's fore-feet from the ground, he
slewed him round on the pivot of his hind-legs, so
as to plant the little equipage in a position nearly at
right angles to ours. Thus far his condition was not
improved, except as a first step had been taken towards the possibility of a second. If no more were
done, nothing was done ; for the little carriage still
occupied the very centre of our path, though in an
altered direction. Yet even now it may not be too
late : fifteen of the seventy seconds may still be unex-
hausted ; and one almighty bound may avail to clear
the ground. Hurry, then, hurry ! for the flying moments — *they* hurry ! Oh, hurry, hurry, my brave

young man! for the cruel hoofs of our horses — *they*
also hurry! Fast are the flying moments, faster are the
hoofs of our horses. But fear not for *him*, if human
energy can suffice ; faithful was he that drove to his
terrific duty ; faithful was the horse to *his* command.
One blow, one impulse given with voice and hand,
by the stranger, one rush from the horse, one bound
as if in the act of rising to a fence, landed the docile
creature's fore-feet upon the crown or arching centre
of the road. The larger half of the little equipage
had then cleared our overtowering shadow: *that* was
evident even to my own agitated sight. But it mat-
tered little that one wreck should float off in safety,
if upon the wreck that perished were embarked the
human freightage. The rear part of the carriage —
was *that* certainly beyond the line of absolute ruin?
What power could answer the question? Glance of
eye, thought of man, wing of angel, which of these
had speed enough to sweep between the question and
the answer, and divide the one from the other?
Light does not tread upon the steps of light more
indivisibly, than did our all-conquering arrival upon
the escaping efforts of the gig. *That* must the young
man have felt too plainly. His back was now turned
to us; not by sight could he any longer communicate
with the peril ; but by the dreadful rattle of our
harness, too truly had his ear been instructed — that
all was finished as regarded any further effort of *his.*
Already in resignation he had rested from his struggle ;
and perhaps in his heart he was whispering, ' Father,
which art in heaven, do thou finish above what I on
earth have attempted.' Faster than ever mill-race we
ran past them in our inexorable flight. Oh, raving of

hurricanes that must have sounded in their young ears
at the moment of our transit! Even in that moment
the thunder of collision spoke aloud. Either with the
swingle-bar, or with the haunch of our near leader, we
had struck the off-wheel of the little gig, which stood
rather obliquely, and not quite so far advanced, as to
be accurately parallel with the near-wheel. The blow,
from the fury of our passage, resounded terrifically.
I rose in horror, to gaze upon the ruins we might have
caused. From my elevated station I looked down,
and looked back upon the scene, which in a moment
told its own tale, and wrote all its records on my heart
for ever.

Here was the map of the passion that now had
finished. The horse was planted immovably, with his
fore-feet upon the paved crest of the central road.
He of the whole party might be supposed untouched
by the passion of death. The little cany carriage —
partly, perhaps, from the violent torsion of the wheels
in its recent movement, partly from the thundering
blow we had given to it — as if it sympathized with
human horror, was all alive with tremblings and shiv-
erings. The young man trembled not, nor shivered.
He sat like a rock. But *his* was the steadiness of
agitation frozen into rest by horror. As yet he dared
not to look round; for he knew that, if anything
remained to do, by him it could no longer be done.
And as yet he knew not for certain if their safety
were accomplished. But the lady ———

But the lady ———! Oh, heavens! will that spectacle
ever depart from my dreams, as she rose and sank
upon her seat, sank and rose, threw up her arms wildly
to heaven, clutched at some visionary object in the air,

fainting, praying, raving, despairing? Figure to yourself, reader, the elements of the case; suffer me to recall before your mind the circumstances of that unparalleled situation. From the silence and deep peace of this saintly summer night — from the pathetic blending of this sweet moonlight, dawnlight, dreamlight — from the manly tenderness of this flattering, whispering, murmuring love — suddenly as from the woods and fields — suddenly as from the chambers of the air opening in revelation — suddenly as from the ground yawning at her feet, leaped upon her, with the flashing of cataracts, Death the crownéd phantom, with all the equipage of his terrors, and the tiger roar of his voice.

The moments were numbered; the strife was finished; the vision was closed. In the twinkling of an eye, our flying horses had carried us to the termination of the umbrageous aisle; at right angles we wheeled into our former direction; the turn of the road carried the scene out of my eyes in an instant, and swept it into my dreams for ever.

THE ENGLISH MAIL-COACH.

SECTION THE THIRD. — DREAM-FUGUE.

FOUNDED ON THE PRECEDING THEME OF SUDDEN DEATH.

> 'Whence the sound
> Of instruments, that made melodious chime,
> Was heard, of harp and organ ; and who moved
> Their stops and chords, was seen ; his volant touch
> Instinct through all proportions, low and high,
> Fled and pursued transverse the resonant fugue.'
> *Par. Lost*, B. **xi.**

Tumultuosissimamente.

PASSION of sudden death ! that once in youth I read
and interpreted by the shadows of thy averted signs ! [22]
— rapture of panic taking the shape (which amongst
tombs in churches I have seen) of woman bursting
her sepulchral bonds — of woman's Ionic form bending from the ruins of her grave with arching foot, with
eyes upraised, with clasped adoring hands — waiting,
watching, trembling, praying for the trumpet's call to
rise from dust for ever ! Ah, vision too fearful of
shuddering humanity on the brink of almighty abysses !
— vision that didst start back, that didst reel away,
like a shrivelling scroll from before the wrath of fire
racing on the wings of the wind ! Epilepsy so brief
of horror, wherefore is it that thou canst not die ?
Passing so suddenly into darkness, wherefore is it that
still thou sheddest thy sad funeral blights upon the
gorgeous mosaics of dreams ? Fragment of music too

[180]

passionate, heard once, and heard no more, what aileth thee, that thy deep rolling chords come up at intervals through all the worlds of sleep, and after forty years, have lost no element of horror?

I.

Lo, it is summer — almighty summer! The everlasting gates of life and summer are thrown open wide; and on the ocean, tranquil and verdant as a savannah, the unknown lady from the dreadful vision and I myself are floating — she upon a fiery pinnace, and I upon an English three-decker. Both of us are wooing gales of festal happiness within the domain of our common country, within that ancient watery park, within that pathless chase of ocean, where England takes her pleasure as a huntress through winter and summer, from the rising to the setting sun. Ah, what a wilderness of floral beauty was hidden, or was suddenly revealed, upon the tropic islands through which the pinnace moved! And upon her deck what a bevy of human flowers — young women how lovely, young men how noble, that were dancing together, and slowly drifting towards *us* amidst music and incense, amidst blossoms from forests and gorgeous corymbi from vintages, amidst natural carolling and the echoes of sweet girlish laughter. Slowly the pinnace nears us, gaily she hails us, and silently she disappears beneath the shadow of our mighty bows. But then, as at some signal from heaven, the music, and the carols, and the sweet echoing of girlish laughter — all are hushed. What evil has smitten the pinnace, meeting or overtaking her? Did ruin to our friends couch within our own dreadful shadow? Was our shadow the shadow of death? I looked over the bow for an answer, and, behold! the pinnace was dismantled; the revel and the revellers were found no more; the glory of the vintage was dust; and the forests with their beauty were left without a witness upon the seas. 'But where,' and I turned to our crew — 'where are the lovely women that danced beneath the awning of flowers and clustering corymbi! Whither have fled the noble young men that danced with *them*?' Answer there was none. But suddenly the man at the masthead, whose countenance darkened with alarm, cried out, 'Sail on the weather beam! Down she comes upon us: in seventy seconds she also will founder.'

II.

I looked to the weather side, and the summer had departed. The sea was rocking, and shaken with gathering wrath. Upon its surface sat mighty mists, which grouped themselves into arches and long cathedral aisles. Down one of these, with the fiery pace of a quarrel from a cross-bow, ran a frigate right athwart our course. 'Are they mad?' some voice exclaimed from our deck. 'Do they woo their ruin?' But in a moment, she was close upon us, some impulse of a heady current or local vortex gave a wheeling bias to her course, and off she forged without a shock. As she ran past us, high aloft amongst the shrouds stood the lady of the pinnace. The deeps opened ahead in malice to receive her, towering surges of foam ran after her, the billows were fierce to catch her. But far away she was borne into desert spaces of the sea: whilst still by sight I followed her as she ran before the howling gale, chased by angry sea-birds and by maddening billows; still I saw her, as at the moment when she ran past us, standing amongst the shrouds, with her white draperies streaming before the wind. There she stood, with hair dishevelled, one hand clutched amongst the tackling — rising, sinking, fluttering, trembling, praying — there for leagues I·saw her as she stood, raising at intervals one hand to heaven, amidst the fiery crests of the pursuing waves and the raving of the storm; until at last, upon a sound from afar of malicious laughter and mockery, all was hidden for ever in driving showers; and afterwards, but when I know not, nor how.

III.

Sweet funeral bells from some incalculable distance, wailing over the dead that die before the dawn, awakened me as I slept in a boat moored to some familiar shore. The morning twilight even then was breaking; and, by the dusky revelations which it spread, I saw a girl, adorned with a garland of white roses about her head for some great festival, running along the solitary strand in extremity of haste. Her running was the running of panic; and often she looked back as to some dreadful enemy in the rear. But when I leaped ashore, and followed on her steps to warn her of a peril in front, alas! from me she fled as from another peril, and vainly I shouted to her of quicksands that lay ahead. Faster and faster she ran; round a promontory of rocks she wheeled out of sight; in an instant I also wheeled round it, but only to see the treacherous sands gathering above her head. Already her person was buried; only the fair young head and the diadem

of white roses around it were still visible to the pitying heavens: and, last of all, was visible one white
marble arm. I saw by the early twilight this fair
young head, as it was sinking down to darkness — saw
this marble arm, as it rose above her head and her
treacherous grave, tossing, faltering, rising, clutching
as at some false deceiving hand stretched out from the
clouds — saw this marble arm uttering her dying hope,
and then uttering her dying despair. The head, the
diadem, the arm — these all had sunk; at last over
these also the cruel quicksand had closed; and no
memorial of the fair young girl remained on earth,
except my own solitary tears, and the funeral bells
from the desert seas, that, rising again more softly,
sang a requiem over the grave of the buried child, and
over her blighted dawn.

I sat, and wept in secret the tears that men have
ever given to the memory of those that died before
the dawn, and by the treachery of earth, our mother.
But suddenly the tears and funeral bells were hushed
by a shout as of many nations, and by a roar as from
some great king's artillery, advancing rapidly along
the valleys, and heard afar by echoes from the mountains. 'Hush!' I said, as I bent my ear earthwards
to listen — 'hush! — this either is the very anarchy
of strife, or else' — and then I listened more profoundly, and whispered as I raised my head — 'or
else, oh heavens! it is *victory* that is final, victory that
swallows up all strife.'

IV.

Immediately, in trance, I was carried over land and
sea to some distant kingdom, and placed upon a tri-

umphal car, amongst companions crowned with laurel.
The darkness of gathering midnight, brooding over all
the land, hid from us the mighty crowds that were
weaving restlessly about ourselves as a centre: we
heard them, but saw them not. Tidings had arrived,
within an hour, of a grandeur that measured itself
against centuries; too full of pathos they were, too
full of joy, to utter themselves by other language than
by tears, by restless anthems, and *Te Deums* reverbe-
rated from the choirs and orchestras of earth. These
tidings we that sat upon the laurelled car had it for
our privilege to publish amongst all nations. And
already, by signs audible through the darkness, by
snortings and tramplings, our angry horses, that knew
no fear of fleshy weariness, upbraided us with delay.
Wherefore *was* it that we delayed? We waited for a
secret word that should bear witness to the hope of
nations, as now accomplished for ever. At midnight
the secret word arrived; which word was — Waterloo
and Recovered Christendom! The dreadful word
shone by its own light; before us it went; high above
our leaders' heads it rode, and spread a golden light
over the paths which we traversed. Every city, at the
presence of the secret word, threw open its gates. The
rivers were conscious as we crossed. All the forests,
as we ran along their margins, shivered in homage to
the secret word. And the darkness comprehended it.

Two hours after midnight we approached a mighty
Minster. Its gates, which rose to the clouds, were
closed. But when the dreadful word, that rode before
us, reached them with its golden light, silently they
moved back upon their hinges; and at a flying gallop
our equipage entered the grand aisle of the cathedral.

16

Headlong was our pace; and at every altar, in the little chapels and oratories to the right hand and left of our course, the lamps, dying or sickening, kindled anew in sympathy with the secret word that was flying past. Forty leagues we might have run in the cathedral, and as yet no strength of morning light had reached us, when before us we saw the aerial galleries of organ and choir. Every pinnacle of the fretwork, every station of advantage amongst the traceries, was crested by white-robed choristers, that sang deliverance; that wept no more tears, as once their fathers had wept; but at intervals that sang together to the generations, saying,

'Chant the deliverer's praise in every tongue,'

and receiving answers from afar,

'Such as once in heaven and earth were sung.'

And of their chanting was no end; of our headlong pace was neither pause nor slackening.

Thus, as we ran like torrents — thus, as we swept with bridal rapture over the Campo Santo [23] of the cathedral graves — suddenly we became aware of a vast necropolis rising upon the far-off horizon — a city of sepulchres, built within the saintly cathedral for the warrior dead that rested from their feuds on earth. Of purple granite was the necropolis; yet, in the first minute, it lay like a purple stain upon the horizon, so mighty was the distance. In the second minute it trembled through many changes, growing into terraces and towers of wondrous altitude, so mighty was the pace. In the third minute already, with our dreadful gallop, we were entering its suburbs. Vast sarcophagi rose on every side, having towers and turrets that, upon the limits of the central aisle, strode forward

with haughty intrusion, that ran back with mighty
shadows into answering recesses. Every scarcophagus
showed many bas-reliefs — bas-reliefs of battles and
of battle-fields; battles from forgotten ages — battles
from yesterday — battle-fields that, long since, nature
had healed and reconciled to herself with the sweet
oblivion of flowers — battle-fields that were yet angry
and crimson with carnage. Where the terraces ran,
there did *we* run; where the towers curved, there did
we curve. With the flight of swallows our horses
swept round every angle. Like rivers in flood, wheeling round headlands — like hurricanes that ride into
the secrets of forests — faster than ever light unwove
the mazes of darkness, our flying equipage carried
earthly passions, kindled warrior instincts, amongst
the dust that lay around us — dust oftentimes of our
noble fathers that had slept in God *from* Créci to Trafalgar. And now had we reached the last sarcophagus,
now were we abreast of the last bas-relief, already had
we recovered the arrow like flight of the illimitable
central aisle, when coming up this aisle to meet us we
beheld afar off a female child, that rode in a carriage
as frail as flowers. The mists, which went before her,
hid the fawns that drew her, but could not hide the
shells and tropic flowers with which she played.— but
could not hide the lovely smiles by which she uttered
her trust in the mighty cathedral, and in the cherubim
that looked down upon her from the mighty shafts of
its pillars. Face to face she was meeting us; face to
face she rode, as if danger there were none. ' Oh,
baby ! ' I exclaimed, ' shalt thou be the ransom for
Waterloo ? Must we, that carry tidings of great joy
to every people, be messengers of ruin to thee ! ' In

horror I rose at the thought; but then also, in horror
at the thought, rose one that was sculptured on a bas-
relief — a Dying Trumpeter. Solemnly from the field
of battle he rose to his feet; and, unslinging his stony
trumpet, carried it, in his dying anguish, to his stony
lips — sounding once, and yet once again; proclamation that, in *thy* ears, oh baby! spoke from the battlements of death. Immediately deep shadows fell
between us, and aboriginal silence. The choir had
ceased to sing. The hoofs of our horses, the dreadful
rattle of our harness, the groaning of our wheels,
alarmed the graves no more. By horror the bas-relief
had been unlocked into life. By horror we, that were
so full of life, we men and our horses, with their fiery
fore-legs rising in mid air to their everlasting gallop,
were frozen to a bas-relief. Then a third time the
trumpet sounded; the seals were taken off all pulses;
life, and the frenzy of life, tore into their channels
again; again the choir burst forth in sunny grandeur,
as from the muffling of storms and darkness; again
the thunderings of our horses carried temptation into
the graves. One cry burst from our lips, as the clouds,
drawing off from the aisle, showed it empty before us
— 'Whither has the infant fled? — is the young child
caught up to God?' Lo! afar off, in a vast recess,
rose three mighty windows to the clouds; and on a
level with their summits, at height insuperable to man,
rose an altar of purest alabaster. On its eastern face
was trembling a crimson glory. A glory was it from
the reddening dawn that now streamed *through* the
windows? Was it from the crimson robes of the
martyrs painted *on* the windows? Was it from the
bloody bas-reliefs of earth? There, suddenly, within

that crimson radiance, rose the apparition of a woman's head, and then of a woman's figure. The child it was — grown up to woman's height. Clinging to the horns of the altar, voiceless she stood — sinking, rising, raving, despairing; and behind the volume of incense, that, night and day, streamed upwards from the altar, dimly was seen the fiery font, and the shadow of that dreadful being who should have baptized her with the baptism of death. But by her side was kneeling her better angel, that hid his face with wings; that wept and pleaded for *her;* that prayed when *she* could *not;* that fought with Heaven by tears for *her* deliverance; which also, as he raised his immortal countenance from his wings, I saw, by the glory in his eye, that from Heaven he had won at last.

V.

Then was completed the passion of the mighty fugue. The golden tubes of the organ, which as yet had but muttered at intervals — gleaming amongst clouds and surges of incense — threw up, as from fountains unfathomable, columns of heart-shattering music. Choir and anti-choir were filling fast with unknown voices. Thou also, Dying Trumpeter! — with thy love that was victorious, and thy anguish that was finishing — didst enter the tumult; trumpet and echo — farewell love, and farewell anguish — rang through the dreadful *sanctus.* Oh, darkness of the grave! that from the crimson altar and from the fiery font wert visited and searched by the effulgence in the angel's eye — were these indeed thy children? Pomps of life, that, from the burials of centuries, rose again to the voice of perfect joy, did ye indeed mingle with the festivals of Death? Lo! as I looked back for seventy leagues through the mighty cathedral, I saw the quick and the dead that sang together to God, together that sang to the generations of man. All the hosts of jubilation, like armies that ride in pursuit, moved with one step. Us, that, with laurelled heads, were passing from the cathedral, they overtook, and, as with a garment, they wrapped us round with thunders greater than our own. As brothers we moved together; to the dawn that advanced — to the stars that fled; rendering thanks to God in the highest — that, having hid his face through one generation behind thick clouds of War, once again was ascending — from the Campo Santo of Waterloo was ascending — in the visions of Peace; rendering thanks for thee, young girl! whom, having overshadowed with his ineffable passion of death, suddenly did God relent; suffered thy angel to turn aside his arm; and even in thee, sister unknown! shown to me for a moment only to be hidden for ever, found an occasion to glorify his goodness. A thousand times, amongst the phantoms of sleep, have I seen thee entering the gates of the golden dawn — with the secret word riding before thee — with the armies of the grave behind thee: seen thee sinking, rising, raving, despairing; a thousand times in the worlds of sleep have seen thee followed by God's angel through storms; through desert seas; through the darkness of quicksands; through dreams, and the dreadful revelations that are in dreams — only that at the last, with one sling of his victorious arm, he might snatch thee back from ruin, and might emblazon in thy deliverance the endless resurrections of his love!

NOTES.

Note 1. Page 125.

Lady Madeline Gordon.

Note 2. Page 125.

' *The same thing :* '—Thus, in the calendar of the Church Festivals, the discovery of the true cross (by Helen, the mother of Constantine) is recorded (and one might think — with the express consciousness of sarcasm) as the *Invention* of the Cross.

Note 3. Page 125.

' *Vast distances :* '—One case was familiar to mail-coach travellers, where two mails in opposite directions, north and south, starting at the same minute from points six hundred miles apart, met almost constantly at a particular bridge which bisected the total distance.

Note 4. Page 129.

De non apparentibus, &c.

Note 5. Page 129.

' *Snobs,*' and its antithesis, ' *nobs,*' arose among the internal factions of shoemakers perhaps ten years later. Possibly enough, the terms may have existed much earlier; but they were then first made known, picturesquely and effectively, by a trial at some assizes which happened to fix the public attention.

Note 6. Page 134.

' *Von Troil's Iceland :* '—The allusion to a well-known chapter in Von Troil's work, entitled, ' Concerning the Snakes of

Iceland.' The entire chapter consists of these six words — '*There are no snakes in Iceland.*'

Note 7.   Page 134.

'*Forbidden seat:*' — The very sternest code of rules was enforced upon the mails by the Post-office. Throughout England, only three outsides were allowed, of whom one was to sit on the box, and the other two immediately behind the box; none, under any pretext, to come near the guard; an indispensable caution; since else, under the guise of passenger, a robber might by any one of a thousand advantages — which sometimes are created, but always are favored, by the animation of frank, social intercourse — have disarmed the guard. Beyond the Scottish border, the regulation was so far relaxed as to allow of *four* outsides, but not relaxed at all as to the mode of placing them. One, as before, was seated on the box, and the other three on the front of the roof, with a determinate and ample separation from the little insulated chair of the guard. This relaxation was conceded by way of compensating to Scotland her disadvantages in point of population. England, by the superior density of her population, might always count upon a large fund of profits in the fractional trips of chance passengers riding for short distances of two or three stages. In Scotland, this chance counted for much less. And therefore, to make good the deficiency, Scotland was allowed a compensatory profit upon one *extra* passenger.

Note 8.   Page 136.

'*False echoes:*' — Yes, false! for the words ascribed to Napoleon, as breathed to the memory of Desaix, never were uttered at all. They stand in the same category of theatrical fictions as the cry of the foundering line-of-battle ship Vengeur, as the vaunt of General Cambronne at Waterloo, ' *La Garde meurt, mais ne se rend pas,*' or as the repartees of Talleyrand.

Note 9.   Page 142

' *Wore the royal livery:*' — The general impression was, that the royal livery belonged of right to the mail-coachmen as their professional dress. But that was an error. To the guard it *did* belong, I believe, and was obviously essential as an official warrant, and as a means of instant identification for his person, in the discharge of his important public duties. But the coachman, and especially if his place in the series did not connect him immediately with London and the General Post-office, obtained the scarlet coat only as an honorary distinction after long (or, if not long, trying and special) service

Note 10.   Page 144.

' *Turrets :* ' — As one who loves and venerates Chaucer for his unrivalled merits of tenderness, of picturesque characterization, and of narrative skill, I noticed with great pleasure that the word *torrettes* is used by him to designate the little devices through which the reins are made to pass. This same word, in the same exact sense, I heard uniformly used by many scores of illustrious mail-coachmen, to whose confidential friendship I had the honor of being admitted in my younger days.

Note 11.   Page 145.

' *Mr. Waterton :* ' — Had the reader lived through the last generation, he would not need to be told that some thirty or thirty-five years back, Mr. Waterton, a distinguished country gentleman of ancient family in Northumberland, publicly mounted and rode in top-boots a savage old crocodile, that was restive and very impertinent, but all to no purpose. The crocodile jibbed and tried to kick, but vainly. He was no more able to throw the squire, than Sinbad was to throw the old scoundrel who used his back without paying for it, until he discovered a mode (slightly immoral, perhaps, though some think not) of murdering the old fraudulent jockey, and so circuitously of unhorsing him.

Note 12.   Page 146.

' *Households :* ' — Roe-deer do not congregate in herds like the fallow or the red deer, but by separate families, parents and children; which feature of approximation to the sanctity of human hearths, added to their comparatively miniature and graceful proportions, conciliate to them an interest of peculiar tenderness, supposing even that this beautiful creature is less characteristically impressed with the grandeurs of savage and forest life.

17

Note 13. Page 148.

' *Audacity :* ' — Such the French accounted it; and it has struck me that Soult would not have been so popular in London, at the period of her present Majesty's coronation, or in Manchester, on occasion of his visit to that town, if they had been aware of the insolence with which he spoke of us in notes written at intervals from the field of Waterloo. As though it had been mere felony in our army to look a French one in the face, he said in more notes than one, dated from two to four P. M., on the field of Waterloo, ' Here are the English — we have them; they are caught *en flagrant delit.*' Yet no man should have known us better; no man had drunk deeper from the cup of humiliation than Soult had in 1809, when ejected by us with headlong violence from Oporto, and pursued through a long line of wrecks to the frontier of Spain; subsequently at Albuera, in the bloodiest of recorded battles, to say nothing of Toulouse, he should have learned our pretensions.

Note 14. Page 148.

' *At that time :* ' — I speak of the era previous to Waterloo.

Note 15. Page 150.

' *Three hundred :* ' — Of necessity, this scale of measurement, to an American, if he happens to be a thoughtless man, must sound ludicrous. Accordingly, I remember a case in which an American writer indulges himself in the luxury of a little fibbing, by ascribing to an Englishman a pompous account of the Thames, constructed entirely upon American ideas of grandeur, and concluding in something like these terms : — ' And, sir, arriving at London, this mighty father of rivers attains a breadth of at least two furlongs, having, in its winding course, traversed the astonishing distance of one hundred and seventy miles. ' And this the candid American thinks it fair to contrast with the scale of the Mississippi. Now, it is hardly worth while to answer a pure fiction gravely, else one might say that no Englishman out of Bedlam ever thought of looking in an island for the rivers of a continent; nor, consequently could have thought of looking for the peculiar grandeur of the Thames in the length of its course, òr in the extent of soil which it drains; yet, if he *had* been so absurd, the American might have recollected that a river, not to be compared with the Thames even as to volume of water — viz , the Tiber — has contrived to make itself heard of in this world for twenty-five centuries to an extent not reached as yet by any river, however corpulent, of his own land. The glory of the Thames is measured by the destiny of the population to which it ministers, by the commerce which it supports, by the grandeur of the empire in which, though far from the largest, it is the most influential stream. Upon some such scale, and not by a transfer of Columbian standards, is the course of our English mails to be valued. The American may fancy the effect of his own valuations to our English ears, by supposing the case of a Siberian glorifying his country in these terms : — 'These wretches, sir, in France and England, cannot march half a mile in any direction without finding a house where food can be had and lodging; whereas, such is the noble desolation of our magnificent country, that in many a direction for a thousand miles, I will engage that a dog shall not find shelter from a snow-storm, nor a wren find an apology for breakfast.'

Note 16.   Page 154.

'*Glittering laurels :*'— I must observe, that the color of *green* suffers almost a spiritual change and exaltation under the effect of Bengal lights.

Note 17.   Page 167.

'*Confluent :*'— Suppose a capital Y (the Pythagorean letter) : Lancaster is at the foot of this letter; Liverpool at the top of the *right* branch; Manchester at the top of the *left ;* proud Preston at the centre, where the two branches unite. It is thirty-three miles along either of the two branches; it is twenty-two miles along the stem — viz., from Preston in the middle, to Lancaster at the root. There's a lesson in geography for the reader.

Note 18.   Page 168.

'*Twice in the year :* ' — There were at that time only two assizes even in the most populous counties — viz., the Lent Assizes, and the Summer Assizes.

Note 19. Page 169.

' *Sigh-born :* ' — I owe the suggestion of this word to an obscure remembrance of a beautiful phrase in ' Giraldus Cambrensis ' — viz., *suspiriosæ cogitationes.*

Note 20. Page 172.

It is true that, according to the law of the case as established by legal precedents, all carriages were required to give way before Royal equipages, and therefore before the mail as one of them. But this only increased the danger, as being a regulation very imperfectly made known, very unequally enforced, and therefore often embarrassing the movements on both sides.

Note 21. Page 172.

' *Quartering :* ' — This is the technical word, and, I presume, derived from the French *cartayer*, to evade a rut or any obstacle.

Note 22. Page 180.

' *Averted signs :* ' —I read the course and changes of the lady's agony in the succession of her involuntary gestures ; but it must be remembered that I read all this from the rear, never once catching the lady's full face, and even her profile imperfectly.

Note 23. Page 186.

' *Campo Santo :* ' — It is probable that most of my readers will be acquainted with the history of the Campo Santo (or cemetery) at Pisa, composed of earth brought from Jerusalem for a bed of sanctity, as the highest prize which the noble piety of crusaders could ask or imagine. To readers who are unacquainted with England, or who (being English) are yet unacquainted with the cathedral cities of England, it may be right to mention that the graves within-side the cathedrals often form a flat pavement over which carriages and horses *might* run ; and perhaps a boyish remembrance of one particular cathedral, across which I had seen passengers walk and burdens carried, as about two centuries back they were through the middle of St. Paul's in London, may have assisted my dream.

DINNER, REAL, AND REPUTED.

GREAT misconceptions have always prevailed about the Roman *dinner*. Dinner [*cœna*] was the only meal which the Romans as a nation took. It was no accident, but arose out of their whole social economy. This I shall endeavor to show, by running through the history of a Roman day. *Ridentem dicere verum quid vetat ?* And the course of this review will expose one or two important truths in ancient political economy, which have been too much overlooked.

With the lark it was that the Roman rose. Not that the earliest lark rises so early in Latium as the earliest lark in England ; that, is, during summer : but then, on the other hand, neither does it ever rise so late. The Roman citizen was stirring with the dawn — which, allowing for the shorter longest-day and longer shortest-day of Rome, you may call about four in summer — about seven in winter. Why did he do this ? Because he went to bed at a very early hour. But why did he do that ? By backing in this way, we shall surely back into the very well of truth : always, where it is possible, let us have the *pourquoi* of the *pourquoi*. The Roman went to bed early for two remarkable reasons. 1st, Because in Rome, built for a martial destiny, every habit of life had reference to

the usages of war. Every citizen, if he were not a
mere proletarian animal kept at the public cost, with a
view to his *proles* or offspring, held himself a soldier-
elect: the more noble he was, the more was his lia-
bility to military service; in short, all Rome, and at
all times, was consciously 'in procinct.' [1] Now it was
a principle of ancient warfare, that every hour of daylight had a triple worth, as valued against hours of
darkness. That was one reason — a reason suggested
by the understanding. But there was a second reason,
far more remarkable; and this was a reason suggested
by a blind necessity. It is an important fact, that this
planet on which we live, this little industrious earth of
ours, has developed her wealth by slow stages of increase. She was far from being the rich little globe in
Cæsar's days that she is at present. The earth in our
days is incalculably richer, as a whole, than in the
time of Charlemagne; and at that time she was richer,
by many a million of acres, than in the era of Augustus. In that Augustan era we descry a clear belt of
cultivation, averaging perhaps six hundred miles in
depth, running in a ring-fence about the Mediterranean. This belt, *and no more*, was in decent cultivation. Beyond that belt, there was only a wild Indian
cultivation; generally not so much. At present, what
a difference! We have that very belt, but much richer, all things considered, *æquatis æquandis*, than in the
Roman era and much beside. The reader must not
look to single cases, as that of Egypt or other parts of
Africa, but take the whole collectively. On that
scheme of valuation, we have the old Roman belt, the
circum Mediterranean girdle not much tarnished, and
we have all the rest of Europe to boot. Such being

the case, the earth, being (as a whole) in that Pagan
era so incomparably poorer, could not in the Pagan
era support the expense of maintaining great empires
in cold latitudes. Her purse would not reach that
cost. Wherever she undertook in those early ages to
rear man in great abundance, it must be where nature
would consent to work in partnership with herself;
where *warmth* was to be had for nothing ; where
clothes were not so entirely indispensable, but that a
ragged fellow might still keep himself warm ; where
slight *shelter* might serve ; and where the *soil*, if not
absolutely richer in reversionary wealth, was more
easily cultured. Nature, in those days of infancy,
must come forward liberally, and take a number of
shares in every new joint-stock concern before it could
move. Man, therefore, went to bed early in those
ages, simply because his worthy mother earth could not
afford him candles. She, good old lady (or good
young lady, for geologists know not [2] whether she is
in that stage of her progress which corresponds to
gray hairs, or to infancy, or to ' a *certain* age ') — she,
good lady, would certainly have shuddered to hear any
of her nations asking for candles. ' Candles, indeed!'
she would have said, ' who ever heard of such a thing?
and with so much excellent daylight running to waste,
as I have provided *gratis !*   What will the wretches
want next ? '

The daylight, furnished *gratis*, was certainly ' unde-
niable ' in its quality, and quite sufficient for all purposes that were honest. Seneca, even in his own
luxurious period, called those men ' *lucifugæ*,' and by
other ugly names, who lived chiefly by candle-light.
None but rich and luxurious men, nay, even amongst

these, none but idlers, *did* live or *could* live by candle-
light. An immense majority of men in Rome never
lighted a candle, unless sometimes in the early dawn.
And this custom of Rome was the custom also of all
nations that lived round the great lake of the Mediterranean. In Athens, Egypt, Palestine, Asia Minor,
everywhere, the ancients went to bed, like good boys,
from seven to nine o'clock.[3] The Turks and other
people, who have succeeded to the stations and the
habits of the ancients, do so at this day.

The Roman, therefore, who saw no joke in sitting
round a table in the dark, went off to bed as the darkness began. Everybody did so. Old Numa Pom-
pilius himself was obliged to trundle off in the dusk.
Tarquinius might be a very superb fellow; but I doubt
whether he ever saw a farthing rushlight. And,
though it may be thought that plots and conspiracies
would flourish in such a city of darkness, it is to be
considered, that the conspirators themselves had no more
candles than honest men: both parties were in the dark.

Being up, then, and stirring not long after the lark,
what mischief did the Roman go about first? Now-a-
days, he would have taken a pipe or a cigar. But,
alas for the ignorance of the poor heathen creatures!
they had neither the one nor the other. In this point,
I must tax our mother earth with being really *too*
stingy. In the case of the candles, I approve of her
parsimony. Much mischief is brewed by candle-
light. But it was coming it too strong to allow no
tobacco. Many a wild fellow in Rome, your Gracchi,
Syllas, Catilines, would not have played 'h— and
Tommy' in the way they did, if they could have
soothed their angry stomachs with a cigar: a pipe

has intercepted many an evil scheme. But the thing is past helping now. At Rome, you must do as 'they does' at Rome. So, after shaving (supposing the age of the *Barbati* to be past), what is the first business that our Roman will undertake? Forty to one he is a poor man, born to look upwards to his fellow-men — and not to look down upon anybody but slaves. He goes, therefore, to the palace of some grandee, some top-sawyer of the senatorian order. This great man, for all his greatness, has turned out even sooner than himself. For he also has had no candles and no cigars; and he well knows, that before the sun looks into his portals, all his halls will be overflowing and buzzing with the matin susurrus of courtiers — the 'mane salutantes.' 4 It is as much as his popularity is worth to absent himself, or to keep people waiting. But surely, the reader may think, this poor man he might keep waiting. No, he might not; for, though poor, being a citizen, the man is a gentleman. That was the consequence of keeping slaves. Wherever there is a class of slaves, he that enjoys the *jus suffragii* (no matter how poor) is a gentleman. The true Latin word for a gentleman is *ingenuus* — a freeman and the son of a freeman.

Yet even here there were distinctions. Under the emperors, the courtiers were divided into two classes: with respect to the superior class, it was said of the sovereign — that he *saw* them ('*videbat*'); with respect to the other — that he *was seen* ('*videbatur*'). Even Plutarch mentions it as a common boast in his times, *ἡμας ειδεν ὁ βασιλευς* — *Cæsar is in the habit of seeing me;* or, as a common plea for evading a suit, *ἑτερης ὁρα μαλλον* — *I am sorry to say he is more inclined to look upon others.* And this usage derived itself

(mark that well!) from the *republican* era. The aulic
spirit was propagated by the empire, but from a republican root.

Having paid his court, you will suppose that our
friend comes home to breakfast. Not at all : no such
discovery as ' breakfast' had then been made : breakfast
was not invented for many centuries after that. I have
always admired, and always shall admire, as the very
best of all human stories, Charles Lamb's account of
roast-pork, and its traditional origin in China. Ching
Ping, it seems, had suffered his father's house to be
burned down : the outhouses were burned along with
the house : and in one of these the pigs, by accident,
were roasted to a turn. Memorable were the results
for all future China and future civilization. Ping, who
(like all China beside) had hitherto eaten his pig raw,
now for the first time tasted it in a state of torrefac-
tion. Of course he made his peace with his father by
a part (tradition says a leg) of the new dish. The
father was so astounded with the discovery, that he
burned his house down once a-year for the sake of
coming at an annual banquet of a roast pig. A curious prying sort of a fellow, one Chang Pang, got to
know of this. He also burned down a house with a
pig in it, and had his eyes opened. The secret was
ill kept — the discovery spread — many great conver-
sions were made — houses were blazing in every part
of the Celestial Empire. The insurance offices took
the matter up. One Chong Pong, detected in the very
act of shutting up a pig in his drawing-room, and then
firing a train, was indicted on a charge of arson.
The chief justice of Pekin, on that occasion, requested an officer of the court to hand him up a piece

óf the roast pig, the *corpus delicti:* pure curiosity it
was, liberal curiosity, that led him to taste; but within
two days after, it was observed, says Lamb, that his
lordship's town-house was on fire. In short, all China
apostatized to the new faith; and it was not until
some centuries had passed, that'a man of prodigious
genius arose, viz., Chung Pung, who, established the
second era in the history of roast pig by showing that
it could be had without burning down a house.

No such genius had yet arisen in Rome. Breakfast
was not suspected. No prophecy, no type of breakfast, had been published. In fact, it took as much
time and research to arrive at that great discovery as
at the Copernican system. True it is, reader, that
you have heard of such a word as *jentaculum;* and
your dictionary translates that old heathen word by
the Christian word *breakfast.* But dictionaries are
dull deceivers. Between *jentaculum* and *breakfast* the
differences are as wide as between a horse-chestnut
and a chestnut horse; differences in the *time when,* in
the *place where,* in the *manner how,* but pre-eminently
in the *thing which.*

Galen is a good authority upon such a subject, since,
if (like other Pagans) he ate no breakfast himself, in
some sense he may be called the cause of breakfast to
other men, by treating of those things which could
safely be taken upon an empty stomach. As to the
time, he (like many other authors) says, περι τριτην, η
(το μαχροτερω) περι τιταρτην, about the third, or at far-
thest about the fourth hour: and so exact is he, that
he assumes the day to lie exactly between six and six
o'clock, and to be divided into thirteen equal portions.
So the time will be a few minntes before nine, or a

few minutes before ten, in the forenoon. That seems
fair enough. But it is not time in respect to its location
that we are concerned with, so much as time in respect
to its duration. Now, heaps of authorities take it
for granted, that you are not to sit down — you are to
stand; and, as to the place, that any place will do —
'any corner of the forum,' says Galen, 'any corner
that you fancy:' which is like referring a man for his
salle à manger to Westminster Hall or Fleet Street.
Augustus, in a letter still surviving, tells us that he
jentabat, or took his *jentaculum*, in his carriage; sometimes in a wheel carriage (*in essedo*), sometimes in a
litter or palanquin (*in lecticâ*). This careless and dis-
orderly way as to time and place, and other circumstances of haste, sufficiently indicate the quality of the
meal you are to expect. Already you are 'sagacious
of your quarry from so far.' Not that we would presume, excellent reader, to liken you to Death, or to
insinuate that you are a 'grim feature.' But would
it not make a saint 'grim' to hear of such prepara-
tions for the morning meal? And then to hear of
such consummations as *panis siccus*, dry bread; or (if
the learned reader thinks it will taste better in Greek),
αϱτος ξηϱος! And what may this word *dry* happen
to mean? 'Does it mean *stale*?' says Salmasius.
'Shall we suppose,' says he, in querulous words,
'*molli et recenti opponi*,' that it is placed in antithesis
to soft and new bread, what English sailors call '*soft
tommy*?' and from that antithesis conclude it to be,
'*durum et non recens coctum, eoque sicciorem*?' Hard
and stale, and in that proportion more arid? Not
quite so bad as that, we hope. Or again — '*siccum
pro biscocto, ut hodie vocamus, sumemus?*' [5] By *hodie*

Salmasius means, amongst his countrymen of France,
where *biscoctus* is verbatim reproduced in the word *bis*
(twice), *cuit* (baked) ; whence our own *biscuit*. Biscuit might do very well, could we be sure that it was
cabin biscuit ; but Salmasius argues that — in this case
he takes it to mean ' *buccellatum, qui est panis nauti-*
cus ; ' that is, the ship company's biscuit, broken with
a sledge-hammer. In Greek, for the benefit again of
the learned reader, it is termed διπυρος, indicating that
it has passed twice under the action of fire.

'Well,' you say, 'no matter if· it had passed
through the fires of Moloch; only let us have this
biscuit, such as it is.' In good faith, then, fasting
reader, you are not likely to see much more than you
have seen. It is a very Barmecide feast, we do assure
you — this same ' jentaculum ; ' at which abstinence
and patience are much more exercised than the teeth :
faith and hope are the chief graces cultivated, together
with that species of the *magnificum* which is founded
on the *ignotum*. Even this biscuit was allowed in the
most limited quantities ; for which reason it is that
the Greeks called this apology for a meal by the name
of βυγκισμος, a word formed (as many words were in
the Post-Augustan ages) from a Latin word — viz.,
buccea, a mouthful ; not literally such, but so much as
a polished man could allow himself to put into his
mouth at once. 'We took a mouthful,' says Sir
William Waller, the parliamentary general — ' took
a mouthful ; paid our reckoning ; mounted ; and were
off.' But there Sir William means, by his plausible
' mouthful,' something very much beyond either nine
or nineteen ordinary quantities of that denomination,
whereas the Roman ' jentaculum ' was literally such ;

and, accordingly, one of the varieties under which the ancient vocabularies express this model of evanescent quantities is *gustatio*, a mere tasting; and again, it is called by another variety *gustus*, a mere taste [whence comes the old French word *gouster* for a refection or luncheon, and then (by the usual suppression of the *s*) *gouter*]. Speaking of his uncle, Pliny the Younger says: 'Post solem plerumque lavabatur: deinde gustabat; dormiebat minimum; mox, quasi alio die, studebat in cœnæ tempus.' 'After taking the air, generally speaking, he bathed; after that he broke his fast on a morsel of biscuit, and took a very slight *siesta :* which done, as if awaking to a new day, he set in regularly to his studies, and pursued them to dinner-time.' *Gustabat* here meant that nondescript meal which arose at Rome when *jentaculum* and *prandium* were fused into one, and that only a *taste* or mouthful of biscuit, as we shall show farther on.

Possibly, however, most excellent reader, like some epicurean traveller, who, in crossing the Alps, finds himself weather-bound at St. Bernard's on Ash-Wednesday, you surmise a remedy: you descry some opening from 'the loopholes of retreat,' through which a few delicacies might be insinuated to spread verdure on this arid wilderness of biscuit. Casuistry can do much. A dead hand at casuistry has often proved more than a match for Lent with all his quarantines. But sorry I am to say that, in this case, no relief is hinted at in any ancient author. A grape or two (not a bunch of grapes), a raisin or two, a date, an olive — these are the whole amount of relief[6] which the chancery of the Roman kitchen granted in such cases. All things here hang together, and prove each other

— the time, the place, the mode, the thing. Well
might man eat standing, or eat in public, such a trifle
as this. Go home, indeed, to such a breakfast? You
would as soon think of ordering a cloth to be laid in
order to eat a peach, or of asking a friend to join you
in an orange. No man in his senses makes ' two bites
of a cherry.' So let us pass on to the other stages of
the day. Only, in taking leave of this morning's
stage, throw your eyes back with me, Christian reader,
upon this truly heathen meal, fit for idolatrous dogs
like your Greeks and your Romans ;. survey, through
the vista of ages, that thrice-accursed biscuit, with
half a fig, perhaps, by way of garnish, and a huge
hammer by its side, to secure the certainty of mastica-
tion, by previous comminution. Then turn your eyes
to a Christian breakfast — hot rolls, eggs, coffee, beef;
but down, down, rebellious visions; we need say no
more! You, reader, like myself, will breathe a male-
diction on the Classical era, and thank your stars for
making you a Romanticist. Every morning I thank
mine for keeping me back from the Augustan age, and
reserving me to a period in which breakfast had been
already invented. In the words of Ovid, I say : —

'Prisca juvent alios : ego me nunc denique natum
Gratulor. Hæc ætas moribus apta meis.'

Our friend, the Roman cit, has therefore thus far, in
his progress through life, obtained no breakfast, if he
ever contemplated an idea so frantic. But it occurs to
you, my faithful reader, that perhaps he will not
always be thus unhappy. I could bring wagon-loads
of sentiments, Greek as well as Roman, which prove,
more clearly than the most eminent pikestaff, that, as

the wheel of fortune revolves, simply out of the fact
that it has carried a man downwards, it must subsequently carry him upwards, no matter what dislike
that wheel, or any of its spokes, may bear to that
man : 'non si male nunc sit, et olim sic erit : ' and
that if a man, through the madness of his nation,
misses coffee and hot rolls at nine, he may easily run
into a leg of mutton at twelve. True it is he may do
so : truth is commendable ; and I will not deny that a
man may sometimes, by losing a breakfast, gain a
dinner. Such things have been in various ages, and
will be again, but not at Rome. There were reasons
against it. We have heard of men who consider life
under the idea of a wilderness — dry as a ' remainder
biscuit after a voyage : ' and who consider a day under
the idea of a little life. Life is the macrocosm, or
world at large ; day is the microcosm, or world in miniature. Consequently, if life is a wilderness, then day,
as a little life, is a little wilderness. And this wilderness can be safely traversed only by having relays of
fountains, or stages for refreshment. Such stages,
they conceive, are found in the several meals which
Providence has stationed at due intervals through the
day, whenever the perverseness of man does not break
the chain, or derange the order of succession.

These are the anchors by which man rides in that
billowy ocean between morning and night. The first
anchor, viz., breakfast, having given way in Rome, the
more need there is that he should pull up by the
second ; and that is often reputed to be dinner. And
as your dictionary, good reader, translated *breakfast* by
that vain word *jentaculum*, so doubtless it will translate
dinner by that still vainer word *prandium*. Sincerely

I hope that your own dinner on this day, and through all time coming, may have a better root in fact and substance than this most visionary of all baseless things — the Roman *prandium*, of which I shall presently show you that the most approved translation is *moonshine*.

Reader, I am anything but jesting here. In the very spirit of serious truth, I assure you that the delusion about 'jentaculum' is even exceeded by this other delusion about 'prandium.' Salmasius himself, for whom a natural prejudice of place and time partially obscured the truth, admits, however, that *prandium* was a meal which the ancients rarely took; his very words are — '*raro prandebant veteres.*' Now, judge for yourself of the good sense which is shown in translating by the word *dinner*, which must of necessity mean the chief meal, a Roman word which represents a fancy meal, a meal of caprice, a meal which few people took. At this moment, what is the single point of agreement between the noon meal of the English laborer and the evening meal of the English gentleman? What is the single circumstance common to both, which causes us to denominate them by the common name of *dinner*? It is, that in both we recognize the *principal* meal of the day, the meal upon which is thrown the *onus* of the day's support. In everything else they are as wide asunder as the poles; but they agree in this one point of their function. Is it credible now, that, to represent such a meal amongst ourselves, we select a Roman word so notoriously expressing a mere shadow, a pure apology, that very few people ever tasted it — nobody sat down to it — not many washed their hands after it, and gradually the very name of it

18

became interchangeable with another name, implying
the slightest possible act of tentative tasting or sipping? ' *Post lavationem sine mensâ prandium,*' says
Seneca, ' *post quod non sunt lavandæ manus ;* ' that is,
' after bathing, I take a *prandium* without sitting down
to table, and such a *prandium* as brings after itself no
need of washing the hands.' No ; moonshine as little
soils the hands as it oppresses the stomach.

Reader ! I, as well as Pliny, had an uncle, an East
Indian uncle ; doubtless you have such an uncle ;
everybody has an Indian uncle. Generally such a
person is ' rather yellow, rather yellow' (to quote
Canning *versus* Lord Durham), that is the chief fault
with his physics ; but, as to his morals, he is universally a man of princely aspirations and habits. He is
not always so orientally rich as he is reputed ; but he
is always orientally munificent. Call upon him at any
hour from two to five, he insists on your taking *tiffin* :
and such a tiffin ! The English corresponding term is
luncheon ; but how meagre a shadow is the European
meal to its glowing Asiatic cousin ! Still, gloriously as
tiffin shines, does anybody imagine that it is a vicarious
dinner, or ever meant to be the substitute and *locum
tenens* of dinner ? Wait till eight, and you will have
your eyes opened on that subject. So of the Roman
prandium : had it been as luxurious as it was simple,
still it was always viewed as something meant only to
stay the stomach, as a prologue to something beyond.
The *prandium* was far enough from giving the feeblest
idea even of the English luncheon ; yet it stood in the
same relation to the Roman day. Now to English-
men that meal scarcely exists ; and were it not for
women, whose delicacy of organization does not allow

them to fast so long as men, would probably be abolished. It is singular in this, as in other points, how nearly England and ancient Rome approximate. We all know how hard it is to tempt a man generally into spoiling his appetite, by eating before dinner. The same dislike of violating what they called the integrity of the appetite (*integram famem*), existed at Rome. *Integer* means what is *intact*, unviolated by touch. Cicero, when protesting against spoiling his appetite for dinner, by tasting anything beforehand, says, *integram famem ad cœnam afferam;* I intend bringing to dinner an appetite untampered with. Nay, so much stress did the Romans lay on maintaining this primitive state of the appetite undisturbed, that any prelusions with either *jentaculum* or *prandium* were said, by a very strong phrase indeed, *polluere famem*, to pollute the sanctity of the appetite. The appetite was regarded as a holy vestal flame, soaring upwards towards dinner throughout the day : if undebauched, it tended to its natural consummation in *cœna :* expiring like a phœnix, to rise again out of its own ashes. On this theory, to which language had accommodated itself, the two prelusive meals of nine or ten o'clock A. M., and of one P. M., so far from being ratified by the public sense, and adopted into the economy of the day, were regarded gloomily as gross irregularities, enormities, debauchers of the natural instinct ; and, in so far as they thwarted that instinct, lessened it, or depraved it, were almost uniformly held to be full of pollution ; and, finally, to *profane* a sacred motion of nature. Such was the language.

But we guess what is passing in the reader's mind. He thinks that all this proves the *prandium* to have been a meal of little account; and in very many cases absolutely 'unknown. But still he thinks all this might happen to the English dinner — *that* also might be neglected; supper might be generally preferred; and, nevertheless, dinner would be as truly entitled to the name of dinner as before. Many a student neglects his dinner; enthusiasm in any pursuit must often have extinguished appetite for all of us. Many a time and oft did this happen to Sir Isaac Newton. Evidence is on record, that such a deponent at eight o'clock A. M. found Sir Isaac with one stocking on, one off; at two, said deponent called him to dinner. Being interrogated whether Sir Isaac had pulled on the *minus* stocking, or gartered the *plus* stocking, witness replied that he had not. Being asked if Sir Isaac came to dinner, replied that he did not. Being again asked, ' At sunset, did you look in on Sir Isaac?' witness replied, ' I did.' . ' And now, upon your conscience, sir, by the virtue of your oath, in what state were the stockings?' *Ans.* — ' *In statu quo ante bellum.*' It seems Sir Isaac had fought through that whole battle of a long day, so trying a campaign to many people — he had traversed that whole sandy Zaarah, without calling, or needing to call, at one of those fountains, stages, or *mansiones*,[7] by which (according to our former explanation) Providence has relieved the continuity of arid soil, which else disfigures that long dreary level. This happens to all; but was dinner not dinner, and did supper become dinner, because Sir Isaac Newton ate nothing at the first, and threw the whole day's support upon the last? No, you will say, a rule is not defeated by one casual deviation, nor by one person's constant deviation.

Everybody. else was still dining at two, though Sir Isaac might not; and Sir Isaac himself on most days no more deferred his dinner beyond two, than he sat in public with one stocking off.' But what if everybody, Sir Isaac included, had deferred his substantial meal until night, and taken a slight refection only at two? The question put does really represent the very case which has happened with us in England. In 1700, a large part of London took a meal at two P. M., and another at seven or eight P. M. At present, a large part of London is still doing the very same thing, taking one meal at two, and another at seven or eight. But the names are entirely changed: the two o'clock meal used to be called *dinner*, whereas at present it is called *luncheon ;* the seven o'clock meal used to be called *supper*, whereas at present it is called *dinner ;* and in both cases the difference is anything but *verbal :* it expresses a translation of that main meal, on which the day's support rested, from mid-day to evening.

Upon reviewing the idea of dinner, we soon perceive that time has little or no connection with it: since, both in England and France, dinner has travelled, like the hand of a clock, through *every* hour between ten A. M. and ten P. M. We have a list, well attested, of every successive hour between these limits having been the known established hour for the royal dinner-table within the last three hundred and fifty years. Time, therefore, vanishes from the problem ; it is a quantity regularly exterminated. The true elements of the idea are evidently these : — 1. That dinner is that meal, no matter when taken, which is the principal meal ; *i. e.,* the meal on which the day's support is

thrown. .2. That it is *therefore* the meal of hospitality.
3. That it is the meal (with reference to both Nos. 1
and 2) in which animal food predominate. 4. That it
is that meal which, upon a necessity arising for the
abolition of all *but* one, would naturally offer itself as
that one. Apply these four tests to *prandium*: —
How could that meal *prandium* answer to the first
test, as *the day's support*, which few people touched?
How could that meal *prandium* answer to the second
test, as the *meal of hospitality*, at which nobody sat
down? How could that meal *prandium* answer to the
third test, as the meal of animal food, which consisted
exclusively and notoriously of bread? Or answer to
the fourth test, as the privileged meal *entitled to sur-
vive the abolition of the rest*, which was itself abolished
at all times in practice?

Tried, therefore, by every test, *prandium* vanishes.
But I have something further to communicate about
this same *prandium*.

1. It came to pass, by a very natural association of
feeling, that *prandium* and *jentaculum*, in the latter
centuries of Rome, were generally confounded. This
result was inevitable. Both professed the same basis.
Both came in the morning. Both were fictions. Hence
they melted and collapsed into each other.

That fact speaks for itself — the modern breakfast
and luncheon never could have been confounded; but
who would be at the pains of distinguishing two
shadows? In a gambling-house of that class, where
you are at liberty to sit down to a splendid banquet,
anxiety probably prevents your sitting down at all;
but, if you do, the same cause prevents you noticing
what you eat. So of the two *pseudo* meals of Rome,

they came in the very midst of the Roman business —
viz., from nine A. M. to two P. M. Nobody could give
his mind to them, had they been of better quality.
There lay one cause of their vagueness — viz., in their
position. Another cause was, the common basis of
both. Bread was so notoriously the predominating
' feature ' in each of these prelusive banquets, that all
foreigners at Rome, who communicated with Romans
through the Greek language, knew both the one and
the other by the name of αϱτοσιτος, or the *bread repast.*
Originally, this name had been restricted to the earlier
meal. But a distinction without a difference could not
sustain itself; and both alike disguised their emptiness
under this pompous quadrisyllable. All words are
suspicious, there is an odor of fraud about them, which
— being concerned with common things — are so base
as to stretch out to four syllables. What does an honest
word want with more than two ? In the identity of
substance, therefore, lay a second ground of confusion
And then, thirdly, even as to the time, which had ever
been the sole real distinction, there arose from accident
a tendency to converge. For it happened that, while
some had *jentaculum* but no *prandium,* others had
prandium but no *jentaculum;* a third party had both ;
a fourth party, by much the largest, had neither. Out
of which four varieties (who would think that a non-
entity could cut up into so many somethings ?), arose a
fifth party of compromisers, who, because they could
not afford a regular *cœna,* and yet were hospitably dis-
posed, fused the two ideas into one; and so, because
the usual time for the idea of a breakfast was nine to
ten, and for the idea of a luncheon twelve to one, compromised the rival pretensions by what diplomatists

call a *mezzo termine*; bisecting the time at eleven, and melting the two ideas into one. But, by thus merging the separate times of each, they abolished the sole real difference that had ever divided them. Losing that, they lost all.

Perhaps, as two negatives make one affirmative, it may be thought that two layers of moonshine might coalesce into one pancake; and two Barmecide banquets might be the square root of one poached egg. Of that the company were the best judges. But, probably, as a rump and dozen, in our land of wagers, is construed with a very liberal latitude as to the materials, so Martial's invitation, ' to take bread with him at eleven,' might be understood by the συνετοι (the knowing ones) as significant of something better than ἀρτοσιτος. Otherwise, in good truth, ' moonshine and turn-out ' at eleven A. M. would be even worse than ' tea and turn-out ' at eight P. M., which the ' fervida juventus ' of Young England so loudly deprecates. But, however that might be, in this convergement of the several frontiers, and the confusion that ensued, one cannot wonder that, whilst the two bladders collapsed into one idea, they actually expanded into four names — two Latin and two Greek, *gustus* and *gustatio*, γευσις and γευσμα — which all alike express the merely tentative or exploratory act of a *prægustator* or professional ' taster ' in a king's household: what, if applied to a fluid, we should denominate sipping.

At last, by so many steps all in one direction, things had come to such a pass — the two prelusive meals of the Roman morning, each for itself separately vague from the beginning, had so communicated and interfused their several and joint vaguenesses, that at last no man knew or cared to know what any other man included in his idea of either; how much or how little. And you might as well have hunted in the woods of Ethiopia for Prester John, or fixed the parish of the Everlasting Jew,[8] as have attempted to say what 'jentaculum' certainly *was*, or what 'prandium' certainly was *not*. Only one thing was clear, that neither was anything that people cared for. They were both empty shadows; but shadows as they were, we find from Cicero that they had a power of polluting and profaning better things than themselves.

We presume that no rational man will heceforth look for 'dinner' — that great idea according to Dr. Johnson — that sacred idea according to Cicero — in a bag of moonshine on one side, or a bag of pollution on the other. *Prandium*, so far from being what our foolish dictionaries pretend — dinner itself — never in its palmiest days was more or other than a miserable attempt at being *luncheon*. It was a *conatus*, what physiologists call a *nisus*, a struggle in a very ambitious spark, or *scintilla*, to kindle into a fire. This *nisus* went on for some centuries; but finally evaporated in smoke. If *prandium* had worked out its ambition, had 'the great stream of tendency' accomplished all its purposes, *prandium* never could have been more than a very indifferent luncheon. But now,

2. I have to offer another fact, ruinous to our dictionaries on another ground. Various circumstances have disguised the truth, but a truth it is, that 'prandium,' in its very origin and *incunabula*, never was a meal known to the Roman *culina*. In that court it was never recognized except as an alien. It had no

19

original domicile in the city of Rome. It was a *vox castrensis*, a word and an idea purely martial, and pointing to martial necessities. Amongst the new ideas proclaimed to the recruit, this was one — 'Look for no " *cœna*," no regular dinner, with us. Resign these unwarlike notions. It is true that even war has its respites; in these it would be possible to have our Roman *cœna* with all its equipage of ministrations. But luxury untunes the mind for doing and suffering. Let us voluntarily renounce it; that, when a necessity of renouncing it arrives, we may not feel it among the hardships of war. From the day when you enter the gates of the camp, reconcile yourself, tiro, to a new fashion of meal, to what in camp dialect we call *prandium*.' This *prandium*, this essentially military meal, was taken standing, by way of symbolizing the necessity of being always ready for the enemy. Hence the posture in which it was taken at Rome, the very counter-pole to the luxurious posture of dinner. A writer of the third century, a period from which the Romans naturally looked back upon everything connected with their own early habits, with much the same kind of interest as we extend to our Alfred (separated from us, as Romulus from them, by just a thousand years), in speaking of *prandium*, says, ' Quod dictum est *parandium*, ab eo quod milites ad bellum *paret*.' Isidorus again says, ' Proprie apud veteres prandium vocatum fuisse omnem militum cibum ante pugnam : ' *i. e.*, ' that, properly speaking, amongst our ancestors every military meal taken before battle was termed *prandium*.' According to Isidore, the proposition is reciprocating ; viz., that, as every *prandium* was a military meal, so every military meal was called

prandium. But, in fact, the reason of that is apparent.
Whether in the camp or the city, the early Romans
had probably but one meal in a day. That is true of
many a man amongst ourselves by choice ; it is true
also, to our knowledge, of some horse regiments in our
service, and may be of all. This meal was called *cœna,*
or dinner in the city — *prandium* in camps. In the
city, it would always be tending to one fixed hour.
In the camp, innumerable accidents of war would
make it very uncertain. On this account it would be
an established rule to celebrate the daily meal at noon,
if nothing hindered; not that a later hour would not
have been preferred, had the choice been free ; but it
was better to have a certainty at a bad hour, than by
waiting for a better hour to make it an uncertainty.
For it was a camp proverb — *Pransus, paratus ;* armed
with his daily meal, the soldier is ready for service.
It was not, however, that all meals, as Isidore imagined,
were indiscriminately called *prandium ;* but that the
one sole meal of the day, by accidents of war, might,
and did, revolve through all hours of the day.

The first introduction of this military meal into
Rome itself would be through the honorable pedantry
of old centurions, &c., delighting (like the Commodore
Trunnions of our navy) to keep up in peaceful life
some image or memorial of their past experience, so
wild, so full of peril, excitement, and romance, as
Roman warfare must have been in those ages. Many
non-military people for health's sake, many as an
excuse for eating early, many by way of interposing
some refreshment between the stages of forensic business, would adopt this hurried and informal meal.
Many would wish to see their sons adopting such a

meal, as a training for foreign service in particular, and for temperance in general. It would also be maintained by a solemn and very interesting commemoration of this camp repast in Rome.

This commemoration, because it has been grossly misunderstood by Salmasius (whose error arose from not marking the true point of a particular antithesis), and still more, because it is a distinct confirmation of all I have said as to the military nature of *prandium*, I shall detach from the series of my illustrations, by placing it in a separate paragraph.

On a set day the officers of the army were invited by Cæsar to a banquet; it was a circumstance expressly noticed in the invitation, that the banquet was not a 'cœna,' but a 'prandium.' What did *that* imply? Why, that all the guests must present themselves in full military accoutrement; whereas, observes the historian, had it been a *cœna*, the officers would have unbelted their swords; for he adds, even in Cæsar's presence the officers are allowed to lay aside their swords. The word *prandium*, in short, converted the palace into the imperial tent; and Cæsar was no longer a civil emperor and *princeps senatûs*, but became a commander-in-chief amongst a council of his staff, all belted and plumed, and in full military fig.

On this principle we come to understand why it is, that, whenever the Latin poets speak of an army as taking food, the word used is always *prandens* and *pransus*; and when the word used is *prandens*, then always it is an army that is concerned. Thus Juvenal in a well-known passage : —

> ' Credimus altos
> Desiccasse amnes, epotaque flumina, Medo
> *Prandente* ' —

that rivers were drunk up, when the Mede [*i. e.*, the Median army under Xerxes] took his daily meal: *prandente*, observe, not *cœnante:* you might as well talk of an army taking tea and buttered toast, as taking *cœna*. Nor is that word ever applied to armies. It is true that the converse is not so rigorously observed; nor ought it, from the explanations already given. Though no soldier dined (*cœnabat*), yet the citizen sometimes adopted the camp usage, and took a *prandium*. But generally the poets use the word merely to mark the time of day. In that most humorous appeal of Perseus — ' Cur quis non prandeat, hoc est ?' — is this a sufficient reason for losing one's *prandium?* — he was obliged to say *prandium*, because no exhibitions ever could cause a man to lose his *cœna*, since none were displayed at a time of day when nobody in Rome would have attended. Just as, in alluding to a parliamentary speech notoriously delivered at midnight, an English satirist might have said, Is this a speech to furnish an argument for leaving one's bed? — not as what stood foremost in his regard, but as the only thing that *could* be lost at that time of night.

On this principle, also — viz. by going back to the military origin of *prandium* — we gain the interpretation of all the peculiarities attached to it: viz. — 1, its early hour ; 2, its being taken in a standing posture; 3, in the open air ; 4, the humble quality of its materials — bread and biscuit (the main articles of military fare). In all these circumstances of the meal, we read most legibly written, the exotic (or non-civic) character of the meal, and its martial character.

Thus I have brought down our Roman friend to noonday, or even one hour later than noon, and to this moment the poor man has had nothing to eat. For supposing him to be not *impransus*, and supposing him *jentásse* beside; yet it is evident (I hope) that neither one nor the other means more than what it was often called — viz., βυχχισμος, or, in plain English, a mouthful. How long do we intend to keep him waiting? Reader, he will dine at three, or (supposing dinner put off to the latest) at four. Dinner was never known to be later than the tenth hour at Rome, which in summer would be past five; but for a far greater proportion of days would be near four in Rome. And so entirely was a Roman the creature of ceremonial usage, that a national mourning would probably have been celebrated, and the ' sad augurs' would have been called in to expiate the prodigy, had the general dinner lingered beyond four.

But, meantime, what has our friend been about since perhaps six or seven in the morning? After paying his little homage to his *patronus*, in what way has he fought with the great enemy Time since then? Why, reader, this illustrates one of the most interesting features in the Roman character. The Roman was the idlest of men. ' Man and boy,' he was ' an idler in the land.' He called himself and his pals, ' rerum dominos, gentemque togatam' — ' *the gentry that wore the toga.*' Yes, a pretty set of *gentry* they were, and a pretty affair that ' toga' was. Just figure to yourself, reader, the picture of a hard-working man, with horny hands, like our hedgers, ditchers, porters, &c., setting to work on the high road in that vast sweeping toga, filling with a strong gale like the mainsail of a frigate. Conceive the roars with which this magnificent figure would be received into the bosom of a

modern poor-house detachment sent out to attack the
stones on some line of road, or a fatigue party of dust-
men sent upon secret service. Had there been nothing
left as a memorial of the Romans but that one relic —
their immeasurable toga [9] — I should have known that
they were born and bred to idleness. In fact, except
in war, the Roman never did anything at all but sun
himself. *Uti se apricaret* was the final cause of peace
in his opinion ; in literal truth, that he might make an
apricot of himself. The public rations at all times
supported the poorest inhabitant of Rome if he were a
citizen. Hence it was that Hadrian was so astonished
with the spectacle of Alexandria, ' *civitas opulenta,
fœcunda, in quâ nemo vivat otiosus.*' Here first he
saw the spectacle of a vast city, second only to Rome,
where every man had something to do ; *podagrosi
quod agant habent ; habent cœci quod faciant ; ne chi-
ragrici* ' (those with gout in the fingers) ' *apud eos
otiosi vivunt.*' No poor rates levied upon the rest of
the world for the benefit of their own paupers were
there distributed *gratis.* The prodigious spectacle
(such it seemed to Hadrian) was exhibited in Alexandria, of all men earning their bread in the sweat of
their brow. In Rome only (and at one time in some
of the Grecian states), it was the very meaning of *citizen* that he should vote and be idle. Precisely those
were the two things which the Roman, the *fæx Romuli,*
had to do — viz., sometimes to vote, and always to be
idle.

In these circumstances, where the whole sum of
life's duties amounted to voting, all the business a
man *could* have was to attend the public assemblies,
electioneering ·or ·factious. These, and any judicial

trial (public or private) that might happen to interest
him for the persons concerned, or for the questions at
stake, amused him through the morning; that is, from
eight till one. He might also extract some diversion
from the *columnæ*, or pillars of certain porticoes to
which they pasted advertisements. These *affiches* must
have been numerous; for all the girls in Rome who
lost a trinket, or a pet bird, or a lap-dog, took this
mode of angling in the great ocean of the public for
the missing articles.

But all this time I take for granted that there were
no shows in a course of exhibition, either the dreadful
ones of the amphitheatre, or the bloodless ones of the
circus. If there were, then that became the business
of all Romans; and it was a business which would
have occupied him from daylight until the light began
to fail. Here we see another effect from the scarcity
of artificial light amongst the ancients. These magnificent shows went on by daylight. But how incomparably more gorgeous would have been the splendor
by lamp-light! What a gigantic conception! Two
hundred and fifty thousand human faces all revealed
under one blaze of lamp-light! Lord Bacon saw the
mighty advantage of candle-light for the pomps and
glories of this world. But the poverty of the earth
was the original cause that the Pagan shows proceeded
by day. Not that the masters of the world, who
rained Arabian odors and perfumed waters of the
most costly description from a thousand fountains,
simply to cool the summer heats, would, in the *latter*
centuries of Roman civilization, have regarded the expense of light; cedar and other odorous woods burning
upon vast altars, together with every variety of fragrant

torch, would have created light enough to shed a new day stretching over to the distant Adriatic. But precedents derived from early ages of poverty, ancient traditions, overruled the practical usage.

· However, as there may happen to be no public spectacles, and the courts of political meetings (if not closed altogether by superstition) would at any rate be closed in the ordinary course by twelve or one o'clock, nothing remains for him to do, before returning home, except perhaps to attend the *palæstra*, or some public recitation of a poem written by a friend,· but in any case to attend the public baths. For these the time varied; and many people have thought it tyrannical in some of the Cæsars that they imposed restraints on the time open for the baths; some, for instance, would not suffer them to open at all before two; and in any case, if you were later than four or five in summer, you would have to pay a fine, which most effectually cleaned out the baths of all raff, since it was a sum that *John Quires* could not have produced to save his life. But it should be considered that the emperor was the steward of the public resources for maintaining the baths in fuel, oil, attendance, repairs. And certain it is, that during the long peace of the first Cæsars, and after the *annonaria provisio* (that great pledge of popularity to a Roman prince) had been increased by the corn tribute from the Nile, the Roman population took a vast expansion ahead. The subsequent increase of baths, whilst no old ones were neglected, proves *that* decisively. And as citizenship expanded by means of the easy terms on which it could be had, so did the bathers multiply. The population of Rome in the century after Augustus, was far greater than during that era; and this, still acting as a vortex to the rest of the world, may have been one great motive with Constantine for translating the capital eastwards; in reality, for breaking up one monster capital into two of more manageable dimensions. Two o'clock was sometimes the earliest hour at which the public baths were opened. But in Martial's time a man could go without blushing (*salvâ fronte*) at eleven; though even then two o'clock was the meridian hour for the great uproar of splashing, and swimming, and 'larking' in the endless baths of endless Rome.

And now, at last, bathing finished, and the exercises of the *palæstra,* at half-past two, or three, our friend finds his way home — not again to leave it for that day. He is now a new man; refreshed, oiled with perfumes, his dust washed off by hot water, and ready for enjoyment. These were the things that determined the time for dinner. Had there been no other proof that *cœna* was the Roman dinner, this is an ample one. Now first the Roman was fit for dinner, in a condition of luxurious ease; business over — that day's load of anxiety laid aside — his *cuticle,* as he delighted to talk, cleansed and polished — nothing more to do or to think of until the next morning: he might now go and dine, and get drunk with a safe conscience. Besides, if he does not get dinner now, when will he get it? For most demonstrably he has taken nothing yet which comes near in value to that basin of soup which many of ourselves take at the Roman hour of bathing. No; we have kept our man fasting as yet. It is to be hoped, that something is coming at last.

Yes, something *is* coming; dinner is coming, the great meal of '*cœna*;' the meal sacred to hospitality and genial pleasure comes now to fill up the rest of the day, until light fails altogether.

Many people are of opinion that the Romans only understood what the capabilities of dinner were. It is certain that they were the first great people that discovered the true secret and meaning of dinner, the great office which it fulfils, and which we in England are now so generally acting on. Barbarous nations — and none were, in that respect, more barbarous than our own ancestors — made this capital blunder: the brutes, if you asked them what was the use of dinner, what it was meant for, stared at you, and replied — as a horse would reply, if you put the same question about his provender — that it was to give him strength for finishing his work! Therefore, if you point your telescope back to antiquity about twelve or one o'clock in the daytime, you will descry our most worthy ancestors all eating for their very lives, eating as dogs eat — viz., in bodily fear that some other dog will come and take their dinner away. What swelling of the veins in the temples (see Boswell's natural history of Dr. Johnson at dinner)! what intense and rapid deglutition! what odious clatter of knives and plates! what silence of the human voice! what gravity! what fury in the libidinous eyes with which they contemplate the dishes! Positively it was an *indecent* spectacle to see Dr. Johnson at dinner. But, above all, what maniacal haste and hurry, as if the fiend were waiting with red-hot pincers to lay hold of the hindermost!

Oh, reader, do you recognize in this abominable picture your respected ancestors and ours? Excuse me for saying, ' What monsters !' I have a right to

call my own ancestors . monsters ; and, if so, I must
have the same right over yours. For Southey has shown
plainly in the 'Doctor,' that every man having four
grandparents in the second stage of ascent, consequently. (since each of those four will have had four
grandparents) sixteen in the third stage, consequently
sixty-four in the fourth, consequently two hundred
and fifty-six in the fifth, and so on, it follows that,
long before you get to the Conquest, every man and
woman then living in England will be wanted to make
up the sum of my separate ancestors ; consequently
you must take your ancestors out of the very same
fund, or (if you are too proud for that) you must go
without ancestors.   So that, your ancestors being
clearly mine, I have a right in law to call the whole
'kit' of them monsters.   *Quod erat demonstrandum.*
Really and upon my honor, it makes one, for the moment, ashamed of one's descent ; one would wish to
disinherit one's-self backwards, and (as Sheridan says
in the 'Rivals') to 'cut the connection.' Wordsworth
has an admirable picture in 'Peter Bell' of 'a snug
party in a parlor' removed into *limbus patrum* for their
offences in the flesh : —

> 'Cramming as they on earth were cramm'd ;
> All sipping wine, all sipping tea ;
> But, as you by their faces see,
> All *silent*, and all d——d.'

How well does that one word *silent* describe those
venerable ancestral dinners — 'All silent !'   Contrast
this infernal silence of voice, and fury of eye, with the
'*risus ambilis*,' the festivity, the social kindness, the
music, the wine, the '*dulcis insania*,' of a Roman
'*cœna*.'   I mentioned four tests for determining what

meal is, and what is not, dinner : we may now add a
fifth — viz., the spirit of festal joy and elegant enjoyment, of anxiety laid aside, and of honorable social
pleasure put on like a marriage garment.

And what caused the difference between our ances-
tois and the Romans ?   Simply this — the error of interposing dinner in the middle of business, thus court-
ing all the breezes of angry feeling that may happen to
blow from the business yet to come, instead of finishing, absolutely closing, the account with this world's
troubles before you sit down.   That unhappy in-
terpolation ruined all.   Dinner was an ugly little
parenthesis between two still uglier clauses of a tee-
totally ugly sentence.   Whereas, with us, their enlightened posterity, to whom they have the honor to be
ancestors, dinner is a great re-action.   There lies *my*
.conception of the matter.   It grew out of the very excess of the evil.   When business was moderate, dinner
was allowed to divide and bisect it.   When it swelled
into that vast strife and agony, as one may call it, that
boils along the tortured streets of modern London or
other capitals, men begin to see the necessity of an
adequate counter-force to push against this overwhelming torrent, and thus maintain the equilibrium.   Were
it not for the soft relief of a six o'clock dinner, the
gentle demeanor succeeding to the boisterous hubbub
of the day, the soft glowing lights, the wine, the intellectual conversation, life in London is now come to
such a pass, that in two years all nerves would sink
before it.   But for this periodic re-action, the modern
business which draws so cruelly on the brain, and so
little on the hands, would overthrow that organ in all
but those of coarse organization.   Dinner it is —

meaning by dinner the whole complexity of attendant circumstances — which saves the modern brain-working man from going mad.

This revolution as to dinner was the greatest in virtue and value ever accomplished. In fact, those are always the most operative revolutions which are brought about through social or domestic changes. A nation must be barbarous, neither could it have much intellectual business, which dined in the morning. They could not be at ease in the morning. So much *must* be granted : every day has its separate *quantum*, its dose of anxiety, that could not be digested as soon noon. No man will say it. He, therefore, who dined at noon, showed himself willing to sit down squalid as he was, with his dress unchanged, his cares not washed off. And what follows from that? Why, that to him, to such a canine or cynical specimen of the genus *homo*, dinner existed only as a physical event, a mere animal relief, a purely carnal enjoyment. For in what, I demand, did this fleshly creature differ from the carrion crow, or the kite, or the vulture, or the cormorant? A French judge, in an action upon a wager, laid it down as law, that man only had a *bouche*, all other animals a *gueule :* only with regard to the horse, in consideration of his beauty, nobility, use, and in honor of the respect with which man regarded him, by the courtesy of Christendom, he might be allowed to have a *bouche*, and his reproach of brutality, if not taken away, might thus be hidden. But surely, of the rabid animal who is caught dining at noonday, the *homo ferus*, who affronts the meridian sun like Thyestes and Atreus, by his inhuman meals, we are, by parity of reason, entitled to say, that he has a ' maw ' (so has Milton's Death), but nothing resembling a stomach. And to this vile man a philosopher would say — 'Go away, sir, and come back to me two or three centuries hence, when you have learned to be a reasonable creature, and to make that physico-intellectual thing out of dinner which it was meant to be, and is capable of becoming.' In Henry VII.'s time the court dined at eleven in the forenoon. But even that hour was considered so shockingly late in the French court, that Louis XII. actually had his gray hairs brought down with sorrow to the grave, by changing his regular hour of half-past nine for eleven, in gallantry to his young English bride.[10] He fell a victim to late hours in the forenoon. In Cromwell's time they dined at one P. M. One century and a half had carried them on by two hours. Doubtless, old cooks and scullions wondered what the world would come to next. Our French neighbors were in the same predicament. But they far surpassed us in veneration for the meal. They actually dated from it. Dinner constituted the great era of the day. *L'apres diner* is almost the sole date which you find in Cardinal De Retz's memoirs of the *Fronde*. Dinner was their *Hegira* — dinner was their *line* in traversing the ocean of day : they crossed the equator when they dined. Our English Revolution came next ; it made some little difference, I have heard people say, in church and state ; I dare-say it did, like enough, but its great effects were perceived in dinner. People now dine at two. So dined Addison for his last thirty years ; so, through his entire life, dined Pope, whose birth was coeval with the Revolution. Precisely as the Rebellion of 1745 arose, did people (but observe, very great

people) advance to four P. M. Philosophers, who watch
the ' semina rerum,' and the first symptoms of change,
had perceived this alteration singing in the upper air
like a coming storm some little time before. About
the year 1740, Pope complains of Lady Suffolk's
dining so late as four. Young people may bear those
things, he observed ; but as to himself, now turned of
fifty, if such things went on, if Lady Suffolk would
adopt such strange hours, he must really absent himself from Marble Hill. Lady Suffolk had a right to
please herself; he himself loved her. But, if she
would persist, all which remained for a decayed poet
was respectfully to cut his stick, and retire. Whether
Pope ever put up with four ·o'clock dinners again, I
have vainly sought to fathom. Some things advance
continuously, like a flood or a fire, which always make
an end of A, eat and digest it, before they go on to
B. Other things advance *per saltum* — they do not
silently cancer their way onwards, but lie as still as a
snake after they have made some notable conquest,
then, when unobserved, they make themselves up ' for
mischief,' and take a flying bound onwards. Thus
advanced Dinner, and by these fits got into the terri-
tory of evening. And ever as it made a motion onwards, it found the nation more civilized (else the
change could not have been effected), and co-operated
in raising them to a still higher civilization. The next
relay on that line of road, the next repeating frigate,
is Cowper in his poem on ' Conversation.' He speaks
of four o'clock as still the elegant hour for dinner —
the hour for the *lautiores* and the *lepidi homines*.
Now this might be written about 1780, or a little
earlier ; perhaps, therefore, just one generation after

Pope's Lady Suffolk. But then Cowper was living amongst the rural gentry, not in high life; yet, again, Cowper was nearly connected by blood with the eminent Whig house of Cowper, and acknowledged as a kinsman. About twenty-five years after this, we may take Oxford as a good exponent of the national advance. As a magnificent body of 'foundations,' endowed by kings, nursed by queens, and resorted to by the flower of the national youth, Oxford ought to be elegant and even splendid in her habits. Yet, on the other hand, as a grave seat of learning, and feeling the weight of her position in the commonwealth, she is slow to move; she is inert as she should be, having the functions of *resistance* assigned to her against the popular instinct (surely active enough) of *movement*. Now, in Oxford, about 1804–5, there was a general move in the dinner hour. Those colleges who dined at three, of which there were still several, now began to dine at four: those who had dined at four, now translated their hour to five. These continued good general hours till about Waterloo. After that era, six, which had been somewhat of a gala hour, was promoted to the fixed station of dinner-time in ordinary; and there perhaps it will rest through centuries. For a more festal dinner, seven, eight, nine, ten, have all been in requisition since then; but I am not aware of any man's habitually dining later than ten P. M., except in that classical case recorded by Mr. Joseph Miller, of an Irishman who must have dined much later than ten, because his servant protested, when others were enforcing the dignity of their masters by the lateness of their dinner hours, that *his* master invariably dined 'to-morrow.'

20

Were the Romans not as barbarous as our own ancestors at one time? Most certainly they were; in their primitive ages theey took their *cœna* at noon,[11] *that* was before they had laid aside their barbarism; before they shaved; it was during their barbarism, and in consequence of their barbarism, that they timed their *cœna* thus unseasonably. And this is made evident by the fact, that, so long as they erred in the hour, they erred in the attending circumstances. At this period they had no music at dinner, no festal graces, and no reposing on sofas. They sat bolt upright in chairs, and were as grave as our ancestors, as rabid, as libidinous in ogling the dishes, and doubtless as furiously in haste.

With us the revolution has been equally complex. We do not, indeed, adopt the luxurious attitude of semi-recumbency; our climate makes that less requisite; and, moreover, the Romans had no knives and forks, which could scarcely be used in that recumbent posture; they ate with their fingers from dishes already cut up — whence the peculiar force of Seneca's ' post quod non sunt lavandæ manus.' But, exactly in proportion as our dinner has advanced towards evening, have we and has *that* advanced in circumstances of elegance, of taste, of intellectual value. This by itself would be much. Infinite would be the gain for any people, that it had ceased to be brutal, animal, fleshly; ceased to regard the chief meal of the day as a ministration only to an animal necessity; that they had raised it to a higher office; associated it with social and humanizing feelings, with manners, with graces moral and intellectual: moral in the self-restraint; intellectual in the fact, notorious to all men, that the chief arenas for the *easy* display of intellectual power are at our dinner tables. But dinner has *now* even a greater function than this; as the fervor of our day's business increases, dinner is continually more needed in its office of a great *re-action*. I repeat that, at this moment, but for the daily relief of dinner, the brain of all men who mix in the strife of capitals would be unhinged and thrown off its centre.

If we should suppose the case of a nation taking three equidistant meals, all of the same material and the same quantity — all milk, for instance, all bread, or all rice — it would be impossible for Thomas Aquinas himself to say which was or was not dinner. The case would be that of the Roman *ancile* which dropped from the skies; to prevent its ever being stolen, the priests made eleven *fac-similes* of it, in order that a thief, seeing the hopelessness of distinguishing the true one, might let all alone. And the result was, that, in the next generation, nobody could point to the true one. But our dinner, the Roman *cœna*, is distinguished from the rest by far more than the hour; it is distinguished by great functions, and by still greater capacities. It is already most beneficial; *if it* saves (as I say it does) the nation from madness, it may become more so.

In saying this, I point to the lighter graces of music, and conversation *more varied*, by which the Roman *cœna* was chiefly distinguished from our dinner. I am far from agreeing with Mr. Croly, that the Roman meal was more 'intellectual' than ours. On the contrary, ours is the more intellectual by much; we have far greater knowledge, far greater means for making it such. In fact, the fault of our meal is — that it is *too*

intellectual; of too severe a character; too political;
too much tending, in many hands, to disquisition.
Reciprocation of question and answer, variety of topics,
shifting of topics, are points not sufficiently cultivated.
In all else I assent to the following passage from Mr.
Croly's eloquent 'Salathiel:' —

' If an ancient Roman could start from his slumber
into the midst of European life, he must look with
scorn on its absence of grace, elegance, and fancy.
But it is in its festivity, and most of all in its banquets,
that he would feel the incurable barbarism of the
Gothic blood.   Contrasted with the fine displays that
made the table of the Roman noble a picture, and
threw over the indulgence of appetite the colors of the
imagination, with what eyes must he contemplate the
tasteless and commonplace dress, the coarse attendants,
the meagre ornament, the want of mirth, music, and
intellectual interest — the whole heavy machinery that
converts the feast into the mere drudgery of devour-
ing!'

Thus far the reader knows already that I dissent
violently; and by looking back he will see a picture
of our ancestors at dinner, in which they rehearse the
very part in relation to ourselves, that Mr. Croly supposes all moderns to rehearse in relation to the Romans; but in the rest of the beautiful description, the
positive, though not the comparative part, we must all
concur: —

' The guests before me were fifty or sixty splendidly
dressed men' (they were in fact Titus and his staff,
then occupied with the siege of Jerusalem), ' attended
by a crowd of domestics, attired with scarcely less
splendor; for no man thought of coming to the ban-

quet in the robes of ordinary life. The embroidered couches, themselves striking objects, allowed the ease of position at once delightful in the relaxing climates of the south, and capable of combining with every grace of the human figure. At a slight distance, the table loaded with plate glittering under a profusion of lamps, and surrounded by couches thus covered by rich draperies, was like a central source of light radiating in broad shafts of every brilliant hue. The wealth of the patricians, and their intercourse with the Greeks, made them masters of the first performances of the arts. Copies of the most famous statues, and groups of sculpture in the precious metals; trophies of victories; models of temples, were mingled with vases of flowers and lighted perfumes. Finally, covering and closing all, was a vast scarlet canopy, which combined the groups beneath to the eye, and threw the whole into the form that a painter would love.'

Mr. Croly then goes on to insist on the intellectual embellishments of the Roman dinner; their variety, their grace, their adaptation to a festive purpose. The truth is, our English imagination, more profound than the Roman, is also more gloomy, less gay, less *riante*. That accounts for our want of the gorgeous *triclinium*, with its scarlet draperies, and for many other differences both to the eye and to the understanding. But both we and the Romans agree in the main point: we both discovered the true purpose which dinner might serve — 1, to throw the grace of intellectual enjoyment over an animal necessity; 2, to relieve and to meet by a benign antagonism the toil of brain incident to high forms of social life.

My object has been to point the eye to this fact; to

show uses imperfectly suspected in a recurring accident of life; to show a steady tendency to that consummation, by holding up, as in a mirror, a series of changes, corresponding to our own series with regard to the same chief meal, silently going on in a great people of antiquity.

NOTES.

Note 1. Page 198.

'*In procinct :* ' — Milton's translation (somewhere in the 'Paradise Regained') of the technical phrase ' in procinctu.'

Note 2. Page 199.

' *Geologists know not :* ' — In man the sixtieth part of six thousand years is a very venerable age. But as to a planet, as to our little earth, instead of arguing dotage, six thousand years may have scarcely carried her beyond babyhood. Some people think she is cutting her first teeth; some think her in her teens. But, seriously, it is a very interesting problem. Do the sixty centuries of our earth imply youth, maturity, or dotage ?

Note 3. Page 200.

' *Everywhere the ancients went to bed, like good boys, from seven to nine o'clock :* ' — As I am perfectly serious, I must beg the reader, who fancies any joke in all this, to consider what an immense difference it must have made to the earth, considered as a steward of her own resources — whether great nations, in a period when their resources were so feebly developed, did, or did not, for many centuries, require candles; and, I may add, fire. The five heads of human expenditure are — 1. Food; 2. Shelter; 3. Clothing; 4. Fuel; 5. Light. All were pitched on a lower scale in the Pagan era; and the two last were almost banished from ancient housekeeping. What a great relief this must have been to our good mother the earth ! who at *first* was obliged to request of her children that they would settle round the Mediterranean. She could not even afford them water, unless they would come and fetch it themselves out of a common tank or cistern.

NOTE 4. Page 201.

' *The mane salutantes :* ' — There can be no doubt that the *levees* of modern princes and ministers have been inherited from this ancient usage of Rome; one which belonged to Rome republican, as well as Rome imperial. The fiction in our modern practice is — that we wait upon the *lever*, or rising of the prince. In France, at one era, this fiction was realized : the courtiers did really attend the king's dressing. And, as to the queen, even up to the Revolution, Marie Antoinette gave audience at her toilette.

NOTE 5. Page 204.

' *Or again,* "*siccum pro biscocto, ut hodie vocamus, sumemus ?* " ' — It is odd enough that a scholar so complete as Salmasius, whom nothing ever escapes, should have overlooked so obvious an alternative as that of *siccus* in the sense of being without *opsonium* — *Scoticè*, without ' kitchen.'

NOTE 6. Page 206.

' *The whole amount of relief :* ' — From which it appears how grossly Locke (see his ' Education ') was deceived in fancying that Augustus practised any remarkable abstinence in taking only a bit of bread and a raisin or two, by way of luncheon. Augustus did no more than most people did; secondly, he abstained only upon principles of luxury with a view to dinner; and thirdly, for this dinner he never waited longer than up to four o'clock.

NOTE 7. Page 212.

' *Mansiones :* ' — The halts of the Roman legions, the stationary places of repose which divided the marches, were so called.

NOTE 8. Page 217.

' *The Everlasting Jew :* ' — The German name for what we English call the Wandering Jew. The German imagination has been most struck by the duration of the man's life, and his unhappy sanctity from death; the English, by the unrestingness of the man's life, his incapacity of repose.

Note 9. Page 223.

'*Immeasurable toga :* ' — It is very true that in the time of Augustus the *toga* had disappeared amongst the lowest plebs, and greatly Augustus was shocked at that spectacle. It is a very curious fact in itself, especially as expounding the main cause of the civil wars. Mere poverty, and the absence of bribery from Rome, whilst all popular competition for offices drooped, can alone explain this remarkable revolution of dress.

Note 10. Page 231.

'*His young English Bride :* ' — The case of an old man, or one reputed old, marrying a very girlish wife, is always too much for the gravity of history; and, rather than lose the joke, the historian prudently disguises the age, which, after all, in this case was not above fifty-four. And the very persons who insist on the late dinner as the proximate cause of death, elsewhere insinuate something more plausible, but not so decorously expressed. It is odd that this amiable prince, so memorable as having been a martyr to late dining at eleven A. M., was the same person who is so equally memorable for the noble, almost the sublime, answer about a King of France not remembering the wrongs of a Duke of Orleans.

Note 11. Page 234.

'*Took their cœna at noon :* ' — And, by the way, in order to show how little *cœna* had to do with any evening hour (though, in any age but that of our fathers, four in the afternoon would never have been thought an evening hour), the Roman *gourmands* and *bons vivants* continued through the very last ages of Rome to take their *cœna*, when more than usually sumptuous, at noon. This, indeed, all people did occasionally, just as we sometimes give a dinner even now so early as four P. M., under the name of a breakfast. Those who took their *cœna* so early as this, were said *de die cœnare* — to begin dining from high day. That line in Horace — ' Ut jugulent homines, surgunt *de nocte* latrones ' — does not mean that the robbers rise when others are going to bed, viz., at nightfall, but at midnight. For, says one of the three best scholars of this earth, *de die, de nocte*, mean from that hour which was most fully, most intensely day or night, viz., the centre, the meridian. This one fact is surely a clincher as to the question whether *cœna* meant dinner or supper.

ORTHOGRAPHIC MUTINEERS.

WITH A SPECIAL REFERENCE TO THE WORKS OF WALTER
SAVAGE LANDOR.

As we are all of us crazy when the wind sets in
some particular quarter, let not Mr. Landor be angry
·with me for suggesting that he is outrageously crazy
upon one solitary subject of spelling. It occurs to
me, as a plausible solution of his fury upon this point,
that perhaps in his earliest school-days, when it is
understood that he was exceedingly pugnacious, he
may have detested spelling, and (like Roberte the
Deville [1]) have found it more satisfactory for all parties, that when the presumptuous schoolmaster differed
from him on the spelling of a word, the question
between them should be settled by a stand-up fight.
Both parties would have the victory at times : and
if, according to Pope's expression, 'justice rul'd the
ball,' the schoolmaster (who is always a villain) would
be floored three times out of four ; no great matter
whether wrong or not upon the immediate point of
spelling discussed. It is in this way, viz., from the
irregular adjudications upon litigated spelling, which
must have arisen under such a mode of investigating
the matter, that we account for Mr. Landor's being
sometimes in the right, but too often (with regard to

[243]

long words) egregiously in the wrong. As he grew
stronger and taller, he would be coming more and
more amongst polysyllables, and more and more
would be getting the upper hand of the schoolmaster;
so that at length he would have it all his own way;
one round would decide the turn-up; and thencefor-
wards his spelling would become frightful. Now, I
myself detested spelling as much as all people ought
to do, except Continental compositors, who have extra
fees for doctoring the lame spelling of ladies and gentlemen. But, unhappily, I had no power to thump the
schoolmaster into a conviction of his own absurdities;
which, however, I greatly desired to do. Still, my
nature, powerless at that time for any active recusancy,
was strong for passive resistance; and *that* is the
hardest to conquer. I took one lesson of this infernal
art, and then declined ever to take a second; and in
fact, I never *did*. Well I remember that unique morning's experience. It was the first page of Entick's
Dictionary that I had to get by heart; a sweet sentimental task; and not, as may be fancied, the spelling
only, but the horrid attempts of this depraved Entick
to explain the supposed meaning of words that probably had none; many of these, it is my belief, Entick
himself forged. Among the strange, grim-looking
words, to whose acquaintance I was introduced on that
unhappy morning, were *abalienate* and *ablaqueation* —
most respectable words, I am fully persuaded, but so
exceedingly retired in their habits, that I never once
had the honor of meeting either of them in any book,
pamphlet, journal, whether in prose or numerous
verse, though haunting such society myself all my
life. I also formed the acquaintance, at that time, of

the word *abacus,* which, as a Latin word, I have often used, but, as an English one, I really never had occasion to spell, until this very moment. Yet, after all, what harm comes of such obstinate recusancy against orthography? I was an ' occasional conformist; ' I conformed for one morning, and never·more. But, for all that, I spell as well as my neighbors; and I can spell *ablaqueation* besides, which I suspect that some of them can *not.*

My own spelling, therefore, went right, because I was left to nature, with strict neutrality on the part of the authorities. Mr. Landor's too often went wrong, because he was thrown into a perverse channel by his continued triumphs over the prostrate schoolmaster. To toss up, as it were, for the spelling of a word, by the best of nine rounds, inevitably left the impression that chance governed all; and this accounts for the extreme capriciousness of Landor.

It is a work for a separate dictionary in quarto to record *all* the proposed revolutions in spelling through which our English blood, either at home or in America, has thrown off, at times, the surplus energy that consumed it. I conceive this to be a sort of cutaneous affection, like nettle-rash, or ringworm, through which the patient gains relief for his own nervous distraction, whilst, in fact, he does no harm to anybody : for usually he forgets his own reforms, and if *he* should not, everybody else *does.* Not to travel back into the seventeenth century, and the noble army of short-hand writers who have all made war upon orthography, for secret purposes of their own, even in the last century, and in the present, what a list of eminent rebels against the spelling-book might be called up to answer for

their wickedness at the bar of the Old Bailey, if anybody would be kind enough to make it a felony!
Cowper, for instance, too modest and too pensive to
raise upon any subject an open standard of rebellion,
yet, in quiet Olney, made a small *émeute* as to the
word 'Grecian.'· Everybody else was content with
one '*e*;' but ‾he recollecting the cornucopia of *e's*,
which Providence had thought fit to empty upon the
mother word *Greece*, deemed it shocking to disinherit
the poor child of its hereditary wealth, and wrote it,
therefore, *Greecian* throughout his Homer. Such a
modest reform the sternest old Tory could not find in
his heart to denounce. But some contagion must have
collected about this word *Greece;* for the next man,
who had much occasion to use it — viz., Mitford[2] —
who wrote that ' History of Greece ' so eccentric, and
so eccentrically praised by Lord Byron, absolutely
took to spelling like a heathen, slashed right and left
against decent old English words, until, in fact, the
whole of Entick's Dictionary (*ablaqueation* and all)
was ready to swear the peace against him. Mitford,
in course of time, slept with his fathers; his grave, I
trust, not haunted by the injured words whom he had
tomahawked; and, at this present moment, the Bishop
of St. David's reigneth in his stead. · His Lordship,
bound over to episcopal decorum, has hitherto been
sparing in his assaults upon pure old English words:
but one may trace the insurrectionary taint, passing
down from Cowper through the word *Grecian*, in
many of his Anglo-Hellenic forms. For instance, he
insists on our saying — not *Heracleidæ* and *Pelopidæ*,
as we all used to do — but *Heracleids* and *Pelopids*.
A list of my Lord's barbarities, in many other cases,

upon unprotected words, poor shivering aliens that fall into his power, when thrown upon the coast of his diocese, I had — *had*, I say, for, alas! *fuit Ilium*.

Yet, really, one is ashamed to linger on cases so mild as those, coming, as one does, in the order of atrocity, to Elphinstone, to Noah Webster, a Yankee — which word means, not an American, but that separate order of Americans, growing in Massachusetts, Rhode Island, or Connecticut, in fact, a New Englander [3] — and to the rabid Ritson. Noah would naturally have reduced us all to an antediluvian simplicity. Shem, Ham, and Japheth, probably separated in consequence of perverse varieties in spelling; so that orthographical unity might seem to him one condition for preventing national schisms. But as to the rabid Ritson, who can describe his vagaries? What great arithmetician can furnish an index to his absurdities, or what great decipherer furnish a key to the principles of these absurdities? In his very title-pages, nay, in the most obstinate of ancient technicalities, he showed his cloven foot to the astonished reader. Some of his many works were printed in *Pall-Mall* ; now, as the world is pleased to pronounce that word *Pel-Mel*, thus and no otherwise (said Ritson) it shall be spelled for ever. Whereas, on the contrary, some men would have said: The spelling is well enough, it is the public pronunciation which is wrong. This ought to be *Paul-Maul* ; or, perhaps — agreeably to the sound which we give to the *a* in such words as *what, quantity, want* — still better, and with more gallantry, *Poll-Moll*. The word Mr., again, in Ritson's reformation, must have astonished the Post-office. He insisted that this cabalistical-looking form, which might as reasonably be translated into *monster*, was a direct fraud on the national language, quite as bad as clipping the Queen's coinage. How, then, *should* it be written? Reader! reader! that you will ask such a question! *mister*, of course; and mind that you put no capital *m;* unless, indeed, you are speaking of some great gun, some mister of misters, such as Mr. Pitt of old, or perhaps a reformer of spelling. The plural, again, of such words as *romance*, *age*, *horse*, he wrote *romancees*, *agees*, *horsees;* and upon the following equitable consideration, that, inasmuch as the *e* final in the singular is mute, that is, by a general vote of the nation has been allowed to retire upon a superannuation allowance, it is abominable to call it back upon active service — like the modern Chelsea pensioners — as must be done, if it is to bear the whole weight of a separate syllable like *ces*. Consequently, if the nation and Parliament mean to keep faith, they are bound to hire a stout young *e* to run in the traces with the old original *e*, taking the whole work off his aged shoulders. Volumes would not suffice to exhaust the madness of Ritson upon this subject. And there was this peculiarity in his madness, over and above its clamorous ferocity, that being no classical scholar (a meagre self-taught Latinist, and no Grecian at all), though profound as a black-letter scholar, he cared not one straw for ethnographic relations of the words, nor unity of analogy, which are the principles that generally have governed reformers of spelling. He was an attorney, and moved constantly under the *monomaniac* idea that an action lay on behalf of the misused letters, mutes, liquids, vowels, and diphthongs, against somebody or other (John Doe, was

it, or Richard Roe ?) for trespass on any rights of theirs
which an attorney might trace, and of course for any
direct outrage upon their persons. Yet no man was
more systematically an offender in both ways than
himself ; tying up one leg of a quadruped word, and
forcing it to run upon three ; cutting off noses and
ears, if he fancied that equity required it : and living
in eternal hot water with a language which he pretended eternally to protect.

. And yet all these fellows were nothing in comparison of Mr. [4] Pinkerton. The most of these men did
but ruin the national *spelling* ; but Pinkerton — the
monster Pinkerton — proposed a revolution which
would have left us nothing to spell. It is almost in-
credible — if a book regularly printed and published,
bought and sold, did not remain to attest the fact —
that this horrid barbarian seriously proposed, as a
glorious discovery for refining our language, the following plan. All people were content with the compass of the English language : its range of expression
was equal to anything ; but, unfortunately, as compared with the sweet, orchestral languages of the
south — Spanish the stately, and Italian the lovely —
it wanted rhythmus and melody. Clearly, then, the
one supplementary grace, which it remained for modern art to give, is that every one should add at discretion *o* and *a*, *ino* and *ano*, to the end of the English
words. The language, in its old days, should be
taught *struttare struttissimamente*. As a specimen,
Mr. Pinkerton favored us with his own version of a
famous passage in Addison, viz., ' The Vision of
Mirza.' The passage, which begins thus, ' As I sat
on the top of a rock,' being translated into, ' As I satto

on the toppino of a rocko,' &c. But *luckilissime* this *proposalio* of the *absurdissimo Pinkertonio*[5] was not adoptado by *anybody-ini whatever-ano.*

Mr. Landor is more learned, and probably more consistent in his assaults upon the established spelling than most of these elder reformers. But *that* does not make him either learned enough or consistent enough. He never ascends into Anglo-Saxon, or the many cognate languages of the Teutonic family, which is indispensable to a searching inquest upon our language; he does not put forward in this direction even the slender qualifications of Horne Tooke. But Greek and Latin are quite unequal, when disjoined from the elder wheels in our etymological system, to the working of the total machinery of the English language. Mr. Landor proceeds upon no fixed principles in his changes. Sometimes it is on the principle of internal analogy within itself, that he would distort or retrotort the language; sometimes on the principle of external analogy with its roots; sometimes on the principle of euphony, or of metrical convenience. Even within such principles he is not uniform. All well-built English scholars, for instance, know that the word *feälty* cannot be made into a dissyllable: trisyllabic it ever was[6] with the elder poets — Spenser, Milton, &c.; and so it is amongst all the modern poets who have taken any pains with their English studies: *e. g.*

> 'The eagle, lord of land and sea,
> Stoop'd — down to pay him fe-al-ty.'

It is dreadful to hear a man say *feal-ty* in any case; but here it is luckily impossible. Now, Mr. Landor generally is correct, and trisects the word; but once,

at least, he bisects it.   I complain, besides, that Mr.
Landor, in urging the authority of Milton for ortho-
graphic innovations, does not always distinguish as to
Milton's motives.   It is true, as he contends, that, in
some instances, Milton reformed the spelling in obedi-
ence to the Italian precedent: and certainly without
blame; as in *sovran, sdeign,* which ought not to be
printed (as it is) with an elision before the *s*, as if
short for disdain; but in other instances Milton's motive had no reference to etymology.   Sometimes it was
this.   In Milton's day the modern use of italics was
nearly unknown.   Everybody is aware that, in our
authorized version of the Bible, published in Milton's
infancy, italics are never once used for the purpose of
emphasis — but exclusively to indicate such words or
auxiliary forms as, though implied and *virtually* present in the original, are not textually expressed, but
must be so in English, from the different genius of
the language.[7]   Now, this want of a proper technical
resource amongst the compositors of the age, for indicating a peculiar stress upon the word, evidently drove
Milton into some perplexity for a compensatory contri-
vance.   It was unusually requisite for *him*, with his
elaborate metrical system and his divine ear, to have
an art for throwing attention upon his accents, and
upon his muffling of accents.   When, for instance, he
wishes to direct a bright jet of emphasis upon the pos-
sessive pronoun *their*, he writes it as we now write it.
But, when he wishes to take off the accent, he writes
it *thir*.[8]   Like Ritson, he writes *therefor* and *wherefor*
without the final *e;* not regarding the analogy, but
singly the metrical quantity: for it was shocking to
his classical feeling that a sound so short to the ear

should be represented to the eye by so long a combination as *fore;* and the more so, because uneducated people did then, and do now, often equilibrate the accent between the two syllables, or rather make the *quantity* long in both syllables, whilst giving an overbalance of the *accent* to the last. The ' Paradise Lost,' being printed during Milton's blindness, did not receive the full and consistent benefit of his spelling reforms, which (as I have contended) certainly arose partly in the imperfections of typography at that æra; but such changes as had happened most to impress his ear with a sense of their importance, he took a special trouble, even under all the disadvantages of his darkness, to have rigorously adopted. He must have astonished the compositors, though not quite so much as the tiger-cat Ritson or the Mr. (viz. monster) Pinkerton — each after *his* kind — astonished *their* compositors.

But the caprice of Mr. Landor is shown most of all upon Greek names. *Nous autres* say ' Aristotle,' and are quite content with it until we migrate into some extra-superfine world; but this title will not do for *him :* ' Aristotles' it must be. And why so? Because, answers the Landor, if once I consent to say Aristotle, then I am pledged to go the whole hog; and perhaps the next man I meet is Empedocles, whom, in that case, I must call Empedocle. Well, do so. *Call* him Empedocle; it will not break his back, which seems broad enough. But, now, mark the contradictions in which Mr. Landor is soon landed. He says, as everybody says, Terence, and not Terentius, Horace, and not Horatius; but he must leave off such horrid practices, because he dares not call Lucretius by the analogous name of Lucrece, since *that* would be putting a she instead of a he; nor Propertius by the name of Properce, because *that* would be speaking French instead of English. Next he says, and continually he says, Virgil for Virgilius. But, on that principle, he ought to say Valer for Valerius; and yet again he ought not: because as he says Tully and not Tull for Tullius, so also is he bound, in Christian equity, to say Valery for Valer; but he cannot say either Valer or Valery. So here we are in a mess. Thirdly, I charge him with saying Ovid for Ovidius: which *I* do, which everybody does, but which *he* must not do: for if he means to persist in *that*, then, upon his own argument from analogy, he must call Didius Julianus by the shocking name of *Did*, which is the same thing as Tit — since T is D soft. Did was a very great man indeed, and for a very short time indeed. Probably Did was the only man that ever bade for an empire, and no mistake, at a public auction. Think of Did's bidding for the Roman empire; nay, think also of Did's having the lot actually knocked down to him; and of Did's going home to dinner with the lot in his pocket. It makes one perspire to think that, if the reader or myself had been living at that time, and had been prompted by some whim within us to bid against him — that is, he or I — should actually have come down to posterity by the abominable name of Anti-Did. All of us in England say Livy when speaking of the great historian, not Livius. Yet Livius Andronicus it would be impossible to indulge with that brotherly name of Livy. Marcus Antonius is called — not by Shakspeare only, but by all the world — Mark Antony; but who is it that ever called Marcus Brutus by the affectionate name of Mark Brute? 'Keep your distance,' we say to that very doubtful brute, ' and expect no pet names from us.' Finally, apply the principle of abbreviation, involved in the names of Pliny, Livy, Tully, all substituting *y* for *ius*, to Marius — that grimmest of grim visions that rises up to us from the phantasmagoria of Roman history. Figure to yourself, reader, that truculent face, trenched and scarred with hostile swords, carrying thunder in its ominous eye-brows, and frightening armies a mile off with its scowl, being saluted by the tenderest of feminine names, as ' My Mary.'

Not only, therefore, is Mr. Landor inconsistent in these innovations, but the innovations themselves, supposing them all harmonized and established, would but plough up the landmarks of old hereditary feelings. We learn oftentimes, by a man's bearing a good-natured sobriquet amongst his comrades, that he is a kind-hearted, social creature, popular with them all! And it is an illustration of the same tendency, that the scale of popularity for the classical authors amongst our fathers, is registered tolerably well, in a gross general way, by the difference between having and *not* having a familiar name. If we except the first Cæsar, the mighty Caius Julius, who was too majestic to invite familiarity, though too gracious to have repelled it, there is no author whom our forefathers loved, but has won a sort of Christian name in the land. Homer, and Hesiod, and Pindar, we all say; we cancel the alien *us* ; but we never say Theocrit for Theocritus. Anacreon remains rigidly Grecian marble; but *that* is only because his name is not of a plastic form — else everybody loves the sad old fellow. The same bar to familiarity existed in the names of the tragic poets, except perhaps for Æschylus; who, however, like Cæsar, is too awful for a caressing name. But Roman names were, generally, more flexible. Livy and Sallust have ever been favorites with men; Livy with everybody; Sallust, in a degree that may be called extravagant, with many celebrated Frenchmen, as the President des Brosses, and in our own days with M. Lerminier, a most eloquent and original writer (' *Etudes Historiques* '); and two centuries ago, with the greatest of men, John Milton, in a degree that seems to me absolutely mysterious. These writers are baptized into our society — have gained a settlement in our parish: when you call a man Jack, and not Mr. John, it's plain you like him. But, as to the gloomy Tacitus, our fathers liked him not. He was too vinegar a fellow for them; nothing hearty or genial about him; he thought ill of everybody; and we all suspect that, for those times, he was perhaps the worst of the bunch himself. Accordingly, this Tacitus, because he remained so perfectly tacit for our jolly old forefathers' ears, never slipped into the name Tacit for their mouths; nor ever will, I predict, for the mouths of posterity. Coming to the Roman poets, I must grant that three great ones, viz., Lucretius, Statius, and Valerius Flaccus, have not been complimented with the freedom of our city, as they should have been, in a gold box. I regret, also, the ill fortune, in this respect, of Catullus, if he was really the author of that grand headlong dithyrambic, the Atys: he certainly ought to have been ennobled by the title of Catull. Looking to very much of his writings, much more I regret the case of Plautus; and I am sure that if her Majesty would warrant his bearing the name and arms of *Plaut* in all time coming, it would gratify many of us. As to the rest, or those that anybody cares about, Horace, Virgil, Ovid, Lucan, Martial, Claudian, all have been raised to the peerage. Ovid was the great poetic favorite of Milton ; and not without a philosophic ground : his festal gayety, and the brilliant velocity of his *aurora borealis* intellect, forming a deep natural equipoise to the mighty gloom and solemn planetary movement in the mind of the other; like the wedding of male and female counterparts. Ovid was, therefore, rightly Milton's favorite. But the favorite of all the world is Horace. Were there ten peerages, were there three blue ribbons, vacant, he ought to have them all.

Besides, if Mr. Landor could issue decrees, and even harmonize his decrees for reforming our Anglo-Grecian spelling — decrees which no Council of Trent could execute, without first rebuilding the Holy Office of the Inquisition — still there would be little accomplished. The names of all continental Europe are often in confusion, from different causes, when Anglicized : German names are rarely spelled rightly by the *laity* of our isle : Polish and Hungarian never. Many foreign towns have in England what botanists would call *trivial* names ; Leghorn, for instance, Florence, Madrid, Lisbon, Vienna, Munich, Antwerp, Brussels, the Hague, — all unintelligible names to the savage Continental native. Then, if Mr. Landor reads as much of Anglo-Indian books as I do, he must be aware that, for many years back, they have all been at sixes and sevens ; so that now most Hindoo words are in masquerade, and we shall soon require *English* pundits in Leadenhall Street.[9] How does he like, for instance, *Sipahee*, the

modern form for *Sepoy* ? or *Tepheen* for *Tiffin* ? At
this rate of metamorphosis, absorbing even the consecrated names of social meals, we shall soon cease to
understand what that *disjune* was which his sacred
Majesty graciously accepted at Tillietudlem. But even
elder forms of oriental speech are as little harmonized
in Christendom. A few leagues of travelling make
the Hebrew unintelligible to us; and the Bible becomes a Delphic mystery to Englishmen amongst the
countrymen of Luther. Solomon is there called Sala-
mo; Samson is called Simson, though probably he
never published an edition of Euclid. Nay, even in
this native isle of ours, you may be at cross purposes
on the Bible with your own brother. I am, myself,
next door neighbor to Westmoreland, being a Lancashire man; and; one day, I was talking with a
Westmoreland farmer, whom, of course, I ought to
have understood very well; but I had no chance with
him : for I could not make out who that *No* was, concerning *whom* or concerning *which*, he persisted in
talking. It seemed to me, from the context, that *No*
must be a man, and by no means a chair ; but so very
negative a name, you perceive, furnished no positive
hints for solving the problem. I said as much to the
farmer, who stared in stupefaction. ‘What,’ cried
he, ‘ did a far-larn’d man, like you, fresh from Oxford,
never hear of *No*, an old gentleman that should have
been drowned, but was *not*, when all his folk were
drowned ? ’ ‘ Never, so help me Jupiter,’ was my
reply : ‘ never heard of him to this hour, any more
than of *Yes*, an old gentleman that should have been
hanged, but was *not*, when all his folk were hanged.
Populous No — I had read of in the Prophets ; but
22

that was *not* an old gentleman.' It turned out that the farmer and all his compatriots in bonny Martindale had been taught at the parish school to rob the Patriarch Noah of one clear moiety appertaining in fee simple to that ancient name. But afterwards I found that the farmer was not so entirely absurd as he had seemed. The Septuagint, indeed, is clearly against him; for *there,* as plain as a pikestaff, the farmer might have read *Nωε.* But, on the other hand, Pope, not quite so great a scholar as he was a poet, yet still a fair one, *always* made Noah into a monosyllable; and that seems to argue an old English usage; though I really believe Pope's reason for adhering to such an absurdity was with a prospective view to the rhymes *blow,* or *row,* or *stow* (an important idea to the Ark), which struck him as *likely* words, in case of any call for writing about Noah.

The long and the short of it is — that the whole world lies in heresy or schism on the subject of orthography. All climates alike groan under heterography. It is absolutely of no use to begin with one's own grandmother in such labors of reformation. It is toil thrown away : and as nearly hopeless a task as the proverb insinuates that it is to attempt a reformation in that old lady's mode of eating eggs. She laughs at one. She has a vain conceit that she is able, out of her own proper resources, to do both, viz., the spelling and the eating of the eggs. And all that remains for philosophers, like Mr. Landor and myself, is — to turn away in sorrow rather than in anger, dropping a silent tear for the poor old lady's infatuation.

NOTES.

Note 1. Page 243.

' *Roberte the Deville :* ' — See the old metrical romance of that name : it belongs to the fourteenth century, and was printed some thirty years ago, with wood engravings of the illuminations. Roberte, however, took the liberty of murdering *his* schoolmaster. But could he well do less? Being a reigning Duke's son, and after the rebellious schoolmaster had said —

> ' *Sir, ye bee too bolde :*
> *And therewith tooke a rodde hym for to chaste.*'

Upon which the meek Robin, without using any bad language as the schoolmaster had done, simply took out a long dagger ' *hym for to chaste,*' which he did effectually. The schoolmaster gave no bad language after that.

Note 2. Page 246.

Mitford, who was the brother of a man better known than himself to the public eye, viz., Lord Redesdale, may be considered a very unfortunate author. His work upon Greece, which Lord Byron celebrated for its ' wrath and its partiality, really had those merits : choleric it was in excess, and as entirely partial, as nearly perfect in its injustice, as human infirmity would allow. Nothing is truly perfect in this shocking world; absolute injustice, alas ! the perfection of wrong, must not be looked for until we reach some high Platonic form of polity. Then shall we revel and bask in a vertical sun of iniquity. Meantime, I *will* say — that to satisfy all bilious and unreasonable men, a better historian of Greece, than Mitford, could not be fancied. And yet, at the very moment when he was stepping into his harvest

[259]

of popularity, down comes one of those omnivorous Germans that, by reading everything and a trifle besides, contrive to throw really learned men — and perhaps better thinkers than themseves — into the shade. ·Ottfried Mueller, with other archæologists and travellers into Hellas, gave new aspects to the very purposes of Grecian history. Do you hear, reader? not new answers, but new questions And Mitford, that was gradually displacing the unlearned Gillies, &c., was himself displaced by those who intrigued with Germany. His other work on ' the Harmony of Language,' though one of the many that attempted, and the few that accomplished, the distinction between accent and quantity, or learnedly appreciated the metrical science of Milton, was yet, in my hearing, pronounced utterly intelligible by the best *practical* commentator on Milton, viz., the best reproducer of his exquisite effects in blank verse, that any generation since Milton has been able to show. Mr. Mitford was one of the many accomplished scholars that are ill-used. Had he possessed the splendid powers of the Landor, he would have raised á clatter on the armor of modern society, such as Samson threatened to the giant Harapha. For, in many respects, he resembled the Landor : he had much of his learning — he had the same extensive access to books and influential circles in great cities — the same gloomy disdain of popular falsehoods or commonplaces — and the same disposition to run a-muck against all nations, languages, and spelling-books.

Note 3. Page 247.

' *In fact, a New Englander.*' — This explanation, upon a matter familiar to the well-informed, it is proper to repeat occasionally, because we English exceedingly perplex and confound the Americans by calling, for instance, a Virginian or a Kentuck by the name of Yankee, whilst that term was originally introduced as antithetic to these more southern States.

Note 4. Page 249.

Pinkerton published one of his earliest volumes, under this title — ' Rimes, by Mr. Pinkerton,' not having the fear of Ritson before his eyes And, for once, we have reason 'to thank Ritson for his remark — that the form Mr. might just as well be read

Monster. Pinkerton in this point was a perfect monster. As to the word *Rimes,* instead of *Rhymes,* he had something to stand upon; the Greek *rythmos* was certainly the remote fountain; but the proximate fountain must have been the Italian *rima.*

Note 5. Page 250.

. The most extravagant of all experiments on language is brought forward in the ' *Letters of Literature,* by Robert Heron.' But Robert Heron is a *pseudonyme* for John Pinkerton ; and I have been told that Pinkerton's motive for assuming it was — because *Heron* had been the maiden name of his mother. Poor lady, she would have stared to find herself, in old age, transformed into Mistressina Heronilla. What most amuses one in pursuing the steps of such an attempt at refinement, is its reception by ' Jack ' in the navy.

Note 6. Page 250.

' *It ever was* ' — and, of course, being (as there is no need to tell Mr. Landor) a form obtained by contraction from *fidelitas.*

Note 7. Page 251.

Of this a ludicrous illustration is mentioned by the writer once known to the public as *Trinity Jones.* Some young clergyman, unacquainted with the technical use of italics by the original compositors of James the First's Bible, on coming to the 27th verse, chap. xiii. of 1st Kings, ' And he ' (viz., the old prophet of Bethel) ' spake to his sons, saying, Saddle me the ass. And they saddled *him ;* ' (where the italic *him* simply meant that this word was involved, but not expressed, in the original,) read it, ' And they saddled HIM ; ' as though these undutiful sons, instead of saddling the donkey, had saddled the old prophet. In fact, the old gentleman's directions are not quite without an opening for a filial misconception, if the reader examines them as closely as *I* examine words.

Note 8. Page 251.

He uses this and similar artifices, in fact, as the damper in a modern piano-forte, for modify'ng the swell of the intonation.

NOTE 9.   Page 256.

The reasons for this anarchy in the naturalization of Eastern words are to be sought in three causes : 1. In national rivalships : French travellers in India, like Jacquemont, &c., as they will not adopt our English First Meridian, will not, of course, adopt our English spelling. In one of Paul Richter's novels a man assumes the First Meridian to lie generally, not through Greenwich, but through his own skull, and always through his own study. I have myself long suspected the Magnetic Pole to lie under a friend's wine-cellar, from the vibrating movement which I have remarked constantly going on in his cluster of keys towards that particular point. Really, the French, like Sir Anthony Absolute, must ' get an atmosphere of their own,' such is their hatred to holding anything in common with us 2. They are to be sought in local *Indian* differences of pronunciation. 3. In the variety of our own British population — soldiers, missionaries, merchants, who are unlearned or half-learned — scholars, really learned, but often fantastically learned, and lastly (as you may swear) young ladies — anxious, above all things, to mystify us outside barbarians.

SORTILEGE ON BEHALF OF THE GLASGOW ATHENÆUM.

Suddenly, about the middle of February, I received a request for some contribution of my own proper writing to a meditated Album of the Glasgow Athenæum. What was to be done? The 13th of the month had already dawned before the request reached me; 'return of post' was the sharp limitation notified within which my communication must revolve; whilst the request itself was dated Feb. 10: so that already three 'returns of post' had finished their brief career on earth. I am not one of those people who, in respect to bread, insist on the discretionary allowance of Paris; but, in respect to time, I *do*. Positively, for all efforts of thought I must have time *à discrétion*. In this case, now, all *discretion* was out of the question; a mounted jockey, in the *melée* of a Newmarket start, might as well demand time for meditation on the philosophy of racing. There was clearly no resource available but one; and it was this: — In my study I have a bath, large enough to swim in, provided the swimmer, not being an ambitious man, is content with going a-head to the extent of six inches at the utmost. This bath, having been superseded (as regards its original purpose) by another mode of bathing, has yielded a secondary service to me as a reservoir for my

MSS. Filled to the brim it is by papers of all sorts and sizes. "Every paper written *by* me, *to* me, *for* me, *of* or *concerning* me, and, finally, *against* me, is to be found, after an impossible search, in this capacious repertory. Those papers, by the way, that come under the last (or hostile) subdivision, are chiefly composed by shoemakers and tailors — an affectionate class of men, who stick by one to the last like pitch-plasters. One admires this fidelity; but it shows itself too often in waspishness, and all the little nervous irritabilities of attachment too ardent. They are wretched if they do not continually hear what one is 'about,' what one is 'up to,' and which way one is going to travel. Me, because I am a political economist, they plague for my private opinions on the currency, especially on that part of it which consists in bills at two years after date; and they always want an answer by return of post. What the deuce! one can't answer *every*body by return of post. Now, from this reservoir I resolved to draw some paper for the use of the Athenæum. It was my fixed determination that this Institution should receive full justice, so far as human precautions could secure it. Four dips into the bath I decreed that the Athenæum should have; whereas an individual man, however hyperbolically illustrious, could have had but one. On the other hand, the Athenæum must really content itself with what fortune might send, and not murmur at me as if I had been playing with loaded dice. To cut off all pretence for this allegation, I requested the presence of three young ladies, haters of everything unfair, as female attorneys, to watch the proceedings on behalf of the Athenæum, to see that the dipping went on correctly, and also to advise the

court in case of any difficulties arising. At 6 P. M.
all was reported right for starting in my study. The
bath had been brilliantly illuminated from above, so
that no tricks *could* be played in that quarter; and the
young man who was to execute the dips had finished
dressing in a new potato sack, with holes cut through
the bottom for his legs. Now, as the sack was tied
with distressing tightness about his throat, leaving
only a loop-hole for his right arm to play freely, it is
clear that, however sincerely fraudulent in his intentions, and in possible collusion with myself, he could
not assist me by secreting any papers about his person,
or by any other knavery that we might wish to perpe-
trate. The young ladies having taken their seats in
stations admirably chosen for overlooking the movements of the young man and myself, the proceedings
opened. The inaugural step was made in a neat
speech from myself, complaining that I was the object
of unjust suspicions, and endeavoring to re-establish
my character for absolute purity of intentions; but, I
regret to say, ineffectually. This angered me, and I
declared with some warmth, that in the bath, but
whereabouts I could not guess, there lay a particular
paper which I valued as equal to the half of my kingdom; 'but for all that,' I went on, 'if our hon. friend
in the potato sack should chance to haul up this very
paper, I am resolved to stand by the event, yes, in that
case, to the half of my kingdom I will express my interest in the Institution. Should even *that* prize be
drawn, out of this house it shall pack off to Glasgow
this very night.' Upon this, the leader of the attorneys, whom, out of honor to Shakspeare, I may as
well call Portia, chilled my enthusiasm disagreeably by

23

saying — ' There was no occasion for any extra zeal on
my part in such an event, since, as to packing out of
this house to Glasgow, she and her learned sisters
would take good care that it *did ;* ' — in fact, *I* was to
have no merit whatever I did.   Upon this, by way of
driving away the melancholy caused by the obstinate
prejudice of the attorneys, I called for a glass of wine,
and, turning to the west, I drank the health of the
Athenæum, under the allegoric idea of a young lady
about to come of age and enter upon the enjoyment
of her estates.   ' Here's to your prosperity, my dear
lass,' I said ; ' you're very young — but that's a fault
which, according to the old Greek adage, is mending
every day ; and I'm sure you'll always continue as
amiable as you are now towards strangers in distress
for books and journals.   Never grow churlish, my
dear, as some of your sex are ' (saying which, I looked
savagely at Portia).   And then, I made the signal to
the young man for getting to work — Portia's eyes, as
I noticed privately, brightening like a hawk's.   ' *Prepare to dip !*' I called aloud ; and soon after — ' *Dip !* '
At the ' *prepare*,' Potato-sack went on his right knee
(his face being at right angles to the bath) ; at the
' Dip !' he plunged his right arm into the billowy
ocean of papers.   For one minute he worked amongst
them as if he had been pulling an oar ; and then, at
the peremptory order ' *Haul up !*' he raised aloft in
air, like Brutus refulgent from the stroke of Cæsar,
his booty.   It was handed, of course, to the attorneys, who showed a little female curiosity at first, for
it was a letter with the seal as yet unbroken, and
might prove to be some old love-letter of my writing,
recently sent back to me by the Dead-Letter Office.

It still looked fresh and blooming. So, if there was no prize for Glasgow, there might still be an interesting secret for the benefit of the attorneys. What it was, and what each successive haul netted, I will register under the corresponding numbers.

No. 1. — This was a dinner invitation for the 15th of February, which I had neglected to open. It was, as bill-brokers say, 'coming to maturity,' but luckily not *past due* (in which case you have but a poor remedy), for, though twenty days after date, it had still two days to run before it could be presented for payment. A debate arose with the attorneys — Whether this might not do for the *Album*, in default of any better haul? I argued, for the affirmative, — that, although a dinner invitation cannot in reason be looked to for very showy writing, its motto being *Esse quam videri* (which is good Latin for — *To eat rather than make believe to eat*, as at ball suppers or Barmecide banquets), yet, put the case that I should send this invitation to the Athenæum, accompanied with a power-of-attorney to eat the dinner in my stead — might not *that* solid bonus as an enclosure weigh down the levity of the letter considered as a contribution to the *Album*,, and take off the edge of the Athenæum's displeasure? Portia argued *contra* — that such a thing was impossible; because the Athenæum had two thousand mouths, and would therefore require two thousand dinners; — an argument which I admitted to be showy, but, legally speaking, hardly tenable: because the Athenæum had power to appoint a plenipotentiary — some man of immense calibre — to eat the dinner, as representative of the collective two thousand. Portia parried this objection by replying, that if the invita-

.tion had been to a ball there might be something in
what I. said; but as to a mere dinner, and full fifty
miles to travel for it from Glasgow, the plenipotentiary (whatever might be his calibre) would decline to
work so hard for such a trifle. 'Trifle!' I replied —
'But, with submission, a dinner twenty-two days after
date of invitation is not likely to prove a trifle. This,
however is, always the way in which young ladies,
whether attorneys or not, treat the subject of dinner.
And as to the fifty miles, the plenipotentiary could go
in an hour.' 'How?' said Portia, sternly. ' Per
rail,' I replied with equal sternness. What there was
to laugh at, I don't see; but at this hot skirmish between me and Portia concerning that rather visionary
person the plenipotentiary, and what he might choose
to do in certain remote contingencies, and especially
when the gross reality of '*per rail*' came into collision
with his aerial essence, Potato-sack began to laugh so
immoderately, that I was obliged to pull him up by
giving the word rather imperiously — '*Prepare to
dip!*' Before he could obey, I was myself pulled up
by Portia, with a triumph in her eye that alarmed me.
She and her sister attorneys had been examining the
dinner invitation — 'and,' said Portia maliciously to
me, 'it's quite correct — as you observe there are two
days good to the dinner hour on the 15th; " *Prepare
to dine!*" is the signal that *should* be flying at this
moment, and in two days more " *Dine!*" — only, by
misfortune, the letter is in the wrong year — it is four
years old!' Oh! fancy the horror of this; since,
besides the mortification from Portia's victory, I had
perhaps narrowly escaped an indictment from the
plenipotentiary for sending him what might *now* be

considered a swindle. I hurried to cover my confusion, by issuing the two orders ' *Prepare to dip !* ' and '*Dip !* ' almost in the same breath. No. 1, after all the waste of legal learning upon it, had suddenly burst like an air-bubble; and the greater stress of expectation, therefore, had now settled on No. 2. With considerable trepidation of voice, I gave the final order — '*Haul up !* '

No. 2. — It is disagreeable to mention that this haul brought up — 'a dun.' Disgust was written upon every countenance ; and I fear that suspicion began to thicken upon myself — as having possibly (from my personal experience in these waters) indicated to our young friend where to dredge for duns with most chance of success. But I protest fervently my innocence. It is true that I had myself long remarked that part of the channel to be dangerously infested with duns. In searching for literary or philosophic papers, it would often happen for an hour together that I brought up little else than variegated specimens of the dun. And one vast bank there was, which I called the Goodwin Sands, because nothing within the memory of man was ever known to be hauled up from it except eternal specimens of the dun — some gray with antiquity, some of a neutral tint, some green and lively. With grief it was that I had seen our dipper shoaling his water towards that dangerous neighborhood. But what could I do ? If I had warned him off, Portia would have been sure to fancy that there was some great oyster-bed or pearl-fishery in that region ; and all I should have effected by my honesty would have been a general conviction of my treachery. I therefore became as anxious as everybody else for

No. 3, which might set all to rights — *might*, but slight were my hopes that it *would*, when I saw in what direction the dipper's arm was working. Exactly below that very spot where he had dipped, lay, as stationary as if he had been anchored, a huge and ferocious dun of great antiquity. Age had not at all softened the atrocious expression of his countenance, but rather aided it by endowing him with a tawny hue. The size of this monster was enormous, nearly two square feet; and I fancied at times that, in spite of his extreme old age, he had not done growing. I knew him but too well ; because whenever I happened to search in that region of the bath, let me be seeking what I would, and let me miss what I might, always I was sure to haul up *him* whom I never wanted to see again. Sometimes I even found him basking on the very summit of the papers ; and I conceived an idea, which may be a mere fancy, that he came up for air in particular states of the atmosphere. At present he was *not* basking on the surface: better for the Athenæum if he *had:* for then the young man would have been cautious. Not being above, he was certainly below, and underneath the very centre of the dipper's plunge. Unable to control my feelings, I cried out — ' Bear away to the right ! ' But Portia protested with energy against this intermeddling of mine, as perfidy too obvious. ' Well,' I said, ' have it your own way: you'll see what will happen.'

No. 3. — This, it is needless to say, turned out the horrid old shark, as I had long christened him : I knew his vast proportions, and his bilious aspect, the moment that the hauling up commenced, which in *his* case occupied some time. Portia was the more angry, because she had thrown away her right to *express* any anger by neutralizing my judicious interference. She grew even more angry, because I, though sorry for the Athenæum, really could not help laughing when I saw the truculent old wretch expanding his huge dimensions — all umbered by time and ill-temper — under the eyes of the wondering young ladies; so mighty was the contrast between this sallow behemoth and a rose-colored little billet of their own. By the way, No. 2 had been a specimen of the dulcet dun, breathing only zephyrs of request and persuasion; but this No. 3 was a specimen of the polar opposite — the dun horrific and Gorgonian — blowing great guns of menace. As ideal specimens in their several classes, might they not have a value for the *museum* of the Athenæum, if it *has* one, or even for the *Album*? This was *my* suggestion, but overruled, like everything else that I proposed; and on the ground that Glasgow had too vast a conservatory of duns, native and indigenous, to need any exotic specimens. This settled, we hurried to the next dip, which, being by contract the last, made us all nervous.

No. 4. — This, alas! turned out a lecture addressed to myself by an ultra-moral friend; a lecture on procrastination; and not badly written. I feared that something of the sort was coming; for, at the moment of dipping, I called out to the dipper — ' Starboard your helm! you're going smack upon the Goodwins: in thirty seconds you'll founder.' Upon this, in an agony of fright, the dipper forged off, but evidently quite unaware that vast spurs stretched off from the Goodwins — shoals and sand-banks — where it was mere destruction to sail without a special knowledge

of the soundings. He had run upon an ethical sand-
bank. 'Yet, after all, since this is to be the last dip,'
said Portia, 'if the lecture is well written, might it
not be acceptable to the Athenæum?' 'Possibly,' I
replied; 'but it is too personal, besides being founded
in error from first to last. I could not allow myself
to be advertised in a book as a procrastinator on principle, unless the Athenæum would add a postscript
under its official seal, expressing entire disbelief of the
accusation; which I have private reasons for thinking
that the Athenæum may decline to do.'

'Well, then,' said Portia, 'as you wilfully rob the
Athenæum of No. 4, which by contract is the un-
doubted property of that body, in fee simple and not
in fee conditional,' (mark Portia's learning as an attorney,) 'then you are bound to give us a 5th dip;
particularly as you've been so treacherous all along.'
Tears rushed to my eyes at this most unjust assumption. In agonizing tones I cried out, 'Potato-sack!
my friend Potato-sack! will you quietly listen to this
charge upon me, that am as innocent as the child un-
born? If it is a crime in me to know, and in you *not*
to know, where the Goodwins lie, why then, let you
and me sheer off to the other side of the room, and
let Portia try if *she* can do better. I allow her motion
for a fresh trial. I grant a 5th dip: and the more
readily, because it is an old saying — that there is
luck in odd numbers: *numero dues impare gaudet;* —
only I must request of Portio to be the dipper on this
final occasion.' All the three attorneys blushed a
rosy red on this unexpected summons. It was one
thing to criticize, but quite another thing to undertake
the performance; and the fair attorneys trembled for

their professional reputation. Secretly, however, I whispered to Potato-sack, 'You'll see now, such is female address, that whatever sort of monster they haul up, they'll swear it's a great prize, and contrive to extract some use from it that may seem to justify this application for a new trial.'

No. 5. — Awful and thrilling were the doubts, fears, expectations of us all, when Portia ' prepared to dip,' and secondly ' dipped.' She shifted her hand, and ' ploitered' amongst the papers for full five minutes. I winked at this in consideration of past misfortunes; but, strictly speaking, she had no right to ' ploiter' for more than one minute. She contended that she knew, by intuition, the sort of paper upon which 'duns' were written; and whatever else might come up, she was resolved it should not be a dun. ' Don't be too sure,' I said; and, at last, when she seemed to have settled her choice, I called out the usual word of command, '*Haul up.*'

' What is it?' we said; ' what's the prize?' we demanded, all rushing up to Portia. Guess, reader; — it was a sheet of blank paper!

I, for my part, was afraid either to laugh or to cry. I really felt for Portia, and, at the same time, for the Athenæum. Yet I had a monstrous desire to laugh horribly. But, bless you, reader! there was no call for pity to Portia. With the utmost coolness she said, 'Oh! here is *carte blanche* for receiving your latest thoughts. This is the paper on which you are to write an essay for the Athenæum; and thus we are providentially enabled to assure our client the Athenæum of something expressly manufactured for the occasion, and not an old wreck from the Goodwins.

Fortune loves the Athenæum; and her four blanks at starting were only meant to tease that Institution, and to enhance the value of her final favor.' 'Ah, indeed!' I said in an under tone, ' *meant to tease !* there are other ladies who understand that little science beside Fortune !' However, there is no disobeying the commands of Portia; so I sate down to write a paper on ASTROLOGY. But, before beginning, I looked at Potato-sack, saying only, ' You see : I·told you what would happen.'

ASTROLOGY.

As my contribution to their *Album*, I will beg the Athenæum·to accept a single thought on this much-injured subject. Astrology I greatly respect; but it is singular that my respect for the science arose out of my contempt for its professors, — not exactly as a direct logical consequence, but as a casual suggestion from that contempt. I believe in astrology, but not in astrologers; as to *them* I am an incorrigible infidel. First, let me state the occasion upon which my astrological thought arose ; and then, secondly, the thought itself.

When about seventeen years old, I was wandering as a pedestrian tourist in North Wales. For some little time, the centre of my ramblings (upon which I still revolved from all my excursions, whether elliptical, circular, or zig-zag) was Llangollen in Denbighshire, or else Rhuabon, not more than a few miles distant. One morning I was told by a young married woman, at whose cottage I had received some kind

hospitalities, that an astrologer lived in the neighborhood. 'What might be his name?' Very good English it was that my young hostess had hitherto spoken;
and yet, in this instance, she chose to answer me in
Welsh. *Mochinahante*, was her brief reply. I dare
say that my spelling of the word will not stand Welsh
criticism; but what can you expect from a man's first
attempt at Welsh orthography? I am sure that my
written word reflects the *vocal* word which I heard —
provided you pronounce the *ch* as a Celtic guttural;
and I can swear to three letters out of the twelve, viz.
the first, the tenth, and the eleventh, as rigorously correct. Pretty well, I think, *that*, for a mere beginner
— only seventy-five per cent. by possibility wrong!
But what did *Mochinahante* mean? For a man might
as well be anonymous, or call himself X Y Z, as offer
one his visiting card indorsed with a name so frightful
to look at — so shocking to utter — so agonizing to
spell — as *Mochinahante*. And that it had a trans-
latable meaning — that it was not a proper name but
an appellative, in fact some playful *sobriquet*, I felt
certain, from observing the young woman to smile
whilst she uttered it. My next question drew from
her — that this Pagan-looking monster of a name
meant *Pig-in-the-dingle*. But really, now, between
the original monster and this English interpretation,
there was very little to choose; in fact the interpretation, as often happens, strikes one as the harder to
understand of the two. 'To be sure it does,' says a
lady sitting at my elbow, and tormented by a passion
so totally unfeminine as curiosity — 'to be sure — very
much harder; for *Mochina — what-do-you-call-it?*
might, you know, mean something or other, for any-

thing that you or I could say to the contrary ; but as to *Pig-in-the-dingle* — what dreadful nonsense! .what impossible description of an astrologer ! A man that — let me see — does something or other about the stars : how can *he* be described as a pig ? pig in *any* sense, you know — pig in *any* place ? But *Pig-in-a-dingle !* — why, if he's a pig at all, he must be *Pig-on-a-steeple*, or *Pig-on-the-top-of-a-hill*, that he may rise above the mists and vapors. Now I insist, my dear creature, on your explaining all this riddle on the spot. *You* know it — you came to the end of the mystery ; but none of *us* that are sitting here can guess at the meaning ; we shall all be ill, if you keep us waiting — I've a headach beginning already — so say the thing at once, and put us out of torment !'

What's to be done ? I *must* explain the thing to the Athenæum ; and if I stop to premise an oral explanation for the lady's separate use, there will be no time to save the Glasgow post, which waits for no man, and is deaf even to female outcries. By way of compromise, therefore, I request of the lady that she will follow my pen with her radiant eyes, by which means she will obtain the earliest intelligence, and the speediest relief to her headach. I, on my part, will not loiter, but will make my answer as near to a telegraphic answer, in point of speed, as a rigid metallic pen will allow. —— I divide this answer into two heads : the first concerning ' *in the dingle*,' the second concerning ' *pig*.' My philosophic researches, and a visit to the astrologer, ascertained a profound reason for describing him as *in-the-dingle* ; viz. because he *was* in a dingle. He was the sole occupant of a little cove amongst the hills — the sole householder ; and

so absolutely such, that if ever any treason should be
hatched in the dingle, clear it was to my mind that
Mochinahante would be found at the bottom of it; if
ever war should be levied in this dingle, *Mochinahante*
must be the sole belligerent; and if a forced contribution were ever imposed upon this dingle, *Mochinahante*
(poor man!) must pay it all out of his own pocket.
The lady interrupts me at this point to say — ' Well,
I understand all *that* — that's all very clear. But
what I want to know about is — *Pig*. Come to *Pig*.
Why *Pig*? How *Pig*? In what sense *Pig*? You
can't have any profound reason, you know, for *that*.'

Yes I have; a *very* profound reason; and satisfactory to the most sceptical of philosophers, viz. that he
was a Pig. I was presented by my fair hostess to the
great interpreter of the stars, in person; for I was
anxious to make the acquaintance of an astrologer,
and especially of one who, whilst owning to so rare a
profession, owned also to the soft impeachment of so
very significant a name. Having myself enjoyed so
favorable an opportunity for investigating the reasonableness of that name, *Mochinahante*, as applied to the
Denbighshire astrologer, I venture to pronounce it
unimpeachable. About his dress there was a forlorn-
ness, and an ancient tarnish or *ærugo*, which went far
to justify the name; and upon his face there sate that
lugubrious rust (or what medallists technically call
patina) which bears so costly a value when it is found
on the *coined* face of a Syro-Macedonian prince long
since compounded with dust, but, alas! bears no value
at all if found upon the flesh-and-blood face of a living
philosopher. Speaking humanly, one would have insinuated that the star-gazer wanted much washing and

scouring ; but, astrologically speaking, perhaps he
would have been spoiled by earthly waters for his
celestial vigils.

Mochinahante was civil enough ; a pig is not necessarily rude ; and, after seating me in his chair of state,
he prepared for his learned labors by cross-examina-
tions as to the day and hour of my birth. The *day* I
knew to a certainty ; and even about the *hour* I could
tell quite as much as ought in reason to be expected
from one who certainly had not been studying a chro-
nometer when that event occurred. These points settled, the astrologer withdrew into an adjoining room,
for the purpose (as he assured me) of scientifically con-
structing my horoscope ; but unless the drawing of
corks is a part of that process, I should myself incline
to think that the great man, instead of minding my
interests amongst the stars and investigating my horoscope, had been seeking consolation for himself in
bottled porter. Within half-an-hour he returned ;
looking more lugubrious than ever ; more grim ;
more grimy (if *grime* yields any such adjective) ; a
little more rusty ; rather more *patinous*, if numisma-
tists will lend me that word ; and a great deal more in
want of scouring. He had a paper of diagrams in his
hand, which of course contained some short-hand
memoranda upon my horoscope ; but, from its smoki-
ness, a malicious visitor might have argued a possibility
that it had served for more customers than myself. Under his arm he carried a folio book, which (he said) was
a manuscript of unspeakable antiquity. This he was
jealous of my seeing ; and before he would open it, as
if I and the book had been two prisoners at the bar
suspected of meditating some collusive mischief (such

as tying a cracker to the judge's wig), he separated us
as widely from each other as the dimensions of the
room allowed. These solemnities finished, we were all
ready — I, and the folio volume, and Pig-in-the-dingle
— for our several parts in the play. *Mochinahante*
began : — He opened the pleadings in a deprecatory
tone, protesting, almost with tears, that if anything
should turn out amiss in the forthcoming revelations,
it was much against his will ; that *he* was powerless, and could not justly be held responsible for
any part of the disagreeable message which it might
be his unhappiness to deliver. I hastened to assure
him that I was incapable of such injustice ; that I
should hold the stars responsible for the whole ; by
nature, that I was very forgiving ; that any little malice, which I might harbor for a year or so, should all
be reserved for the use of the particular constellations
concerned in the plot against myself; and, lastly, that
I was now quite ready to stand the worst of their
thunders. Pig was pleased with this reasonableness ;
he saw that he had to deal with a philosopher ; and,
in a more cheerful tone, he now explained that my
case was msystically contained in the diagrams ; these
smoke-dried documents submitted, as it were, a series
of questions to the book ; which book it was — a book•
of unspeakable antiquity — that gave the inflexible
answers, like the gloomy oracle that it was. But I
was not to be angry with the book, any more than
with himself, since —— ' Of course not,' I replied, in-
terrupting him, ' the book did but utter the sounds
which were predetermined by the white and black
keys struck in the smoky diagrams ; and I could
no more be angry with the book for speaking what

it conscientiously believed to be the truth than with
a decanter of port wine, or a bottle of porter, for
declining to yield more than one or two wine-glasses
of the precious liquor at the moment when I was looking for a dozen, under a transient forgetfulness, incident to the greatest minds, that I myself, ten minutes
before, had nearly drunk up the whole.' This comparison, though to a critic wide awake it might have
seemed slightly personal, met with the entire approbation of *Pig-in-the-dingle.* A better frame of mind
for receiving disastrous news, he evidently conceived,
could not exist or be fancied by the mind of man
than existed at that moment in myself. *He* was in a
state of intense pathos from the bottled porter. *I* was
in a state of intense excitement (pathos combined with
horror) at the prospect of a dreadful lecture on my
future life, now ready to be thundered into my ears
from that huge folio of unspeakable antiquity, prompted by those wretched smoke-dried diagrams. I believe we were in magnetical rapport. Think of *that,*
reader!— Pig and I in magnetical rapport! Both
making passes at each other! What in the world
would have become of us if suddenly we should have
taken to somnambulizing? Pig would have abandoned
his dingle to me; and I should have dismissed Pig to
that life of wandering which must have betrayed the
unscoured patinous condition of the astrologer to the
astonished eyes of Cambria : —

> ' Stout Glos'ter stood aghast [or *might* have stood] in speechless
> trance.
> *To arms!* cried Mortimer [or at least *might* have cr.ed], and
> couch'd his quivering lance.'

But Pig was a greater man than he seemed. He

yielded neither to magnetism nor to bottled porter;
but commenced reading from the black book in the
most awful tone of voice, and, generally speaking,
most correctly. Certainly he made one dreadful mis-
také; he started from the very middle of a sentence,
instead of the beginning; but then *that* had a truly
lyrical effect, and also it was excused by the bottled
porter. The words of the prophetic denunciation,
from which he started, were these — 'also *he* [that
was myself, you understand] shall have red hair.'
'*There* goes a bounce,' I said in an under tone; 'the
stars it seems, can tell falsehoods as well as other
people.' 'Also,' for Pig went on without stopping,
'he shall have seven-and-twenty-children.' Too hor-
ror-struck I was by this news to utter one word of
protest against it. 'Also,' Pig yelled out at the top
of his voice, 'he shall desert them.' Anger restored
my voice, and I cried out, 'That's not only a lie in
the stars, but a libel; and, if an action lay against a
constellation, I should recover damages.' Vain it
would be to trouble the reader with all the monstrous
prophecies that Pig read against me. He read with a
steady Pythian fury. Dreadful was his voice: dreadful were the starry charges against myself — things
that I *was* to do, things that I *must* do: dreadful was
the wrath with which secretly I denounced all partici-
pation in the acts which these wicked stars laid to my
charge. But this infirmity of good nature besets me,
that, if a man shows trust and absolute faith in any
agent or agency whatever, heart there is not in me to
resist him, or to expose his folly. Pig trusted — oh
how profoundly! — in his black book of unspeakable
antiquity. It would have killed him on the spot to

24

prove that the black book was a hoax, and that he
himself was another. Consequently, I submitted in
silence to pass for the monster that Pig, under coer
cion of the stars, had pronounced me, rather than part
in anger from the solitary man, who after all was not
to blame, acting only in a ministerial capacity, and
reading only what the stars obliged him to read. I
rose without saying one word, advanced to the table,
and paid my fees; for it is a disagreeable fact to
record, that astrologers grant no credit, nor even dis-
count upon prompt payment. I shook hands with
Mochinahante; we exchanged kind farewells — he
smiling benignly upon me, in total forgetfulness that
he had just dismissed me to a life of storms and
crimes; I, in return, as the very best benediction that
I could think of, saying secretly, ' Oh Pig, may the
heavens rain their choicest soap-suds upon thee ! '

Emerging into the open air, I told my fair hostess
of the red hair which the purblind astrologer had
obtained for me from the stars, and which, with *their*
permission, I would make over to *Mochinahante* for a
reversionary wig in his days of approaching baldness.
But I said not one word upon that too bountiful
allowance of children with which *Moch.* had endowed
me. I retreated by nervous anticipation from that
inextinguishable laughter which, I was too certain,
would follow upon *her* part; and yet, when we
reached the outlet of the dingle, and turned round to
take a parting look of the astrological dwelling, I
myself was overtaken by fits of laughter; for suddenly I figured in vision my own future return to this
mountain recess, with the young legion of twenty-
seven children. ' *I* desert them, the darlings ! ' I

exclaimed, ' far from it! Backed by this filial army, I shall feel myself equal to the task of taking vengeance on the stars for the affronts they have put upon me through Pig their servant. It will be like the return of the Heracleidæ to the Peloponnesus. The sacred legion will storm the " dingle," whilst *I* storm Pig; the rising generation will take military possession of " -*inahante*," whilst I deal with " *Moch* " (which I presume to be the part in the long word answering to Pig).' My hostess laughed in sympathy with *my* laughter; but I was cautious of letting her have a look into my vision of the sacred legion. We quitted the dingle for ever; and so ended my first visit, being also my last, to an astrologer.

This, reader, was the true general occasion of my one thought upon astrology; and, before I mention it, I may add that the immediate impulse drawing my mind in any such direction was this : — On walking to the table where the astrologer sat, in order to pay my fees, naturally I came nearer to the folio book than astrological prudence would generally have allowed. But Pig's attention was diverted for the moment to the silver coins laid before him; these he reviewed with the care reasonable in one so poor, and in a state of the coinage so neglected as it then was. By this moment of avarice in Pig, I profited so far as to look over the astrologer's person, sitting and bending forward full upon the book. It was spread open, and at a glance I saw that it was no MS. but a printed book, printed in black-letter types. The month of August stood as a rubric at the head of the broad margin; and below it stood some days of that month in orderly succession. ' So then, Pig,' said I in my thoughts, ' it seems that any person whatever, born on any particular day and hour of August, is to have the same exact fate as myself. But a king and a beggar may chance thus far to agree. And be you assured, Pig, that all the infinite variety of cases lying between these two *termini* differ from each other in fortunes and incidents of life as much, though not so notoriously, as king and beggar.'

Hence arose a confirmation of my contempt for astrology. It seemed as if *necessarily* false — false by an *à priori* principle, viz. that the possible differences in human fortunes, which are infinite, cannot be measured by the possible differences in the particular moments of birth, which are too strikingly finite. It strengthened me in this way of thinking, that subsequently I found the very same objection in Macrobius. Macrobius may have stolen the idea; but certainly not from me — *as* certainly I did not steal it from him; so that here is a concurrence of two people independently, *one* of them a great philosopher, in the very same annihilating objection.

Now comes my one thought. Both of us were wrong, Macrobius and myself. Even the great philosopher is obliged to confess it. The objection truly valued is — to astrologers, not to astrology. No two events ever *did* coincide in point of time. Every event has, and must have, a certain duration; this you may call its *breadth;* and the true *locus* of the event in time is the central point of that breadth, which never was or will be the same for any two separate events, though grossly held to be contemporaneous. It is the mere imperfection of our human means for chasing the infinite subdivisibilities of time which causes us to regard two events as even by possibility concurring in their central moments. This imperfection is crushing to the pretensions of astrologers; but astrology laughs at it in the heavens; and astrology, armed with celestial chronometers, is true!

Suffer me to illustrate the case a little: — It is rare that a metaphysical difficulty can be made as clear as a pikestaff. This can. Suppose two events to occur in the same quarter of a minute — that is, in the same fifteen seconds; then, if they started precisely together, and ended precisely together, they would not only have the same breadth, but this breadth would accurately coincide in all its parts or fluxions; consequently, the central moment, viz., the 8th, would coincide rigorously with the centre of each event. But, suppose that one of the two events, A for instance, commenced a single second before B the other, then, as we are still supposing them to have the same breadth or extension, A will have ended in the second before B ends; and, consequently, the centres will be different, for the 8th second of A will be the 7th of B. The disks of the two events will overlap — A will overlap B at the beginning; B will overlap A at the end. Now, go on to assume that, in a particular case, this overlapping does not take place, but that the two events eclipse each other, lying as truly surface to surface as two sovereigns in a tight *rouleau* of sovereigns, or one dessert-spoon nestling in the bosom of another; in that case, the 8th or central second will be the centre for both. But even here a question will arise as to the degree of rigor in the coincidence; for divide that 8th second into a thousand parts or sub-moments, and perhaps the centre of A will be found to hit the 450th sub-moment, whilst that of B may hit the 600th. Or suppose, again, even this trial surmounted: the two harmonious creatures, A and B, running neck and neck together, have both hit simultaneously the true centre of the thousand sub-moments which lies half-way between the 500th and the 501st. All is right so far — 'all right behind;' but go on, if you please; subdivide this last centre, which we will call X, into a thousand lesser fractions. Take, in fact, a railway express-train of decimal fractions, and give chase to A and B; my word for it that you will come up with them in some stage or other of the journey, and arrest them in the very' act of separating their centres — which is a dreadful crime in the eye of astrology; for, it is utterly impossible that the initial moment, or *sub*-moment, or *sub-sub*-moment of A and B should absolutely coincide. Such a thing as a perfect start was never heard of at Doncaster. Now, this severe accuracy is not wanted on earth. Archimedes, it is well known, never saw a perfect circle, nor even, with his leave, a decent circle; for, doubtless, the reader knows the following fact, viz., that, if you take the most perfect Vandyking ever cut out of paper or silk, by the most delicate of female fingers, with the most exquisite of Salisbury scissors, upon viewing it through a microscope you will find the edges frightfully ragged; but, if you apply the same microscope to one of God's Vandyking on the corolla or calyx of a flower, you will find it as truly cut and as smooth as a moonbeam. We on earth, I repeat, need no such rigorous truth. For instance, you and I, my reader, want little perhaps with circles, except now and then to bore one with an augre in a ship's bottom, when we wish to sink her and to cheat the underwriters; or, by way of variety,

to cut one with a centre-bit through shop-shutters, in
order to rob a jeweller; — so *we* don't care much
whether the circumference is ragged or not. But that
won't do for a constellation! The stars *n'entendent
pas la raillerie* on the subject of geometry. The pen-
dulum of the starry heavens oscillates truly; and if
the Greenwich time of the *Empyreum* can't be repeated
upon earth, without an error, a horoscope is as much a
chimera as the perpetual motion, or as an agreeable
income-tax. In fact, in casting a nativity, to swerve
from the true centre by the trillionth of a centillionth
is as fatal as to leave room for a coach and six to turn
between your pistol shot and the bull's eye. If you
haven't done the trick, no matter how near you've
come to it. And to overlook this, is as absurd as was
the answer of that Lieutenant M., who, being asked
whether he had any connection with another officer of
the same name, replied — ' Oh yes ! a very close one.'
' But in what way ? ' ' Why, you see, I'm in the 50th
regiment of foot, and he's in the 49th : ' walking, in
fact, just behind him ! Yet, for all this, horoscopes
may be calculated very truly by the stars amongst
themselves; and my conviction is — that they are.
They are perhaps even printed hieroglyphically, and
published as regularly as a nautical almanac; only,
they cannot be re-published upon earth by any mode
of piracy yet discovered amongst sublunary book-
sellers. Astrology, in fact, is a very profound, or at
least a very lofty science ; but astrologers are hum-
bugs.

I have finished, and I am vain of my work ; for I
have accomplished three considerable things : — I
have floored Macrobius; I have cured a lady of her

headache; and lastly, which is best of all, I have expressed my sincere interest in the prosperity of the Glasgow Athenæum.

But the Glasgow post is mounting, and this paper will be lost; a fact which, amongst all the dangers besetting me in this life, the wretched Pig forgot to warn me of.

FEB. 24, 1848.

CPSIA information can be obtained
at www.ICGtesting.com
Printed in the USA
LVOW12*2310090417

530219LV00020B/437/P

9 781372 147302